HIGHER ORDER LOGIC AND HARDWARE VERIFICATION

Cambridge Tracts in Theoretical Computer Science

Managing Editor   Professor C.J. van Rijsbergen,
Department of Computing Science, University of Glasgow

Titles in the series

HIGHER ORDER LOGIC
AND HARDWARE VERIFICATION

T. Melham
University of Cambridge

CAMBRIDGE
UNIVERSITY PRESS

CAMBRIDGE UNIVERSITY PRESS
Cambridge, New York, Melbourne, Madrid, Cape Town,
Singapore, São Paulo, Delhi, Mexico City

Cambridge University Press
The Edinburgh Building, Cambridge CB2 8RU, UK

Published in the United States of America by Cambridge University Press, New York

www.cambridge.org
Information on this title: www.cambridge.org/9780521417181

First published 1993

A catalogue record for this publication is available from the British Library

ISBN 978-0-521-41718-1 Hardback
ISBN 978-0-521-11532-2 Paperback

Cambridge University Press has no responsibility for the persistence or
accuracy of URLs for external or third-party internet websites referred to in
this publication, and does not guarantee that any content on such websites is,
or will remain, accurate or appropriate. Information regarding prices, travel
timetables, and other factual information given in this work is correct at
the time of first printing but Cambridge University Press does not guarantee
the accuracy of such information thereafter.

Contents

List of Figures

Preface

This book shows how formal logic can be used to reason about the behaviour of digital hardware designs. The main focus is on a fundamental tool for dealing with the complexity of this activity—namely the use of abstraction in bridging the gaps between logical descriptions of hardware at different levels of detail.

The text of this book was adapted[1] from a Ph.D. dissertation on abstraction mechanisms for reasoning about hardware, written at the University of Cambridge Computer Laboratory. This work was originally motivated by my experience with using the LCF_LSM theorem prover to verify the correctness of an associative memory device intended for use in a local area network. This device comprised 37 SSI and MSI TTL chips, the most complex of which was an AM2910 microprogram controller. Although the design was straightforward, its verification using the LCF_LSM system was remarkably difficult. The main problem was simply the almost intractably large size of the intermediate theorems generated during the proof. Single theorems were generated that were hundreds of lines long, and several minutes or even several hours of CPU time were needed to manipulate them. The proof was completed only with considerable difficulty—unfortunately, some time after the LCF_LSM system had become obsolete.

These difficulties were for the most part due not to problems with the LCF_LSM theorem prover itself, but to deficiencies in the underlying formalism for hardware verification supported by the system. There were two main problems. First, the LCF_LSM formalism (which is described in detail in [43]) limited the extent to which both the associative memory itself and the hardware components used in its design could be described by *abstract*—and therefore concise—specifications. Second, this formalism provided only limited and inflexible *abstraction mechanisms* for relating specifications of hardware behaviour at different levels of abstraction.

These limitations imposed severe restrictions on the extent to which abstraction could be used to simplify specifications at intermediate levels in the hierarchically-structured proof of correctness. For example, a complete description of the effect of executing any of 16 possible opcodes using the AM2910 microprogram controller had to be retained in specifications throughout much of the proof, even though the actual microcode for the associative memory made use of only 5 different opcodes. It became clear from this exercise that more effective abstraction mechanisms were needed for controlling the complexity of specifications and proofs than were made

---

[1]It was adapted, among other things, by the deletion of a long appendix full of technicalities; this is published separately as [88].

available by the LCF_LSM formalism and theorem prover.

The abstraction techniques explained in this book are designed specifically for dealing with these kinds of problems. The formalism used here is a variety of higher order logic which is widely employed for both research and practical applications. The book begins with an introduction to higher order logic and the established techniques for hardware verification using this formalism. A variety of examples is then given; each of these illustrates a specific application of abstraction to reasoning about hardware.

Outline of the book

Chapter 1 briefly introduces the method of hardware design verification by formal proof and discusses its limitations. The importance of abstraction mechanisms for the success of this technique is explained.

Chapter 2 gives an overview of the formulation of higher order logic used in this book for reasoning about hardware. A sketch is also given of the mechanization of this logic in the HOL theorem proving system. The purpose of this chapter is to make the book self-contained, and emphasis is therefore on the features of the logic which are important to an understanding of later chapters.

Chapter 3 introduces the basic techniques for hardware verification using higher order logic. A method for specifying the behaviour of hardware is described, together with a method for constructing behavioural models of composite devices from the specifications of their components. An example proof is given to illustrate the general approach. The techniques described in this chapter are well-established and widely-used; they constitute the essence of hardware verification using higher order logic. The chapter concludes with an overview of some other approaches.

Chapter 4 shows how certain fundamental abstraction mechanisms for hardware specification and verification can be formalized in higher order logic and used to express assertions about hardware correctness and the accuracy of formal models of hardware. Two basic types of abstraction are discussed—abstraction *within* a model of hardware behaviour, and abstraction *between* models of hardware behaviour. This chapter is concerned only with the general ideas behind these abstraction techniques; the technical details are covered later.

The subject of chapter 5 is data abstraction. The emphasis is on the use of *types* to represent 'data' in higher order logic. It is shown how a wide class of concrete data types can be characterized formally in higher order logic. Examples are given to show how these types be used to support formal reasoning about hardware behaviour where data abstraction is involved. A common theme of these examples is the importance of an appropriate choice of data types for use in specifications.

Chapter 6 describes some basic techniques for temporal abstraction in higher order logic and illustrates their use by a case study. Temporal abstraction relates specifications that describe hardware behaviour using different notions of time. A technique is described for constructing *time mappings* in logic, and it is shown how mappings of this kind can be used to formulate the correctness of hardware devices with respect to temporally abstract specifications of required behaviour.

In chapter 7, an example is given to illustrate the concept of an abstraction relationship between two models of hardware behaviour which was introduced in chapter 4. An abstraction relationship of this kind describes the conditions under which correctness results obtained in an abstract or simplified model of hardware behaviour agree with correctness results obtained using a more accurate but less tractable model. Formalization of this relationship leads to a rigorous notion of 'design for verifiability'.

Acknowledgements

I wish to thank my Ph.D. supervisor, Dr Mike Gordon, who allowed me free rein in my early days as a research student, and who spurred me on towards the end. His guidance, advice, and the influence of his ideas have been of great value throughout the development of this work. I should also like to thank Dr Graham Birtwistle for his continued support over many years.

Thanks are also due to the members of the Cambridge hardware verification group, both past and present, for many valuable discussions. I am especially grateful to Albert Camilleri, Avra Cohn, Inder Dhingra, Mike Gordon, and Tim Leonard for their helpful comments on earlier drafts of this book in its dissertation form. Graham Birtwistle also very kindly read an early draft and made several valuable suggestions, and Jim Grundy helped with useful comments on chapter 6. Thanks are also due to Glynn Winskel for discussions about relating transistor models.

Financial support came from several sources. Early work was supported by a scholarship from the Royal Commission for the Exhibition of 1851 and by funding provided by the ORS Awards scheme. The Commissioners for the Exhibition of 1851, Pembroke College, and Graham Birtwistle helped by supplying funding to attend conferences. I am grateful to Gonville and Caius College for support in the form of an unofficial fellowship, during the tenure of which much of this book was written.

Chapter 1

Hardware Verification

Continued advances in microelectronics have allowed hardware designers to build devices of remarkable size and complexity. With increasing size and complexity, however, it becomes increasingly difficult to ensure that these devices are free of design errors. Exhaustive simulation of even moderately-sized circuits is impossible, and partial simulation offers only partial assurance of correctness.

This is an especially serious problem in safety-critical applications, where failure due to design errors may cause loss of life or extensive damage. In these applications, functional errors in circuit designs cannot be tolerated. But even where safety is not the primary consideration, there may be important economic reasons for doing everything possible to eliminate design errors, and to eliminate them early in the design process. A flawed design may mean costly and time-consuming refabrication, and mass-produced devices may have to be recalled and replaced.

A solution to these problems is one of the goals of formal methods for verification of the correctness of hardware designs—sometimes just called *hardware verification*. With this approach, the behaviour of hardware devices is described mathematically, and formal proof is used to verify that they meet rigorous specifications of intended behaviour. The proofs can be very large and complex, so mechanized theorem-proving tools are often used to construct them.

Considerable progress has been made in this area in the past few years. Notable large-scale applications of hardware verification include Graham's verification of the design of an SECD chip using the HOL proof assistant [8], Joyce's verification in HOL [78, 79] of a simple microprocessor originally verified by Gordon using the LCF_LSM theorem prover [44], Hunt's verification of the FM8501 microprocessor using the Boyer-Moore theorem prover [73], and the verification by Narendran and Stillman of an image processing chip using a method based on rewriting [101].

Hardware verification techniques are now considered mature enough to be applied to simple circuits intended for safety-critical applications. Cohn's work on verifying the Viper microprocessor is a preliminary experiment in this area [29, 27]. Viper is a simple microprocessor designed at the Royal Signals and Radar Establishment with formal verification in mind and intended for use in safety-critical applications [31]. Cohn's formal proof of the correctness of Viper is not complete, but it covers some important aspects of the machine's design.

1.1   The hardware verification method

Two things are needed for any method of hardware verification based on rigorous specification and formal proof. The first is a formal language for describing the behaviour of hardware and expressing propositions about it. The ideal language is expressive enough to describe hardware in a natural and concise notation yet still has a well-understood and reasonably simple semantics. The second requirement is a deductive calculus for proving propositions expressed in this language. This must, of course, be logically sound, and it should be powerful enough to allow one to prove all the true propositions about hardware behaviour that arise in practice.

Various formal languages and associated proof techniques have been proposed as a basis for hardware verification. These range from special-purpose hardware description languages with *ad hoc* proof rules to systems of formal logic and subsets of ordinary mathematics. Formal methods for reasoning about hardware behaviour have been based, for example, on algebraic techniques [6, 22, 90], various kinds of temporal logic [11, 33, 80, 100], functional programming techniques [105], predicate calculus [34, 71, 73, 113], and higher order logic [21, 45, 57, 81].

The details of the verification methods based on these different formalisms vary, but many of them share a common general approach. This typically involves the following four steps.

1. Write a formal specification S to describe the behaviour that the device to be verified must exhibit for it to be considered correct.

2. Write a specification for each kind of primitive hardware component used in the device. These specifications are intended to describe the actual behaviour of real hardware components.

3. Define an expression D which describes the behaviour of the device to be proved correct. The definition of D has the general form

   $$D \stackrel{\text{def}}{=} P_1 + \cdots + P_n$$

   where $P_1, \ldots, P_n$ specify the behaviours of the constituent parts of the device and $+$ is a *composition operator* which models the effect of wiring components together. The expressions $P_1, \ldots, P_n$ used here are instances of the specifications for primitive devices defined in step 2.

4. Prove that the device described by the expression D is correct with respect to the specification S. This is done by proving a theorem of the form

   $$\vdash D \text{ satisfies } S$$

   where 'satisfies' is some *satisfaction relation* on specifications of hardware behaviour. This correctness theorem asserts that the behaviour described by D satisfies the specification of intended behaviour S.

When the device to be proved correct is large, this method is usually applied hierarchically. The design is structured into a hierarchy of components and sub-components, and specifications that describe 'primitive components' at one level of the hierarchy then become specifications of intended behaviour at the next level down. The structure of the proof mirrors this hierarchy: the top-level specification is shown to be satisfied by an appropriate connection of components; at the next level down, each of these components is shown to be correctly implemented by a connection of sub-components, and so on—down to the lowest level, where the components used correspond to devices available as hardware primitives.

1.2   Limitations of hardware verification[1]

A correctness proof cannot guarantee that a real device will never malfunction; the *design* of a device may be proved correct, but the hardware actually built can still behave in ways not intended by the designer. There are some obvious reasons for this. There may, for example, be defects in fabrication. Or, since the theorem-proving tools used for hardware verification are not yet integrated with the CAD systems used to generate circuit layouts, the design which is verified may not correspond exactly to the device which is built. But in addition to these pragmatic problems, there are also two more fundamental reasons why a physical device, although built to a verified design, may still fail to behave as intended by the designer. Both are results of obvious but important limits to what can be established by formal proof.

First, a proof can never demonstrate that a circuit will behave 'as intended' by the designer; a proof can show only that its design behaves as prescribed by a written, and possibly inaccurate, specification. A 'verified' device may therefore exhibit unexpected behaviour because its design was proved correct with respect to a specification that fails to reflect the designer's intent. This is an obvious point. But it is an especially important one when the specification is large or the behaviour being specified is complex, for then it may be far from clear to the designer that the specification is itself correct.

Second, a formal proof cannot, of course, demonstrate anything about physical reality. All that can be proved is that a mathematical *model* of a device has the properties prescribed by a specification of required behaviour. But a model may fail to capture important aspects of the real hardware it is intended to describe, and design errors can therefore escape discovery because the undesirable behaviour resulting from them is not reflected in this model.

Because of these fundamental limits to the scope of formal proof, verification can never establish with complete certainty that a physical device will function exactly as intended. A correctness theorem can be only as good as the model and the

---

[1]See also Cohn's discussion of the limitations of hardware verification in the context of the Viper verification project [28]. For a discussion of certain extra-logical aspects of Viper, see [85].

specification it relates. There are, however, two important practical measures that can be taken to help justify confidence in the significance of such results. First, specifications can be made as clear and concise as possible, so that their fidelity to the designer's intent can be evaluated easily. This reduces the likelihood of a proof failing to yield a meaningful result because the specification is itself incorrect.[2] Second, models can be used that describe the empirical behaviour of real devices as accurately as possible. The more accurate the model, the less likely it is that a design error will escape discovery.

Adopting these two measures is essential if design verification by formal proof is to be an effective way of dealing with the problem of hardware correctness. An important consequence is that the notion of *abstraction* must play a central role in effective formal methods for hardware verification.

1.3   Abstraction

Abstraction is the process by which the important properties of a complex object are isolated for further use and the remaining ones ignored as being irrelevant to the task at hand. An example is the process of procedural abstraction in programming. Once a procedure has been defined, it is treated as an atomic operation with only one important attribute, namely *what* the procedure does. The exact sequence of computation steps which achieve this operation—*how* the procedure does it—is ignored [50]. Programming language constructs that support abstraction in this way are fundamental tools for dealing with the complexity of programming. By allowing the attributes of a complex object which are important to be isolated from those which are not, software abstraction mechanisms provide a way of limiting the amount of detail that must be considered at any one time [52].

Abstraction plays a similar role in hardware verification. Here, an abstraction mechanism establishes a relationship of abstraction between a complex description of hardware behaviour and a simpler one. This provides a means for controlling the complexity of both specifications and proofs of correctness. By suppressing the irrelevant information in detailed descriptions of hardware behaviour, and thereby isolating the properties of these descriptions which are most important, effective abstraction mechanisms help reduce the size and complexity of the specifications at each level in a hierarchically-structured correctness proof. Abstraction mechanisms and hierarchical structuring help to control the complexity of proofs in the same way that software abstraction mechanisms are used to manage the complexity of program development.

Considered in the context of the limitations of proof discussed above, it is clear

---

[2]Another approach is to make specifications executable, so that the designer can run them to gain confidence in their accuracy (see, for example, [20, 92, 110]). This is a special case of the more general strategy of evaluating specifications by deriving consequences of them.

that abstraction must play a central role in two areas of hardware verification—first, in formulating meaningful assertions about correctness, and second, in assessing the accuracy of the models on which correctness proofs are based. These two aspects of the role of abstraction in hardware verification are discussed briefly below.

1.3.1 Abstraction and correctness

In proving the correctness of a design, it is generally desirable to use a model whose mathematical properties reflect as accurately as possible the empirical behaviour of the physical device itself. This does not mean that it is always necessary to model the physics of electronic circuits in as much detail as possible; a simplified model can often be justified by the fact that the device to be verified is implemented in a particular technology or design style. But a model should nonetheless reflect as accurately as possible the actual behaviour of a device built using the technology or design style in question.

Specifications, on the other hand, must be clear and concise, so that they are intelligible enough to be seen to reflect the designer's intent. Most of the details about the actual behaviour of a device must therefore be left out the specification of its intended behaviour. Only the essential aspects of its required behaviour can be included. Furthermore, the larger and more complex the device being verified, the more detailed information about its actual behaviour must be ignored in order to keep the specification small.

This means that specifications must, in general, present more abstract views of the behaviour of devices than models do. The concept of a relationship of abstraction between two formal descriptions of hardware behaviour is therefore fundamental to expressing what it means for a device to be 'correct'. Formally, the correctness of a device is stated by a theorem which asserts that a mathematical model of its actual behaviour in some sense 'satisfies' a specification of its intended behaviour. For all but the simplest devices, the satisfaction relation used to formulate this correctness relationship must relate a detailed design model to a more abstract specification. This notion of correctness as a relationship of abstraction is explored in detail in this book.

1.3.2 Abstraction and the accuracy of models

Although the value of a correctness result depends on how accurately a model reflects the actual behaviour of the physical device it represents, a very accurate model of hardware behaviour may be unnecessarily complex. It may be possible to adopt a circuit design style for which a simpler model will do. The functional correctness of a fully complementary CMOS circuit, for example, does not critically depend on transistor size ratios [114]. A very accurate model of CMOS transistor behaviour, which takes into account transistor size ratios, would therefore be inappropriate for this conservative design style. In this case, a less accurate—but also simpler and

more tractable—model can be used. The validity of using this simpler model can
be justified on empirical grounds, in the light of what is known about the actual
behaviour of fully complementary CMOS circuit designs.

In general, a simplified model can often be justified empirically by the fact that
the device which is to be proved correct is implemented in a restricted style of
circuit design. Such a model may be less accurate than a more complex one, but the
restrictions on device behaviour imposed by the design style itself will ensure that
the extra accuracy of a more complex model is not needed. In this case, the simple
model of hardware behaviour will in fact be an abstraction of a more accurate model.
Both models will describe the same design, but the simpler model will describe only
some of the aspects of device behaviour that are captured by the more accurate
model.

Although it may be possible to justify this use of a simplified model of device
behaviour empirically, it is also desirable to assess the accuracy of models by more
rigorous means. This can be done by means of a proof which demonstrates that
a simplified model is sufficiently accurate (with respect to a more complex model)
for the particular circuit design style in question. Such a proof shows that, for a
restricted class of circuit designs, a simple model is in some sense a valid abstraction
of a more complex model. This notion of an abstraction relationship between models
of hardware behaviour and the connection between this idea and the concept of the
relative accuracy of models are discussed in detail in chapters 4 and 7.

1.4   Hardware verification using higher order logic

The choice of a formalism for hardware verification involves a compromise between
expressive power and ease of proof. A simple and restricted formalism may make the
proofs of some devices easy, but it may also make it hard to specify complex devices
easily and concisely. A powerful formalism will be expressive enough for a wide
class of devices but may make proofs difficult. The formalism used for hardware
verification in this book is a version of type theory called *higher order logic* [24, 41].
Higher order logic is a foundational formalism that makes available the results of
general mathematics. This allows one (in principle) to construct within the logic
whatever mathematical tools are needed for the verification task at hand.

Chapters 2 and 3 introduce higher order logic and explain the basics of hardware
verification using this formalism. One of the main aims of this book is to give a
clear account of the role of abstraction in hardware verification and to show how
certain fundamental abstraction mechanisms can be formalized in higher order logic.
Chapter 4 provides a general account of the basic principles of abstraction, and
chapters 5–7 give a selection of examples to illustrate these principles. The aim of
these examples is to provide clear illustrations of some specific aspects of hardware
verification using higher order logic. The examples are therefore generally very
simple. The reader should, however, be able to see how the methods illustrated by

these examples can be applied on a larger scale.

Two fundamental principles underlie the approach taken in this book. The first is that all reasoning about hardware should be done by strictly formal proof, using only the deductive calculus provided by the primitive basis of higher order logic. This provides the greatest possible assurance that only logically sound reasoning is used. The second principle is that any special-purpose notation needed to specify hardware behaviour and to formulate correctness should be introduced by definitional means only. That is, the syntax of the logic is extended with new notation not simply by postulating axioms to give meaning to it, but rather by defining it in terms of existing expressions of the logic that already have the required semantics. This ensures that inconsistency is not introduced by postulating *ad hoc* axioms intended to characterize non-primitive mathematical objects.

An important consequence of adopting these two principles is that mechanized theorem proving support becomes essential in practice, since only for the simplest theorems of higher order logic is it feasible to carry out fully detailed formal proofs manually. The HOL theorem-prover [42, 47] is a proof generating system suitable for conducting large-scale proofs in the version of higher order logic used in this book. The basic ideas behind the HOL system are explained in chapter 2. It is, however, beyond the scope of this book to discuss theorem-proving in HOL in detail; for this, the interested reader should consult the HOL system manual [47]. A substantial case study is described in [49].

Chapter 2

Higher Order Logic and the HOL System

This chapter provides an overview of the formulation of higher order logic used in this book for reasoning about hardware. A brief account is also given of the mechanization of this logic in the HOL theorem proving system.

The version of higher order logic described in this chapter was developed by Mike Gordon at the University of Cambridge [41]. Gordon's version of higher order logic is based on Church's formulation of simple type theory [24], which combines features of the λ-calculus with a simplification of the original type theory of Whitehead and Russell [115]. Gordon's machine-oriented formulation extends Church's theory in two significant ways: the syntax of types includes the polymorphic type discipline developed by Milner for the LCF logic PPλ [48], and the primitive basis of the logic includes rules of definition for extending the logic with new constants and types.

The description of higher order logic given in this chapter is not complete, though it does cover all the aspects of the logic important to an understanding of later chapters. This book is concerned more with specifications than with proofs, and verification of theorems will be left mainly to the reader's logical and mathematical intuition. This chapter therefore deals mostly with notation. See Gordon's paper [41] or the HOL system manual [47] for a full account of higher order logic, including a list of the primitive rules of inference and a set-theoretic semantics.

In this book, the phrase 'higher order logic' should generally be understood to mean the particular formulation described in this chapter. Related versions of higher order logic are discussed by Andrews [2] and Hatcher [64].

2.1 Types

Higher order logic is a typed logic; every term of the logic has an associated logical *type*, which names the kind of value it denotes. A term is syntactically well-formed only if its type is consistent with the types of its subterms. As a syntactic device, types are necessary to eliminate certain 'paradoxical' statements which, if they could be expressed in the logic, would make it inconsistent (e.g. formulations of Russell's paradox). Requiring every term to have a type that is consistent with those of its

subterms makes such paradoxical expressions syntactically ill-formed and thereby
eliminates them from the logic.

But as well as preventing inconsistency, logical types also play an important role
in writing natural and concise propositions about hardware behaviour. Types can
be used in hardware verification, as in mathematics and programming, to organize
data and to make distinctions between variables that range over different kinds of
values (e.g. bits, numbers, pairs, lists, recursive structures). This pragmatic use of
logical types is discussed in chapter 5.

2.1.1   The syntax of types

The syntax of types in higher order logic is given by

$$\sigma \quad ::= \quad c \mid v \mid (\sigma_1, \ldots, \sigma_n)op$$

where $\sigma, \sigma_1, \ldots, \sigma_n$ range over types, c ranges over type *constants*, v ranges over
type *variables*, and *op* ranges over n-ary type *operators* (for $n \geq 1$). Type constants
and type variables are called *atomic* types. Types constructed using type operators
are called *compound* types.

Type constants are identifiers that name fixed sets of values. Examples are the
primitive type constant *bool*, which denotes the two-element set of boolean truth-
values, and the type constant *num*, which denotes the set of natural numbers.

Type variables are used to stand for 'any type'. They are written α, β, γ, etc.
Type expressions that contain type variables are called *polymorphic*. A *substitution
instance* of a polymorphic type σ is a type obtained by substituting types for all
occurrences of one or more of the type variables in σ. Type variables occur in
Church's formulation of higher order logic as metavariables ranging over types; in
the version used here they are part of the object language. This allows a limited
form of implicit universal quantification over types within the logic, since theorems
that contain polymorphic types are also true for any substitution instance of them.

A compound type of the form $(\sigma_1, \ldots, \sigma_n)op$ denotes a set constructed from the
sets denoted by the types σ_1 through σ_n. The n-ary type operator *op* is the name
of the operation that constructs this set. The compound type $(bool, bool)fun$, for
example, denotes the set of all total functions from values of type *bool* to values of
type *bool*. This compound type is constructed using the binary type operator *fun*,
which stands for the function space operation on sets.

2.1.2   Primitive and defined types

There are two primitive type constants in higher order logic, namely *bool* and *ind*.
The type constant *bool* denotes the two-element set of boolean truth-values. The
type constant *ind* denotes the set of 'individuals', which in this formulation of higher
order logic is simply a set with infinitely many distinct elements. There is only one

primitive type operator, the binary type operator *fun*. If σ_1 and σ_2 are any two types, then the compound type $(\sigma_1, \sigma_2)fun$ denotes the set of all total functions from values of type σ_1 to values of type σ_2.

In principle, every type needed for doing proofs can be written using only type variables, the primitive type constants *bool* and *ind*, and the primitive type operator *fun*. But in practice it is desirable to add more type constants and operators to the logic than are strictly necessary to prevent inconsistency. In the version of higher order logic used here, this is done by defining new types and type operators in terms of primitive types or other already-defined types. A type definition extends the language of types by introducing a new type constant or type operator not already present in it. Formally, a type definition is an axiom that is added to the logic to give meaning to a new type expression. The primitive basis of the logic includes an explicitly-stated *rule of definition* for introducing axioms of this kind. This rule is explained in detail in section 2.7.

Two types that can be defined formally using this rule are *num*, the type of natural numbers, and $(\sigma_1, \sigma_2)prod$, the cartesian product of σ_1 and σ_2. A summary of some notation associated with these two basic types is given in section 2.2.6; a full account of how they are defined can be found in [88]. Other types defined specially for hardware verification are also introduced in later chapters.

2.1.3 Notational abbreviations for types

Some notational abbreviations are used to make type expressions more readable. Compound types constructed with the type operators *fun* and *prod* can be written using the infix notation shown below.

Infix Abbreviations for Types	
Type	*Abbreviation*
$(\sigma_1, \sigma_2)fun$	$\sigma_1 \rightarrow \sigma_2$
$(\sigma_1, \sigma_2)prod$	$\sigma_1 \times \sigma_2$

Expressions written using this infix notation are metalinguistic abbreviations for the corresponding object-language types; unlike defined types, they are not part of an extended syntax of object-language type expressions. For example, the type expression $bool \rightarrow (bool \rightarrow bool)$ is simply shorthand for the rather less readable type expression $(bool, (bool, bool)fun)fun$.

By convention, it is assumed that the infix symbols $\rightarrow$ and $\times$ associate to the right. The expression $bool \rightarrow (bool \rightarrow bool)$, for example, can be written without parentheses as $bool \rightarrow bool \rightarrow bool$. In addition, $\times$ is assumed to be more tightly binding than $\rightarrow$. So, for example, the expression $bool \times bool \rightarrow bool$ means $(bool \times bool) \rightarrow bool$.

2.2   Terms

The notation for *terms* in higher order logic can be viewed informally as an extension
of the conventional syntax of predicate calculus in which variables can range over
functions (higher order variables) and functions can take functions as arguments
or yield functions as results (higher order functions). These two extensions are
illustrated by the proposition shown below.

$$\forall x\, f.\, \exists fn.\, (fn\ 0 = x) \wedge \forall n.\, fn\ (n{+}1) = (f\ (fn\ n))\ n$$

This states that functions can be defined on the natural numbers such that they
satisfy primitive-recursive defining equations. It asserts that for any value x and
any function f, there is a function fn that yields x when applied to 0 and satisfies
the recursive equation $fn\ (n{+}1) = (f\ (fn\ n))\ n$ for all natural numbers n. The
quantified variables f and fn are examples of higher order variables; they both
range over functions. The function f is also an example of a higher order function;
when applied to the value $(fn\ n)$, it yields a function as a result.

   The proposition shown above is written in an abbreviated notation. It stands for
a much less readable expression written in the 'pure' syntax of higher order logic
terms. This pure syntax of terms is described in the next section. Some notational
abbreviations for terms are then introduced in the sections that follow. These define
the notation used in the proposition shown above and allow terms to be written in
a form that resembles the conventional syntax of predicate calculus.

2.2.1   The syntax of terms

The syntax of (untyped) terms in higher order logic is given by

$$\text{M} \quad ::= \quad c \mid v \mid (\text{M N}) \mid \lambda v.\,\text{M}$$

where c ranges over constants, v ranges over variables, and M and N range over
terms. Terms of the form (M N) are called *applications*, and terms of the form $\lambda v.\,$M
are called *abstractions*. In this book, sans serif identifiers (e.g. a, b, Dev, Xor) and
non-alphabetical symbols (e.g. $\supset$, $=$, $\forall$) are generally used for constants, and italic
identifiers (e.g. v, x, x_1, f, fn, F) are used for variables. Small roman capitals (e.g.
M, N, P) will be used as syntactical meta-variables ranging over terms.

2.2.2   Free and bound variables and substitution

An occurrence of variable v in a term M is *bound* if it occurs after the dot in a
subterm of M that has the form '$\lambda v.\,$N'. An occurrence of a variable which is not
bound is called *free*. If N_1, ..., N_n are terms and v_1, ..., v_n are distinct variables,
then the metalinguistic notation $M[N_1,\ldots,N_n/v_1,\ldots,v_n]$ stands for the result of
simultaneously substituting N_i for v_i for $1 \leq i \leq n$ at every free occurrence of v_i in

the term M, with the condition that no free variable in any N_i becomes bound in the result of the substitution.

When the notation $M[N_1, \ldots, N_n]$ is used, it should be understood to represent a term obtainable as the result of such a substitution. In particular, '$M[v_1, \ldots, v_n]$' means a term obtainable by a substitution of the form $M[v_1, \ldots, v_n/u_1, \ldots, u_n]$ such that none of the variables $v_1, \ldots, v_n$ becomes bound in the result. Thus $M[v_1, \ldots, v_n]$ represents a term in which there may be free occurrences of the variables $v_1, \ldots, v_n$. This notation should usually be understood simply to mean a term with exactly n distinct free variables $v_1, \ldots, v_n$. Finally, in a context in which a term has been written $M[v_1, \ldots, v_n]$, subsequent use of the notation $M[N_1, \ldots, N_n]$ should be understood to mean $M[N_1, \ldots, N_n/v_1, \ldots, v_n]$.

2.2.3 Well-typed terms

Every term in higher order logic must be *well-typed*. Writing $M{:}\sigma$ indicates explicitly that the term M is well-typed with type σ. The well-typed terms of higher order logic are defined inductively as follows:

- *Constants:* Each constant c has a fixed type called its *generic* type. If the generic type σ of a constant c is polymorphic, then $c{:}\sigma'$ is a well-typed term for any substitution instance σ' of σ.

- *Variables:* Strictly speaking, the term $v{:}\sigma$ is a well-typed variable for any identifier v and type σ. In practice, however, one normally avoids using the same identifier as both a variable and a constant.

- *Applications:* If $M{:}\sigma_1 \rightarrow \sigma_2$ and $N{:}\sigma_1$ are well-typed terms, then the application $(M\ N){:}\sigma_2$ is a well-typed term. It represents the result of applying the function denoted by 'M' to the value denoted by 'N'.

- *Abstractions:* If $v{:}\sigma_1$ is a variable and $N{:}\sigma_2$ is a well-typed term, then the abstraction $(\lambda v.\,N){:}\sigma_1 \rightarrow \sigma_2$ is a well-typed term. It represents the function whose value for an argument $M{:}\sigma_1$ is given by $N[M/v]$.

Only well-typed terms are considered syntactically well-formed. There is an algorithm, due to Milner [96], which can be used to infer the type of a term from the generic types of the constants it contains. The HOL mechanization of higher order logic uses this algorithm to assign consistent types to terms entered by the user. In general, types will not be mentioned explicitly when it is clear from the form or context of a term what its type must be. Where necessary, the notation $M{:}\sigma$ will be used to indicate the types of variables or constants.

2.2.4 Primitive and defined constants

There are three primitive constants in higher order logic:

$$=: \alpha \to \alpha \to bool, \qquad \supset : bool \to bool \to bool \qquad \text{and} \qquad \varepsilon : (\alpha \to bool) \to \alpha.$$

The two constants $=$ and $\supset$ denote the binary relations of equality and material implication respectively. These relations are represented by higher order functions; when applied to a value, both $=$ and $\supset$ yield boolean-valued functions. For example, the application $(\supset P)$ denotes a function of type $bool \to bool$. When applied to a boolean term Q, the resulting term $(\supset P) Q$ expresses the proposition that P implies Q. Likewise, the application $(=x) y$ means x equals y. The third primitive constant, the constant ε, is a *selection* operator for higher order logic [64, 83]. A description of this constant is deferred until section 2.5.

The three symbols $=$, $\supset$, and ε are the only primitive constants in higher order logic; all other constants are introduced by means of constant definitions. These are equations that extend the logic by introducing new constants as atomic abbreviations for specific terms. Formally, constant definitions, like type definitions, are axioms that extend the object-language syntax of higher order logic. The rule of definition which allows these axioms to be added to the logic is explained in section 2.4.

Some basic constants which can be defined using this rule of definition are listed in the table shown below. These constants are part of the conventional notation of mathematical logic. In higher order logic, they need not be taken as primitives but can instead be formally defined so that they have their usual logical properties. The definitions of these basic constants will not be given here, but full details can be found in Gordon's paper [41] or the HOL manual [47].

Basic Defined Constants		
Constant	*Generic Type*	*Description*
¬	$bool \to bool$	negation
∧	$bool \to bool \to bool$	conjunction
∨	$bool \to bool \to bool$	disjunction
∀	$(\alpha \to bool) \to bool$	universal quantification
∃	$(\alpha \to bool) \to bool$	existential quantification
∃!	$(\alpha \to bool) \to bool$	unique existence
T, F	$bool$	truth-values: *true* and *false*

2.2.5 Notational abbreviations for terms

The pure syntax of terms described above can be made to resemble the conventional notation of predicate calculus by means of the following metalinguistic abbreviations.

Infixes. Certain applications of the form $(c\ M)\ N$ are abbreviated by writing the constant c in infix position. These include applications of the constants $=$, $\wedge$, $\vee$, and $\supset$. The expression $(P \wedge Q) \supset P$, for example, should be read as a metalinguistic abbreviation for $(\supset ((\wedge\ P)\ Q))\ P$. Other infix notation will be introduced as needed.

Omission of Parentheses. The following conventions allow parentheses to be omitted when writing terms. Application associates to the left, so terms of the form $(\ldots ((M_1\ M_2)\ M_3) \ldots M_n)$ can also be written $M_1\ M_2\ M_3 \ldots M_n$. When the constants $\supset$, $\wedge$, and $\vee$ occur in infix position, they associate to the right. For example, the expression $P \supset Q \supset R$ means $P \supset (Q \supset R)$. Application of the basic constants $\neg$, $\wedge$, $\vee$, $\supset$, and $=$ binds less tightly than application of other functions. For example, the expression $f\ x \wedge g\ x$ means $(f\ x) \wedge (g\ x)$. These basic constants are themselves ranked in decreasing order of tightness of binding as follows: $\neg$, $\wedge$, $\vee$, $\supset$, $=$. For example, the expression $\neg P \wedge Q \supset R$ means $((\neg P) \wedge Q) \supset R$. Finally, the scope of a lambda binding '$\lambda v.$' is assumed to extend as far to the right as possible. For example, the expression $\lambda f.\ f\ x$ means $\lambda f.\ (f\ x)$ rather than $(\lambda f.\ f)\ x$.

Quantifiers. In higher order logic, the quantifiers $\forall$, $\exists$, and $\exists!$ are functions that map predicates (i.e. boolean-valued functions) to truth-values. For example, the application $\exists\ (\lambda x.\ x{=}x)$ expresses the proposition that there is at least one value for which the predicate $\lambda x.\ x{=}x$ is true. In the usual notation of predicate calculus, this proposition is written $\exists x.\ x{=}x$. In higher order logic, this conventional notation for quantification is defined by means of the metalinguistic abbreviations shown below.

Abbreviations for Quantifiers			
Term	*Abbreviation*	*Term*	*Abbreviation*
$\forall\ (\lambda v.\ M)$	$\forall v.\ M$	$\forall v_1.\ \forall v_2.\ \cdots\ \forall v_n.\ M$	$\forall v_1\ v_2\ \ldots\ v_n.\ M$
$\exists\ (\lambda v.\ M)$	$\exists v.\ M$	$\exists v_1.\ \exists v_2.\ \cdots\ \exists v_n.\ M$	$\exists v_1\ v_2\ \ldots\ v_n.\ M$
$\exists!\ (\lambda v.\ M)$	$\exists! v.\ M$	$\exists! v_1.\ \exists! v_2.\ \cdots\ \exists! v_n.\ M$	$\exists! v_1\ v_2\ \ldots\ v_n.\ M$

A similar abbreviated notation is used for nested λ-abstractions. For example, the expression $\lambda x\ y\ z.\ M$ is an abbreviation for the term $\lambda x.\ \lambda y.\ \lambda z.\ M$.

Other Notation. The expression '$f \circ g$' stands for the composition of the functions f and g and satisfies the usual defining equation $\forall x.\ (f \circ g)\ x = f(g(x))$. The symbol $\circ$ is a defined constant written in infix position. The expression $(P \Rightarrow M\ |\ N)$ means 'if P then M else N' and is an abbreviation for the term $\mathsf{Cond}\ P\ M\ N$, where Cond is an appropriately-defined constant. (See [41] for its definition.) Other metalinguistic abbreviations and notational conventions are introduced in later chapters.

2.2.6   Constants for the defined types num and $\sigma_1 \times \sigma_2$

Some constants associated with the basic defined types num and $\sigma_1 \times \sigma_2$ are shown in the table below. These constants are standard mathematical notation, and they can all be defined using the rule for constant definitions so that they have their conventional mathematical meanings. (See [41] for the actual definitions.) The usual elementary theorems about the natural numbers (e.g. Peano's Postulates), theorems of arithmetic, and theorems about pairs follow from these definitions.

Constants for the Defined Types num and $\sigma_1 \times \sigma_2$			
Type	*Constants*	*Generic Type*	*Description*
num	$0, 1, 2, \ldots$	num	numerals
	Suc	$num{\rightarrow}num$	successor function
	$+, \times, \mathsf{Exp}$	$num{\rightarrow}num{\rightarrow}num$	arithmetic functions
	$<, \leq, >, \geq$	$num{\rightarrow}num{\rightarrow}bool$	ordering relations
$\sigma_1 \times \sigma_2$	,	$\alpha{\rightarrow}\beta{\rightarrow}(\alpha \times \beta)$	pairing (infix)
	Fst Snd	$(\alpha \times \beta){\rightarrow}\alpha$ $(\alpha \times \beta){\rightarrow}\beta$	projection functions for the components of pairs

2.3   Sequents, theorems and inference rules

The style of proof used in Gordon's formulation of higher order logic is a form of natural deduction [64] based on Milner's formulation of PPλ. In this style of proof, *sequents* are used to keep track of assumptions. A sequent is written $\Gamma \vdash P$, where Γ is a set of boolean terms called the assumptions and P is a boolean term called the conclusion. The assumptions and conclusion of a sequent correspond to formulas in predicate calculus. In higher order logic, however, there is no special syntactic class of formulas—these are simply terms of type $bool$.

The sequent notation $\Gamma \vdash P$ can be read as the metalinguistic assertion that there exists a natural deduction proof of the conclusion P from the assumptions in Γ. When the set of assumptions Γ is empty, the notation $\vdash P$ is used. In this case, P is a formal *theorem* of the logic. The same notation is used for the *axioms* of the logic; these are theorems which are just postulated to be true.

The inference rules of higher order logic are stated using the notation illustrated by the rule shown below.

$$\text{MP:} \quad \frac{\Gamma_1 \vdash P \supset Q \qquad \Gamma_2 \vdash P}{\Gamma_1 \cup \Gamma_2 \vdash Q}$$

This is the rule of *modus ponens*, one of the primitive inference rules of the logic;

it states that from the two formulas P ⊃ Q and P one can immediately infer the formula Q.

The formulas occurring as lines in a natural deduction proof can depend on assumptions, in the sense of having been deduced from them. The sequent notation makes this dependence on assumptions explicit. For example, the MP rule states that if P ⊃ Q depends on assumptions Γ_1 and P depends on assumptions Γ_2, then the inferred formula Q depends on the union of Γ_1 and Γ_2. This notation for inference rules resembles a sequent calculus, in which sequents are assertions in the object language. The proof system of higher order logic, however, is essentially natural deduction. Sequents are used merely to keep track of assumptions, and a sequent $\Gamma \vdash$ P should be read as a meta-theorem about provability by natural deduction.

The formulation of higher order logic presented by Gordon in [41] has five axioms, eight inference rules , and two rules of definition. (The later formulation [47] adds a third rule of definition.) All the theorems about hardware in this book follow by formal proof using only this primitive logical basis. Fully detailed proofs, however,

$$\text{ASSUME:} \quad \frac{}{\{P\} \vdash P}$$

$$\text{REFL:} \quad \frac{}{\vdash N = N} \qquad \text{BETA\_CONV:} \quad \frac{}{\vdash (\lambda v. N)\, M = N[M/v]}$$

$$\text{ABS:} \quad \frac{\Gamma \vdash M = N}{\Gamma \vdash (\lambda v. M) = (\lambda v. N)} \qquad (v \text{ not free in } \Gamma)$$

$$\text{INST\_TYPE:} \quad \frac{\Gamma \vdash P}{\Gamma \vdash P[\sigma_1, \ldots, \sigma_n / \alpha_1, \ldots, \alpha_n]}$$

$$\text{DISCH:} \quad \frac{\Gamma \vdash P}{\Gamma - \{Q\} \vdash Q \supset P} \qquad \text{MP:} \quad \frac{\Gamma_1 \vdash P \supset Q \qquad \Gamma_2 \vdash P}{\Gamma_1 \cup \Gamma_2 \vdash Q}$$

$$\text{SUBST:} \quad \frac{\Gamma_1 \vdash N_1 = N_1' \quad \ldots \quad \Gamma_n \vdash N_n = N_n' \quad \Gamma \vdash P}{\Gamma_1 \cup \ldots \cup \Gamma_n \cup \Gamma \vdash P[N_1', \ldots, N_n'/N_1, \ldots, N_n]}$$

Figure 2.1: The primitive inference rules of higher order logic.

will not be given for these theorems—complete proofs are generally very long and complex, and they are therefore best generated by computer.[1] In general, verification of the propositions in this book is left to the reader's intuitive judgement of logical truth. A complete list of the axioms of higher order logic is therefore not given here. For reference, however, the primitive inference rules of higher order logic are summarized in figure 2.1. See the HOL manual [47] for an explanation of these rules.

Of particular relevance to later chapters are the mechanisms provided by higher order logic for making object-language definitions. Definitions allow the logic to be consistently extended with new notation (i.e. with new constants and types) without postulating *ad hoc* axioms to give meaning to this notation. This provides a means for introducing special-purpose notation for hardware verification into the logic in a rigorous and purely formal way. The following sections provide an overview of these definitional mechanisms.

2.4   Constant definitions

The only primitive constants of higher order logic are the three constants $=$, $\supset$, and ε. All other constants must be introduced using the following rule of definition.

> CONSTANT DEFINITIONS: If $M{:}\sigma$ has no free variables, M does not contain the identifier c, there are no type variables in M not also present in σ, and c is not already the name of a constant, then a new constant c with generic type σ can be defined by extending the syntax of the logic to include c as a constant and adding the axiom $\vdash c = M$.

The axiom $\vdash c = M$ introduced by this rule simply makes the new constant c an object-language abbreviation for the term M. Adding a new constant by postulating a definitional axiom of this kind is a *conservative extension* of the logic. That is, for any formula P not containing the new constant c being defined, $\vdash P$ is a theorem of the extended logic if and only if it is a theorem of the original logic. In particular, $\vdash F$ is a theorem of the extended logic only if it is a theorem of the original logic. Thus adding axioms that define new constants to the logic will not introduce inconsistency that was not already there; adding definitional axioms is 'safe'.

2.4.1   Derived constant definitions

The advantage of definitional approach to introducing new notation, as opposed to the axiomatic method, is that the primitive rules of definition in higher order logic admit only sound extensions to the logic. The disadvantage is that this allows one to make definitions of only certain very restricted forms. All other kinds of definitions must be derived by formal proof from equivalent but possibly rather

---

[1]The HOL system, described in section 2.8, is specifically designed to generate such proofs.

complex primitive ones. A *derived* rule of definition is a non-primitive principle of definition that has been justified by giving a general procedure for constructing a certain class of such proofs.

An example is a derived rule for making function definitions of the forms

$$\vdash c\, v_1\, v_2\, \ldots\, v_n = M \qquad \text{and} \qquad \vdash c(v_1, v_2, \ldots, v_n) = M,$$

where c is the constant being defined and all the free variables in M are included among $v_1, v_2, \ldots, v_n$. For every such defining equation, there is a provably equivalent equation of the more basic kind allowed by the primitive rule of constant definition.

For example, every theorem of the form $\vdash c\, x = M[x]$, where c is a constant and x is the only free variable in $M[x]$, is equivalent to a corresponding definitional axiom of the form $\vdash c = \lambda x.\, M[x]$. An equation of the form $\vdash c\, x = M[x]$ can therefore be regarded as a legitimate definition of the function constant c, justified by means of a derived principle of definition based on the primitive rule for constant definitions. Any defining equation of the two forms shown above can be justified in a similar way. The actual proofs of these defining equations are straightforward and can easily be automated in a theorem prover like HOL.

2.5 The primitive constant ε

The primitive constant $\varepsilon{:}(\alpha{\rightarrow}bool){\rightarrow}\alpha$ is a function that maps predicates on values of type α to values of type α. The semantics of ε can be described informally as follows. If $P{:}\sigma{\rightarrow}bool$ is a predicate on values of type σ, then the application '$\varepsilon\, P$' denotes a value of type σ for which P is true. If there is no such value, then the term '$\varepsilon\, P$' denotes a fixed but unknown value of type σ.

This informal semantics is formalized by one of the five axioms of higher order logic, namely the single axiom for ε shown below.

$$\vdash \forall P\, x.\, P\, x \supset P(\varepsilon\, P) \tag{2.1}$$

It follows from this axiom that ε can be used to obtain a term that provably denotes a value having some property P from a theorem stating merely that such a value exists. Formally, if P is a predicate and $\vdash \exists x.\, P\, x$ is a theorem of the logic, then so is $\vdash P(\varepsilon\, P)$. The only axiom for ε is theorem 2.1, so when $\vdash \exists x.\, P\, x$ holds the only (non-trivial) facts that can be proved about $\varepsilon\, P$ are the logical consequences of $\vdash P(\varepsilon\, P)$. In particular, if more than one value satisfies P, then it is not possible to prove which of these values the term '$\varepsilon\, P$' denotes. And if no value satisfies P, then nothing significant can be proved about $\varepsilon\, P$.

In practice, applications of the form $\varepsilon\, P$ are usually treated as atomic names for values having the property P, and it is often convenient to abbreviate such ε-terms by defining new constants that denote them. If $P[x]{:}bool$ is a term with no free variables other than x, and $\vdash \exists x. \mathrm{P}[x]$ is a theorem of the logic, then the equation $\vdash c = (\varepsilon \, \lambda x. \mathrm{P}[x])$ defines a constant c such that $\vdash \mathrm{P}[c/x]$. In presenting proofs, this fact will be used as a derived rule of inference to justify omitting the intermediate inference steps needed to introduce a constant c and prove $\vdash \mathrm{P}[c/x]$, given a theorem of the form $\vdash \exists x. \mathrm{P}[x]$.

Certain applications of the constant ε are abbreviated by notation similar to that introduced for quantifiers on page 15. An application of the form '$\varepsilon \, \lambda v. \mathrm{P}$', in which ε is applied to an abstraction, is written '$\varepsilon v. \mathrm{P}$'. This abbreviated term can be read 'a value v such that P'. Nested applications of the form $\varepsilon v_1 . \varepsilon v_2 . \cdots \varepsilon v_n . \mathrm{P}$ are abbreviated by $\varepsilon v_1 \, v_2 \ldots v_n . \mathrm{P}$.

2.6   Recursive definitions

In a constant definition $\vdash c = \mathrm{M}$, the constant c being defined must not occur in the term M on the right hand side of the equation. This restriction rules out the possibility of making inconsistent recursive definitions, for example $\vdash \mathrm{P} = \neg \, \mathrm{P}$. Constants that satisfy recursive equations are therefore not directly definable by the rule for constant definitions. To define such a constant one must first prove that the desired recursive equation is in fact satisfiable. The constant can then be defined non-recursively using ε, and the required recursive equation can be derived from this definition using the method outlined in the previous section.

Suppose, for example, the aim is to define a constant c such that $\vdash c = \mathrm{M}[c]$, where M[c] is a term that contains c. To ensure that this equation is consistent, one must first show that it can be satisfied by *some* value. This is done by proving the theorem $\vdash \exists x. \, x = \mathrm{M}[x]$. Using ε, the constant c can then be defined non-recursively by the equation

$$\vdash c = (\varepsilon x. \, x = \mathrm{M}[x]).$$

Using the axiom for ε discussed above, the desired recursive equation $\vdash c = \mathrm{M}[c]$ then easily follows from this non-recursive definition of c and the previously-proved consistency theorem $\vdash \exists x. \, x = \mathrm{M}[x]$.

An important application of this method is in defining constants that denote primitive recursive functions on the natural numbers. Many functions that arise in proofs about hardware are primitive recursive, and constants that denote such functions can be defined formally using the *primitive recursion theorem* shown below.

$$\vdash \forall x f. \, \exists! fn{:}num{\rightarrow}\alpha. \, (fn \, 0 = x) \wedge (\forall n. \, fn \, (\mathrm{Suc} \, n) = f \, (fn \, n) \, n) \tag{2.2}$$

An outline of the proof of this theorem is given by Gordon in [41]. The theorem states the validity of function definitions by primitive recursion on the natural numbers: for any x and f there exists a unique total function $fn{:}num{\rightarrow}\alpha$ which satisfies the primitive recursive definition whose form is determined by x and f.

Theorem 2.2 can be used to justify the introduction of a constant to denote any particular function that satisfies primitive recursive defining equations. Choosing appropriate values for x and f in theorem 2.2 yields a theorem that asserts the (unique) existence of the desired function, and a constant can then be introduced to name this function. For example, taking x and f in a suitably type-instantiated version of theorem 2.2 to be $\lambda m.\, m$ and $\lambda f\, x\, m.\, \mathsf{Suc}(f\, m)$ yields, after beta-reduction and other simplifications, the following theorem.

$$\vdash \exists fn.\, (\forall m.\, fn\, 0\, m = m) \wedge (\forall n\, m.\, fn\, (\mathsf{Suc}\, n)\, m = \mathsf{Suc}(fn\, n\, m))$$

This asserts the existence of a recursively-defined addition function on the natural numbers. By using ε and the method discussed in section 2.5, a new constant $+$ can then be introduced to denote this function. This yields the theorem

$$\vdash (\forall m.\, +\, 0\, m = m) \wedge (\forall n\, m.\, +\, (\mathsf{Suc}\, n)\, m = \mathsf{Suc}(+\, n\, m)),$$

which states that the function $+$ satisfies the usual primitive recursive definition of addition. If the constant $+$ is written in infix position, this is equivalent to the two equations shown below.

$$\vdash 0 + m = m$$
$$\vdash (\mathsf{Suc}\, n) + m = \mathsf{Suc}(n + m)$$

There is a procedure by which recursion equations like these can be derived systematically from the primitive recursion theorem. (See [42] for the details.) This justifies the principle of function definition by primitive recursion as a derived rule of definition in the logic. This rule is used in this book, but details of the proofs that underlie these definitions are omitted.

The primitive recursion theorem applies to recursive function definitions on the natural numbers only. Recursive functions defined on other logical types, for example recursive data types such as lists and trees, are discussed in chapter 5.

2.7 Type definitions

The primary function of types in higher order logic is to eliminate inconsistency. For this purpose, all that is needed are the primitive types—type variables, the types *ind* and *bool*, and compound types built from these atomic ones using $\rightarrow$. But there is a pragmatic reason for having a richer syntax of types than is strictly necessary for consistency. Extending the syntax of types allows more natural and concise formulations of propositions about hardware than are possible with only primitive type expressions. For example, introducing new types to name sets of values that arise naturally in specifications of device behaviour helps make these specifications clear and concise. This pragmatic motivation for a rich syntax of types is similar to the motivation for the use of abstract data types in high-level programming languages: using higher-level data types reduces complexity by abstracting away from the details of how values are represented.

The next two sections describe a method for extending the logic with new type constants and type operators. This method is based on a formal rule of definition which allows axioms of a restricted form to be added to the primitive basis of the logic. These axioms are analogous to definitional axioms for new constants; they define new types in terms of other type expressions already present in the logic. Like the rule for constant definitions, the rule for type definitions ensures that adding a new type is a consistent extension of the logic.[2]

2.7.1   The rule for type definitions

The mechanism for defining logical types is analogous to the way in which abstract data types are defined in the programming language Standard ML [116]; new types are defined in terms of the values of already existing ones. More precisely, a type definition is made by adding an axiom to the logic which asserts that there is a bijection between the set of values denoted by a new type and an appropriate subset of the values denoted by a type expression already present in the logic.

Suppose that σ is a type of the logic, and $P{:}\sigma{\to}bool$ is a predicate on values of type σ which defines some useful subset of the set denoted by σ. A type definition introduces a new type expression σ_P that denotes a set of values having exactly the same properties as the subset defined by P. This is done formally by adding an axiom to the logic which states that there is a bijection f from the new type σ_P to the set of values that satisfy P:

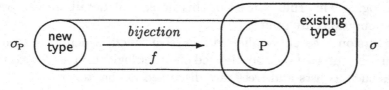

The function f can be thought of as a representation function, a function that maps each value of the new type σ_P to the value of type σ that represents it. Because f is a bijection, it can be shown that the set denoted by σ_P has the same properties as the subset of σ defined by P. The new type σ_P is therefore defined in terms of σ, and its properties are determined by the choice made for the predicate P.

This method is used to define both type constants and type operators. When the representing type σ contains no type variables, the new type being defined is a type constant. But when σ does contain type variables, the new type is an expression of

---

[2]It is not, however, technically a conservative extension. But type definitions do preserve the property of the logic having a standard model—see [47] for the details.

the form $(\alpha_1, \ldots, \alpha_n)op$, where $\alpha_1, \ldots, \alpha_n$ are all the type variables in σ. In this case, the type definition has the effect of introducing a new n-ary type operator op.

The formal rule of definition for adding new types is shown below. For clarity, the rule is stated for the case when the type being defined is a type constant. The general rule, which also allows definitions of type operators, is similar. It will not be shown here, but the details can be found in [41, 47].

> TYPE DEFINITIONS: If $P{:}\sigma{\rightarrow}bool$ has no free variables, both σ and P contain no type variables, $\vdash \exists x. P\,x$ is a theorem of the logic, and σ_P is not already the name of a type constant, then a new type constant σ_P can be defined by extending the syntax of types to include σ_P and adding the axiom
>
> $$\vdash \exists f{:}\sigma_P{\rightarrow}\sigma.$$
> $$(\forall a_1\, a_2.\,(f\,a_1 = f\,a_2) \supset (a_1 = a_2)) \wedge (\forall r. P\,r = (\exists a.\,r = f\,a))$$
>
> to the primitive basis of the logic.

The axiom introduced by this rule simply states that there is a bijection from σ_P to the values of type σ that satisfy P. The restriction that P satisfies $\vdash \exists x. P\,x$ ensures that the defined type constant σ_P denotes a non-empty set. This restriction is necessary because all type expressions in the logic must denote non-empty sets.

2.7.2 Deriving abstract characterizations of defined types

A type definition merely states that the values of a new type are in a one-to-one correspondence with the values in a particular subset of an existing type. This is a logically sufficient but not particularly useful form of characterization; in practice, one needs theorems that describe a new type more abstractly. The idea is to prove a collection of theorems that state the essential properties of a new type without reference to how it is defined. These theorems constitute a derived 'axiomatization' of the type; once they have been proved, they become the basis for all further reasoning about it.

With this approach, introducing a new type (or type operator) in higher order logic involves two steps:

1. Find an appropriate representation for the new type, and make a type definition based on this representation.

2. Use the definition of the new type and the properties of its representation to prove a set of theorems that abstractly characterizes it.

The motivation for first defining a new type and then deriving abstract 'axioms' for it is that this process guarantees consistency. Simply postulating plausible-looking axioms to express the properties of a new type can inadvertently make the logic inconsistent.[3] But deriving abstract 'axioms' from a type definition amounts to giving a formal proof of their consistency by showing that there is a model for them.

The usual axioms for the cartesian product type $\sigma_1 \times \sigma_2$ are a simple example of the result of this two-step process. The essential properties of this type are captured formally by the three theorems shown below.

$$\vdash \forall a{:}\alpha.\ \forall b{:}\beta.\ \mathsf{Fst}(a,b) = a$$

$$\vdash \forall a{:}\alpha.\ \forall b{:}\beta.\ \mathsf{Snd}(a,b) = b$$

$$\vdash \forall p{:}(\alpha \times \beta).\ p = (\mathsf{Fst}\ p, \mathsf{Snd}\ p)$$

These three theorems can be derived by formal proof from an appropriate definition for the type operator $\times$ and suitable definitions of the three constants ',' (the infix pairing operator), Fst, and Snd. All the usual properties of pairs follow from these theorems, and once they have been proved it becomes unnecessary to know how the type $\sigma_1 \times \sigma_2$ was represented and defined.

All the non-primitive types and type operators used in this book can be defined formally using the primitive rule of type definition and the two-step 'methodology' discussed above. Full details of the definitions of these types (including the basic types *num* and $\sigma_1 \times \sigma_2$) and outline proofs of the abstract characterizations for them can be found in [88].

2.8   The HOL system

The HOL system is a mechanized proof-assistant developed by Mike Gordon at the University of Cambridge for conducting proofs in higher order logic [42]. It has been used primarily to reason about the correctness of hardware, but much of what has been developed in HOL for hardware verification—the theory of arithmetic, for example—is also fundamental to many other applications. The underlying logic and basic facilities of the system are completely general and can in principle be used to support reasoning in any area that can be formalized in higher order logic.

HOL is based on the LCF approach to interactive theorem proving and has many features in common with the LCF systems developed at Cambridge and Edinburgh.[4] Like LCF, the HOL system supports secure theorem proving by representing its logic in the strongly-typed functional programming language ML (not Standard ML, but

---

[3]The axioms for the list type $(\sigma)list$ in the early definition of higher order logic given in [41] illustrate this danger. These axioms are inconsistent, and this survived notice for several years after they first appeared in print.

[4]The implementation of HOL is a modified version of Cambridge LCF [102], which is itself a development of the Edinburgh LCF system [48]. The basic approach to mechanized theorem proving used in all these systems is due to Milner.

an earlier version of the language [30]). Propositions and theorems of the logic are
represented by ML abstract data types, and interaction with the theorem prover
takes place by executing ML procedures that operate on values of these data types.
Because HOL is built on top of a general-purpose programming language, the user
can write arbitrarily complex programs to implement proof strategies. Furthermore,
because of the way the logic is represented in ML, such user-defined proof strategies
are guaranteed to perform only valid logical inferences.

2.8.1   The representation of higher order logic in ML

ML is a strongly-typed language. All expressions in the language have types, and
only consistently-typed expressions are syntactically well-formed. The syntax of
types in ML resembles that of types in higher order logic. For example, the ML type
`int->bool` is the type of functions (i.e. functional programs) that take an integer
as a parameter and return a boolean as a result. The rules for type-checking ML
expressions are similar to the rules for well-typed logical terms given on page 13.
An ML function call '`f(x)`', for example, will be accepted by the type-checker only
if there are ML types ty_1 and ty_2 such that the function `f` has type ty_1-> ty_2 and
the value `x` has type ty_1.

This type discipline is the basis for the soundness of proofs in the HOL system.
HOL is built on top of ML by extending the set of built-in ML data types with an
abstract data type `thm`, values of which are theorems of higher order logic. There are
no literals of type `thm`, i.e. it is not possible to obtain a value of type `thm` simply by
typing one in. There are, however, certain ML identifiers which are given values of
type `thm` when the system is built. These values correspond to the axioms of higher
order logic. In addition, HOL makes available several built-in ML functions that take
theorems as arguments and return theorems as results. Each of these corresponds
to one of the primitive inference rules of the logic and returns only theorems that
logically follow from its input theorems using the corresponding inference rule. The
ML type-checker ensures that values of type `thm` can be generated only by applying
these functions, either to previously-generated values of type `thm`, or to the values
of type `thm` that represent axioms. Every value of type `thm` must therefore be an
axiom or have been obtained by computation using the functions that represent the
primitive inference rules of the logic—i.e. every theorem in HOL must be generated
from the axioms using the inference rules. The ML type-checker guarantees the
soundness of the HOL theorem prover; a theorem can be generated in the system
only by valid formal proof.

In addition to the primitive inference rules, there are many *derived inference rules*
available in HOL. These are ML procedures that perform commonly-used sequences
of primitive inferences by calling the appropriate ML functions which represent the
primitive inference rules. Derived inference rules relieve the HOL user of the need to
give explicitly all the primitive inference steps of a proof. The ML code for a derived

rule can be arbitrarily complex; but it will never return a theorem that does not follow by valid logical inference, since a theorem can be obtained only by a series of calls to the primitive inference rules.

Among the derived inference rules in HOL are several derived *rules of definition*. These are ML programs that automatically carry out the proofs necessary to derive non-primitive forms of definition from equivalent primitive ones. The HOL system's derived rules of definition include recursive concrete type definitions and primitive recursive function definitions over these types as well as certain forms of inductive definition [88, 89].

2.8.2   Efficiency in HOL

The LCF approach to theorem proving used in HOL ensures the soundness of any proof done in the system. This approach, however, is computationally expensive. Completely formal proofs of even simple theorems can take thousands of primitive inferences, and when these proofs are done in the HOL system, all the inferences involved must actually be carried out by executing the corresponding ML procedures.

There are, however, two important features of the HOL system which, together, allow efficient proof strategies to be programmed. The first of these is a feature inherited from LCF: theorems proved in HOL (or LCF) can be saved on disk and therefore do not have to be generated each time they are needed in future proofs. The second is the expressive power of higher order logic itself, which allows useful and very general lemmas to be stated in the logic. The amount of inference that a programmed proof rule must do can therefore be reduced by appeal to pre-proved general theorems from which the desired results follow by a relatively small amount of deduction. These theorems can then be saved and used by the derived inference rule in future proofs. This strategy of replacing run-time inference by pre-proved theorems is possible in HOL because type polymorphism and higher-order variables make the logic expressive enough to yield theorems of sufficient generality.

This simple strategy for making derived rules efficient is illustrated by the method for automating recursive type definitions described in [88], where a theorem is given from which an abstract characterization for any concrete recursive type can be deduced with relatively little inference.

2.8.3   Interactive proof in HOL

HOL supports two styles of interactive proof: *forward* proof and *backward* proof. In the forward style, inference rules are simply applied in sequence to previously proved theorems until the desired theorem is obtained. The user specifies which rule is applied at each step of the proof, either interactively or by writing an ML program that calls the appropriate sequence of procedures. This is usually not the easiest way of doing a proof in the system, since the exact details of a proof are rarely known in advance.

It is often simpler to find the proof by working backwards from the statement to be proved (called a *goal*) to previously proved theorems that imply it. This is the backward, or goal-directed, proof style. The HOL system, following LCF, supports this style of proof by means of ML functions called *tactics*. These break goals down into increasingly simple subgoals, until the subgoals obtained can be proved directly from theorems already derived. Again, the user specifies which tactic to use at each step. In addition to breaking a goal down into subgoals, a tactic also constructs a sequence of forward inference steps which can be used to prove the goal, once the subgoals have themselves been proved. This is necessary because all theorems in the system must ultimately be obtained by forward proof. This approach to proof using tactics is due to Milner. It is described in detail in [42, 48, 97, 102].

2.8.4 Hardware verification using HOL

Machine-assisted theorem proving is essential for large-scale formal verification of hardware correctness. The HOL system is widely used for hardware verification, and several substantial and well-documented projects have been done using it. A notable example is Cohn's (partial) verification of the Viper microprocessor using HOL. Cohn's proof employs a mixture of the forward and backward proof styles and is described in full detail in the papers [29, 27]. Joyce has also verified the design of a microprocessor used higher order logic and the HOL system [78, 79]. Birtwistle and Graham describe a verification using HOL of the design of an SECD chip [8]. This device, designed by a team at the University of Calgary, is a custom CMOS chip that implements Henderson's version of Landin's abstract architecture for evaluating expressions in the λ-calculus. HOL has also been used for many smaller verification exercises—for example Herbert's proof of correctness for a component of the Cambridge Fast Ring Network [65], and the verification of a CMOS cell library by Gordon, Loewenstein and Shahaf [46].

Chapter 3

Hardware Verification using Higher Order Logic

This chapter describes the basic techniques for using higher order logic to specify hardware behaviour and to prove the correctness of hardware designs.

The advantages of higher order logic as a formalism for hardware verification are discussed by Gordon in [45] and by Hanna and Daeche in [57, 58]. Higher order logic makes available the results of general mathematics, and this allows one to construct any mathematical tools needed for the verification task in hand. Its expressive power permits hardware behaviour to be described directly in logic; a specialized hardware description language is not needed. In the formulation used here, new constants and types can be introduced by purely definitional means. This allows special-purpose notation for hardware verification to be introduced without the danger associated with postulating *ad hoc* axioms. In addition, the inference rules of the logic provide a secure basis for proofs of correctness; a specialized deductive calculus for reasoning about hardware behaviour is not required.

Although higher order logic has all these pragmatic advantages, to say that it is the only feasible formalism for hardware verification would be an exaggeration. Some other approaches are briefly discussed at the end of this chapter. Furthermore, higher order logic does not make traditional hardware description languages (HDLs) obsolete. A major problem with these languages is that they usually lack a formal semantics, which precludes using them to reason about hardware behaviour. But the definition of semantics for HDLs in higher order logic and other formalisms is an active area of research, which promises to combine the familiar syntax of hardware description languages and the rigour of logic in one framework [13, 15, 36, 112].

3.1 Specifying hardware behaviour

The approach to specifying hardware behaviour explained in this section is well-known (see, for example, [21, 45, 57, 71]). The idea is to specify the behaviour of a device by describing the combinations of values that can be observed on its external wires. A specification is expressed formally in logic by a boolean-valued term whose free variables correspond to these external wires. This term imposes a constraint on the values of these variables. To reflect the behaviour of the device it specifies, the term is chosen so that the combinations of values that satisfy this constraint are precisely those which can be observed simultaneously on the corresponding external wires of the device itself.

As an example, consider the device Dev shown below.

This device has four external wires: a, b, c, and d. A specification of its behaviour in logic is therefore a boolean-valued term of the form $S[a, b, c, d]$, constructed so that for all values of the free variables a, b, c, and d:

$$S[a, b, c, d] = \begin{cases} \mathsf{T} & \text{if the values } a, b, c, \text{ and } d \text{ could occur} \\ & \text{simultaneously on the corresponding} \\ & \text{external wires of the device Dev} \\ \\ \mathsf{F} & \text{otherwise} \end{cases}$$

There is no restriction on the form this specification must take; any notation needed to describe the behaviour of Dev may be used, provided it can be defined formally. Since higher order logic is designed as a foundation for mathematics, it has the advantage that it is possible (in principle) to define in the logic all the mathematical concepts required to describe the behaviour of any particular device.

This approach to specifying hardware describes its behaviour only in terms of the values that can be observed externally. No information about internal state is used in a specification. Furthermore, there is no distinction between the inputs and the outputs of a device; the constraint imposed by a specification on its free variables need not be a functional one. Of course, the free variables in a specification need not stand for the values on the physical 'wires' of an actual circuit; they may represent more abstract externally observable quantities. Both specifications of hardware primitives and specifications of the intended behaviour of designs can therefore be expressed by this method.

The logical types of the free variables in a specification model the range of values that a device operates on. These variables very commonly have the type $bool$,[1] which represents the two-valued set of boolean logic levels. But many other types are also used in specifications.

Specifications can describe either the purely combinational behaviour or the time-dependent (sequential) behaviour of hardware. These two possibilities are discussed below in sections 3.1.2 and 3.1.3. Specifications may also only partially describe the behaviour of a device. This is discussed in section 3.1.4.

---

[1]or, in specifications of time-dependent behaviour, the type $num \rightarrow bool$; see section 3.1.3.

3.1.1 Abbreviating specifications

The primitive and derived rules for constant definitions provide a simple mechanism for abbreviating hardware specifications in logic. A specification is just a boolean-valued term with free variables, and an object-language abbreviation for it can be introduced by defining a constant to name the constraint it imposes on these variables. This is sometimes called the 'relational' method of specifying hardware, because specifications are then just n-place relations in logic.

For example, the specification of the device shown in the previous section can be abbreviated using a constant Dev defined by

$$\vdash \mathsf{Dev}(a, b, c, d) = \mathsf{S}[a, b, c, d].$$

This introduces a 4-place relation symbol 'Dev' into the logic and makes the term 'Dev(a, b, c, d)' an object-language abbreviation for the specification 'S$[a, b, c, d]$'. The constant Dev can be regarded as an atomic name for a class of devices, each of which exhibits the same kind of behaviour as the others but has differently labelled external wires. Any particular device in this class is specified by an application of Dev to an appropriate 4-tuple of variables; for example, the term 'Dev(w, x, y, z)' specifies a device with external wires named w, x, y, and z. This can be viewed as providing an object-language notation for 'parameterized' specifications of hardware.

An alternative way of abbreviating the specification S$[a, b, c, d]$ is to define the constant Dev by the equation

$$\vdash \mathsf{Dev}\ a\ b\ c\ d = \mathsf{S}[a, b, c, d].$$

This makes Dev a higher order function, rather than a predicate on 4-tuples. This *curried* representation of relations in logic is equivalent to the more usual tupled form; it is largely a matter of syntactic convenience which form is used.

3.1.2 Specifying combinational behaviour

The most direct application of formal specification in logic is in describing the purely combinational behaviour of hardware. A highly simplified view is taken of hardware behaviour; only the static behaviour of a device is specified, and the possibility that its behaviour may change over time is ignored. An example is the following combinational specification of an exclusive-or gate.

$$\vdash \mathsf{Xor}(i_1, i_2, o) = (o = \neg(i_1 = i_2))$$

The variables i_1, i_2, and o in this specification have logical type *bool*; they range over the two boolean truth-values T and F, which are used to represent the two logic levels 'true' and 'false'. The term $\mathsf{Xor}(i_1, i_2, o)$ describes a relationship between these variables that corresponds to the way an exclusive-or gate works in practice: the output o is true exactly when either i_1 or i_2 is true but not both.

The output of the exclusive-or gate shown above is a function of its two inputs. The full generality of the relational method of specifying behaviour is therefore not needed; the combinational behaviour of this gate could be specified equally well by the function Xor defined below.

$$\begin{array}{c} i_1 \\ i_2 \end{array} \Rrightarrow\!\!D\!\!\!\longrightarrow \quad \neg(i_1 = i_2) \qquad \vdash \mathsf{Xor}(i_1, i_2) = \neg(i_1 = i_2)$$

In general, however, a hardware device may have bidirectional external wires, used for both input and output. And one advantage that relational specifications have over functional ones is that they easily allow one to describe such devices. This is illustrated by the N-type transistor and its formal specification shown below.

$$\begin{array}{c} g \\ \mid \\ s \!-\!\!\sqcap\!\!-\! d \end{array} \qquad\qquad \vdash \mathsf{Ntran}(g, s, d) = (g \supset (d = s))$$

In this specification, the source s and the drain d of the transistor are bidirectional. It follows from the specification that if the gate g has the value T then s and d must have the same boolean value—the source and drain are connected. But the direction of signal flow (if any) between s and d is not expressed by the term 'T $\supset (d = s)$', which merely states that the values on s and d must be equal.

Because relational specifications do not distinguish between inputs and outputs, they can be interpreted in ambiguous ways. For example, Hoare [71] has pointed out that the transistor specification shown above might lead one to conclude that if opposite values are supplied to the source and drain, then this will cause the gate to have the value F. The exclusive-or specification defined above also admits of ambiguous interpretation. It can be viewed as the specification of a gate with output o and inputs i_1 and i_2. But it can also be viewed as the specification of an exclusive-or gate with output i_2 and inputs i_1 and o. The purely logical properties of the term 'Xor(i_1, i_2, o)' are appropriate to both interpretations.

This problem of ambiguous interpretation is partly due to the inadequacy of combinational specifications in general. Real hardware has delay: a change of value on the inputs takes time to produce a change on the output. But a combinational specification presents only a static view of behaviour, and it cannot suggest the temporal relationship between a change of input and a change of output. For this, another way of describing behaviour is needed.

3.1.3 Specifying sequential behaviour

The sequential behaviour of hardware devices can be specified in logic by using functions to model the sequences of values that appear on their external wires at successive moments of time. Time is represented by the natural numbers, which in higher order logic are denoted by the defined logical type *num*. The sequence of values that appears on a wire is represented by a function $f{:}num{\rightarrow}\sigma$, so that the value present on the wire at any particular time t is given by the application $f(t)$. A specification of the time-dependent behaviour of a device is then a constraint on variables that range over such functions.

The type σ in the type of a function $f{:}num{\rightarrow}\sigma$ models the range of possible values of the externally-observable quantity represented by f. Very commonly, this is just the type *bool* of boolean truth-values; in this case we call f a *signal*. Of course other types may also be used.

The behaviour of a rising-edge triggered D-type flip-flop can be specified in logic by the term $\mathsf{Dtype}(ck, d, q)$ defined, together with an auxiliary function Rise, as shown below.

$$\vdash \mathsf{Rise}\ ck\ t = \neg ck(t) \wedge ck(t{+}1)$$

$$\vdash \mathsf{Dtype}(ck, d, q) = \forall t.\, q(t{+}1) = (\mathsf{Rise}\ ck\ t \Rightarrow d\ t \mid q\ t)$$

In this specification, instants of discrete time are represented by natural numbers, and the variables ck, d, and q range over functions of logical type $num{\rightarrow}bool$. The term $\mathsf{Dtype}(ck, d, q)$ specifies the sequential behaviour of a flip-flop by imposing constraints on the functions ck, d, and q. Whenever the clock ck rises, the value on the input d is sampled and appears on the output q one time unit later. When the clock does not rise, the output q remains stable over time.[2]

This example illustrates why it is advantageous to use *higher order* logic, rather than first order logic, to specify hardware behaviour. In general, a specification of sequential behaviour is a term that imposes constraints on higher order variables. In the D-type specification, for example, the variables ck, d, and q are higher order variables; they range over functions of logical type $num{\rightarrow}bool$. The constant Rise is also higher order. It denotes a function that both takes a function as an argument and yields a function as a result. Higher order logic directly supports these higher order entities, and this expressive power allows natural and direct specifications of sequential behaviour.

3.1.4 Partial specifications

A *partial* specification is one that does not completely describe the behaviour of a device but only selected aspects of it. The ability to write such specifications

---

[2]This is, of course, a highly simplified view of the behaviour of a D-type flip-flop. More realistic formal specifications of this device can be found in [45, 58, 66, 109].

is essential if formal verification is to be applied to very large or complex designs. To be intelligible, the specification of intended behaviour for such a design must concentrate on only its most important features—a complete description may be too complex to understand.

Partial specifications can be expressed in logic in a particularly natural and direct way. Specifications are just terms that describe constraints on the values that can appear on the external wires of a device. A partial specification simply constrains these values in only the situations that are regarded as significant or relevant. In all other situations, it leaves them unconstrained.

The specification of a D-type flip-flop given above is a simple example. The equation for the output wire q constrains the value of $q(t+1)$ for all times t, but the value of $q(0)$ is left unconstrained. This is therefore only a partial specification of behaviour; the value of the output q at time zero is not specified. If time zero is thought of as the time at which the D-type is 'switched on', then this specification says that it may be in any state at this initial time.

This D-type example is a somewhat special case; the output is unspecified at only a single point in time. A more general application of partial specifications is illustrated by the schematic specification shown below.

$$\vdash \mathsf{Dev}(i, o) = (\mathrm{P}[i] \supset (o = \mathrm{E}[i]))$$

Here, a partial specification is used to leave undefined the value on the output o for certain values on the input i. The term $\mathrm{P}[i]$ is a condition on this input value, and the output o is required to take the value $\mathrm{E}[i]$ only for inputs that satisfy this condition. This is reflected formally by the fact that if $\mathrm{P}[i] = \mathrm{F}$ then the implication '$\mathrm{P}[i] \supset (o = \mathrm{E}[i])$' is satisfied for any value o. This is a very common technique for writing partial specifications that define the behaviour a device is required to exhibit only for selected input values (examples can be found in [45, 58, 65, 87]). Such specifications are appropriate when it is known that the device will be used in an environment where only these input values arise and it is therefore unnecessary to specify its required behaviour for all possible inputs.

Another important application of partial specifications is in constructing realistic models of hardware designs. The value of a proof of correctness depends on the accuracy of the model used, and this model must therefore not make unrealistic assumptions about the behaviour of the design. Using partial specifications for the components of a design can sometimes avoid this danger.

For example, the partial specification of a D-type flip-flop shown above provides a convenient way of constructing a model that does not presuppose that the device it describes starts operating in a well-defined initial state. If a different instance of the D-type specification is used for each memory element in the model of a device, then at time zero each bit of state can be either true or false. A proof of correctness will therefore have to show that the device can be reset from *any* initial state. This is a significant result, because it shows that the device can be made to work when started in an unknown or random initial state (for example, when switched on).

A less valuable result is obtained if a total specification is used—for example one in which the output of every flip-flop has the value F at time zero. A model in which this total specification is used includes a hidden (and perhaps unjustifiable) assumption, namely that the device starts off in a state in which every memory element is storing F. A similar problem arises even if the output of each flip-flop at time zero is some fixed but unknown boolean value arb,[3] rather than the particular value F. In this case, it is assumed that at time zero the device is in a state in which every memory element stores the *same* value. A proof based on this model will show only that the device is correct if starts off in such a state. But this may be an unrealistic assumption—there may be no way to get from the initial state of the device (its state when switched on) into a state satisfying the assumption. The problem is that using a total specification gives a model that assumes too much about the initial state of the device it describes. Using a partial specification avoids this problem.

3.2   Deriving behaviour from structure

Both the actual behaviour of hardware primitives (e.g. gates, or transistors) and the required behaviour of hardware devices can be specified directly in logic using the methods explained above. The aim of verification, however, to prove the correctness of hardware designs—that is, to verify that devices built by connecting components together behave as intended. A method is therefore also needed for constructing descriptions of composite devices from the specifications of their parts. This is done by first writing a specification for each kind of primitive hardware component used in a design. Instances of these specifications are then combined syntactically to obtain a term that describes the net behaviour of the entire device. This term is called a *model* of the composite device.

Two syntactic operations on terms, called *composition* and *hiding*, are used to construct models. These represent two ways in which a physical device can be constructed from its components: composition represents the operation of wiring parts together; and hiding represents the operation of 'insulating' wires from the environment by designating them as unavailable for further connection to other wires. A model is constructed syntactically by applying these two operations to the logical terms that describe the constituent parts of a device. This approach is based on the algebraic method of modelling concurrent systems, originally proposed by Milne and Milner in [93]. The next two sections describe how these operations can be represented in higher order logic for modelling hardware.

---

[3] Such a value can be defined formally by $\vdash$ arb $= \varepsilon x.$ F. See section 2.5.

3.2.1   Composition

Composition models the effect of joining two devices together by connecting them at all identically-labelled external wires. Syntactically, composition is done by forming the *conjunction* of the logical terms that specify the devices to be connected together.

For example, suppose that the two devices D_1 and D_2 are specified by the boolean terms $S_1[a, x]$ and $S_2[x, b]$ respectively, as shown below.

$$a \underline{\quad\boxed{D_1}\quad} x \qquad\qquad x \underline{\quad\boxed{D_2}\quad} b$$

$$S_1[a, x] \qquad\qquad\qquad S_2[x, b]$$

The terms $S_1[a, x]$ and $S_2[x, b]$ describe the values that can be observed independently on the external wires of the devices D_1 and D_2. If these two devices are connected together by the wire x, the values that can be observed on the external wires of resulting composite device are just those that can be observed simultaneously on the wires of *both* its components. A model of the resulting behaviour is therefore given by the logical conjunction of the terms which specify these components:

$$a \underline{\quad\boxed{D_1}\quad} x \underline{\quad\boxed{D_2}\quad} b$$

$$S_1[a, x] \wedge S_2[x, b]$$

The result is a term with three free variables a, x, and b. This term constrains the values on the wires of the composite device to be exactly those allowed by the constraints imposed by both $S_1[a, x]$ and $S_2[x, b]$.

3.2.2   Hiding

A model constructed by composition will usually have free variables that correspond to wires used only for internal communication between components. Hiding models the effect of insulating these wires from the environment, making them internal to the device. Syntactically, hiding is done by *existentially quantifying* the free variables in a term that correspond to internal wires. This results in a term in which these variables are bound and no longer represent externally observable values.

For example, consider the term

$$S_1[a, x] \wedge S_2[x, b],$$

which describes the device shown in the previous section. Suppose that the wire corresponding to the free variable x is used for internal communication only. A model in which this wire is internal to the device, hidden from the environment, is given by existentially quantifying over this variable:

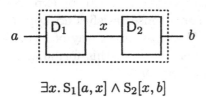

$$\exists x. \, S_1[a, x] \wedge S_2[x, b]$$

The result is a term in which only the variables a and b, corresponding to the external wires of the device, are free. This term expresses the constraint that two values a and b can be observed on the external wires of the device exactly when there is *some* internal value x such that the constraints for the components of the device are satisfied.

Hiding is thus achieved 'syntactically' by variable binding (in the example above, making x a bound variable) and 'semantically' by existential quantification (over the values x could have).

3.2.3   A note on terminology

A specification constructed by the methods explained above is called a *model* of the device it describes. What is meant by a 'model' is a logical expression that describes the behaviour of a particular device. Such an expression models the device in the sense that its purely formal properties are intended to reflect at least some aspects of how the physical hardware itself really behaves. For example, the term 'Dtype(ck, d, q)' defined above is a model of the behaviour of a D-type flip-flop. A term constructed by composition and hiding from the specifications of the parts used in a design is also referred to as a model. Such a term models the behaviour of a device built from smaller components.

The word 'model' is also used in another sense. It is sometimes used to mean the mathematical model of a particular technology for building hardware—for example TTL or CMOS. A model in this sense consists of a set of specifications for the primitive components from which all devices implemented in a certain technology are built. For example, a collection of specifications for the primitive components used in CMOS circuits (i.e. transistors) is called a CMOS 'transistor model'. Such a model consists of a particular choice of specifications for the primitive components used in all CMOS designs.

Both senses of the word 'model' are used in the literature on hardware verification. In this book, the sense in which the term is used is always indicated explicitly if it may not be clear from the context in which it occurs. In particular, 'design model' is used to mean the model of an individual device, and 'hardware model' is used to mean the model of a technology.

3.3   Formulating correctness

Once a model of a design has been constructed, its correctness can be expressed by a proposition which asserts that this model in some sense satisfies an appropriate specification of required or intended behaviour. The most direct way of formulating this satisfaction relationship is by logical equivalence. With this formulation, the correctness of a design is asserted by a theorem of the form

$$\vdash M[v_1, \ldots, v_n] = S[v_1, \ldots, v_n],$$

where the term $M[v_1, \ldots, v_n]$ is the model of the device asserted to be correct and the term $S[v_1, \ldots, v_n]$ is the specification of required behaviour. This theorem states that the truth-values denoted by these two terms are the same for any assignment of values to the free variables v_1, ..., v_n. Indeed, one may generalize over these variables to obtain the logically equivalent theorem

$$\vdash \forall v_1 \ldots v_n. M[v_1, \ldots, v_n] = S[v_1, \ldots, v_n].$$

For simplicity of presentation, however, correctness theorems are usually written without the universal quantifiers. Equivalence gives a formal notion of correctness in which the design is clearly 'correct' with respect to the specification, since the behaviour described by the model is identical to that required by the specification.

Formulating correctness by equivalence is usually appropriate only for small or relatively simple hardware designs; for more complex devices, it is often impractical to express correctness this way. Indeed, for all but the simplest devices, it is clear that satisfaction must not be logical equivalence. If correctness is formulated by an equivalence of the form shown above, then the specification must impose the same constraint on the free variables v_1, ..., v_n as the model does. But if the device to be proved correct is large or complex, and if the model of the device is at all realistic, then both the model and *any logically equivalent specification* are likely to be large and complex as well.[4] This means that the specification of intended behaviour may be too complex to be seen to reflect the designer's intent—the correctness of the *specification* may be no more obvious than the correctness of the design itself.

For the specification of a complex device to be intelligible to the designer, it must generally be limited to a more abstract view of its behaviour than is given by the model of its design. The satisfaction relation used to express correctness must usually be one of *abstraction*, rather than strict equivalence. The formalization of this notion of correctness in logic is discussed in detail in chapter 4.

---

[4]The specification may, of course, be expressed in a more concise notation than the model, but the perspicuity obtainable in this way is limited.

3.4   An example correctness proof

In this section, a very simple example is given to illustrate the basic approach to verification introduced above. The example is the formal verification of the standard CMOS circuit design for an inverter. The purpose of this example is to provide a very simple preliminary illustration of hardware verification using higher order logic; it is not suggested that the particular correctness result demonstrated here has any significant practical value. More realistic examples are given in later chapters.

3.4.1   The specification of required behaviour

The first step in the verification of an inverter is to write a formal specification of required behaviour for the design. A specification of the combinational behaviour that a correctly implemented inverter is required to exhibit is given by the term Not(i, o) defined below.

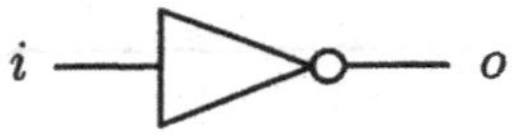

$\vdash \mathsf{Not}(i, o) = (o = \neg i)$

This specification simply states that the boolean value on the output o must be the logical negation of the value on the input i.

3.4.2   Specifications of the primitive components

The specifications shown in figure 3.1 describe the four different kinds of primitive components used in CMOS circuit designs. The terms Pwr p and Gnd g specify the behaviour of power (VDD) and ground (VSS) nodes. The terms Ntran(g, s, d) and Ptran(g, s, d) specify the behaviour of N-type and P-type transistors. These are modelled as ideal switches controlled by the boolean values present on their gates. For example, Ntran(g, s, d) acts as an ideal switch which is closed when g=T and open when g=F. This is, of course, a highly simplified model of CMOS transistor behaviour.

$\vdash$ Gnd $g = (g = \mathsf{F})$ 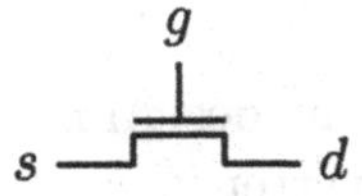 $\vdash \mathsf{Ntran}(g, s, d) = (g \supset (d = s))$

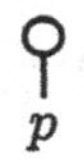

$\vdash$ Pwr $p = (p = \mathsf{T})$ 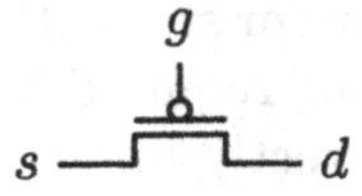 $\vdash \mathsf{Ptran}(g, s, d) = (\neg g \supset (d = s))$

Figure 3.1: CMOS primitives.

These four specifications constitute a model of the CMOS technology in general, in the sense that a formal description of the behaviour of any particular circuit implemented in CMOS can be constructed from instances of these primitives using composition and hiding. This is an example of a 'model' in the second sense discussed above in section 3.2.3.

3.4.3   The design model

Given the CMOS primitives defined in the previous section, the model $\mathsf{Inv}(i, o)$ shown in figure 3.2 can be constructed using conjunction '$\wedge$' to compose specifications that describe the four constituent parts of a standard CMOS inverter. The variables p and g in the definition represent wires that are internal to the inverter's design. They are therefore hidden from the environment using the existential quantifier '$\exists$'. The result is that the term $\mathsf{Inv}(i, o)$ is satisfied precisely when the values i and o satisfy the constraint imposed by the specifications of the parts used in the design, for some internal values p and g.

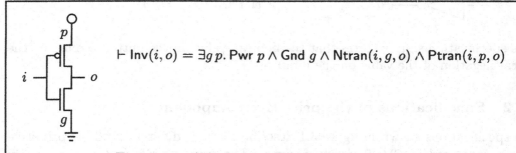

$$\vdash \mathsf{Inv}(i, o) = \exists g\, p.\ \mathsf{Pwr}\ p \wedge \mathsf{Gnd}\ g \wedge \mathsf{Ntran}(i, g, o) \wedge \mathsf{Ptran}(i, p, o)$$

Figure 3.2: A formal model of a CMOS inverter.

3.4.4   The proof of correctness

The correctness of the inverter design is expressed formally by the following theorem.

$$\vdash \forall i\, o.\ \mathsf{Inv}(i, o) = \mathsf{Not}(i, o)$$

Here, the satisfaction relation between the design model and the specification is just logical equivalence; the design of an inverter is easily simple enough for correctness to be formulated in this way. The theorem states that the behaviour described by the model exactly matches the behaviour required by the specification. The CMOS circuit shown in figure 3.2 therefore correctly implements the specified behaviour.

An outline of the proof of this correctness theorem is given below. Each step in this proof can be justified formally using only the primitive and derived inference rules of higher order logic. Only an informal sketch of the proof is given here. A completely formal proof of this particular correctness result is trivial to generate using the HOL theorem proving system.

Proof Outline:

1. The definition of the constant Inv is:

    $\vdash \mathsf{Inv}(i, o) = \exists g\, p.\, \mathsf{Pwr}\, p \wedge \mathsf{Gnd}\, g \wedge \mathsf{Ntran}(i, g, o) \wedge \mathsf{Ptran}(i, p, o)$

2. Expanding with the definitions of **Pwr, Gnd, Ntran,** and **Ptran** yields:

    $\vdash \mathsf{Inv}(i, o) = \exists g\, p.\, (p = \mathsf{T}) \wedge (g = \mathsf{F}) \wedge (i \supset (o = g)) \wedge (\neg i \supset (o = p))$

3. By the meta-theorem $\vdash (\exists v.\, (v = E) \wedge P) = P[E/v]$ this is equivalent to:

    $\vdash \mathsf{Inv}(i, o) = (i \supset (o = \mathsf{F})) \wedge (\neg i \supset (o = \mathsf{T}))$

4. Simplifying using the laws $\vdash (o = \mathsf{F}) = \neg o$ and $\vdash (o = \mathsf{T}) = o$ gives:

    $\vdash \mathsf{Inv}(i, o) = (i \supset \neg o) \wedge (\neg i \supset o)$

5. Replacing $i \supset \neg o$ by its contrapositive $o \supset \neg i$ yields:

    $\vdash \mathsf{Inv}(i, o) = (o \supset \neg i) \wedge (\neg i \supset o)$

6. By the definition of boolean equality, this is equivalent to:

    $\vdash \mathsf{Inv}(i, o) = (o = \neg i)$

7. Abbreviating the right hand side using the definition of **Not** gives:

    $\vdash \mathsf{Inv}(i, o) = \mathsf{Not}(i, o)$

8. Generalizing the free variables i and o gives:

    $\vdash \forall i\, o.\, \mathsf{Inv}(i, o) = \mathsf{Not}(i, o)$

Steps 1–3 of this proof illustrate a procedure which is commonly used in proofs of hardware correctness. This consists of first expanding with the definitions of the parts used in the model and then eliminating the equations for internal wires using the meta-theorem shown in step 3. For other examples of the use of this technique, see [8, 21, 45, 87]. Step 4 of the proof makes use of the fact that formulas in higher order logic are just boolean terms. Steps 5–8 amount to an elementary proof in propositional calculus.

This example, although trivial in itself, is a typical illustration of the general approach to proving a design correct in higher order logic. First, a specification of intended behaviour is written. A specification is then written for each different kind of primitive device used in the design, and instances of these specifications are composed to obtain a formal model of the design. Finally, a theorem is proved which asserts that this model satisfies the specification of required behaviour. In the example given above, satisfaction is just logical equivalence. Ways of expressing satisfaction by a relationship of abstraction, rather than simply by equivalence, are discussed in detail in the next chapter.

3.5   Other approaches

Various approaches to hardware design verification have been proposed based on specification and proof in formal logic. These include methods based on first order logic, higher order logic, and temporal logic. A brief outline of some of this work is given below. For an excellent survey of research in the field generally, including many topics not discussed in this book, see the proceedings of the conferences, workshops, and summer schools in hardware verification organized in cooperation with the IFIP [12, 25, 91, 106, 107], the proceedings of the DCC workshops [77, 108] and the Banff Higher Order Workshops [7, 9, 10], and the proceedings of the Royal Society discussion meeting [70] and the hardware verification workshops held at Edinburgh [94], Leeds [84], and Cornell [82]. See also the survey article by Gupta [51] and the tutorial volume edited by Yoeli [120].

Early work using first order logic

Early work using first order logic for hardware verification was done at Stanford by T. J. Wagner [113]. Wagner uses a mechanized proof checker for first order logic to verify the correctness of clocked sequential circuits. The approach is based on an *ad hoc* axiomatization in logic of an algebra of signal transitions. Device specifications are conjunctions of first order terms that describe conditional register-transfer operations. A similar approach, based on resolution and a clausal form for conditional assignments to registers, is discussed by Wojcik in [119].

The Boyer-Moore logic and theorem prover

A notable application of first order logic is W. Hunt's verification of the FM8501 16-bit microprocessor using the Boyer-Moore theorem prover [73]. The Boyer-Moore logic, described in detail in [14], is quantifier-free first order logic with equality and axiom-schemes of induction. Hunt specifies hardware in this logic using a functional approach: the behaviour of a device is modelled by a function from its inputs to its output. Sequential behaviour is modelled by recursive functions on lists, the elements of which represent the values that appear as inputs or outputs at successive moments of time. Specifications of required behaviour are also functions, and correctness is formulated by (conditional) function equality. Structural induction on lists is used to prove the equality of functions that describe sequential behaviour.

The verification using the Boyer-Moore system of a 32-bit microprocessor with a richer instruction set than FM8501—the 'FM8502' microprocessor—is discussed by Hunt in [74]. Other recent work on hardware verification using the Boyer-Moore system includes the embedding of HDLs reported in [15, 16].

Conlan CHDLs and first order theories

Hans Eveking uses the standard notion of a logical *theory* to formalize hardware descriptions in first order logic [34, 37]. This approach was originally developed in connection with the Conlan project, which provides a family of computer hardware description languages (CHDLs) for describing digital systems [103].

Eveking's approach is to associate a first order theory with each device description written in one of these languages. Such a theory consists of the predicate calculus augmented with a collection of extra constants and axioms. The axioms are of two kinds: CHDL-specific axioms, and description-specific axioms. The CHDL-specific axioms describe the various constructs of the CHDL in which device descriptions are written. These axioms are analogous to the theorems of higher order logic that characterize the defined entities used in specifications of hardware, for example the type *num* and the constants $+$ and $\times$.

The description-specific axioms of a theory formalize the CHDL description of the particular device associated with the theory. Taken as a group, these axioms are analogous to a model in the higher order approach described in this chapter. Each axiom constrains the values that can be observed at certain points in a circuit. A typical example, taken from [34], is shown below.

$$\vdash \forall t.\, ((0 < t) \wedge (a(t{-}1) = \mathsf{T})) \supset (x(t) = y(t{-}1))$$

The functions a, x, and y represent the sequences of values that can be observed over time at three particular points in a circuit. With the higher order approach described in section 3.1.3, these sequences would be represented by variables ranging over functions; in Eveking's first order approach, they are represented by function constants. The description-specific axiom shown above characterizes the relationship that holds between the values observed at the three points of the circuit represented by these constants. In Eveking's work, both specifications of required behaviour and models of designs are theories that contain description-specific axioms of this kind.

Eveking formulates design correctness using the notion of one theory being an *extension* of another.[5] A theory T_2 is an extension of a theory T_1 if every axiom of T_2 is a theorem of T_1. Correctness is demonstrated by showing that a theory

---

[5]The notion of *interpreting* one theory in another is also used. A discussion of this way of formulating the correctness of designs is deferred until section 4.8.

describing the behaviour that a device is intended to have is an extension of a theory that models the actual behaviour of the device. This is similar to formulating correctness in higher order logic by an implication ⊢ M ⊃ S, where M is a design model and S is the specification of required behaviour.

As presented in [34], the approach described above is based on *first order* logic only. But certain concepts that often arise in reasoning about hardware behaviour are most naturally represented by higher order entities. The function Rise defined on page 33 is a typical example. In later papers (for example [37]) Eveking extends the logic he uses by including certain higher order constructs, so that such naturally higher order entities can be represented. These extensions include second order functions (i.e. 'functionals') and λ-abstractions.

First order theories for asynchronous devices

Barros and Johnson [3] use first order logic to reason about the ideal behaviour of four commonly-used asynchronous devices: the arbiter, the synchronizer, the latch, and the inertial delay. The approach taken is axiomatic; each device is described by a collection of first order axioms (i.e. a first order theory). These axioms are of three kinds: *output* axioms, *forward* axioms, and *reverse* axioms. Output axioms express idealizing assumptions about the values on the output wires of a device. The formal description of each device includes, for example, an output axiom which asserts that every transition between boolean values on its output wires takes a bounded amount of time. Forward axioms specify the effect that a particular sequence of values at the inputs of a device has on the values at the outputs. These axioms stipulate conditions on the inputs which are *sufficient* for a certain kind of output behaviour to occur. Reverse axioms specify the conditions that the inputs of a device *must* satisfy for a particular output behaviour to occur; that is, reverse axioms express *necessary* conditions on the inputs for a certain kind of output behaviour to be observed. One of the notable features of this approach is this systematic method of describing asynchronous hardware.

Barros and Johnson use equivalence of theories[6] to formalize a notion of functional equivalence for the four asynchronous devices mentioned above. Two of these devices are considered to be equivalent if they can be used to implement, or simulate, each other. More precisely, two devices D_1 and D_2 are equivalent if a circuit that behaves like D_1 can be built using instances of D_2 as primitive components, and vice versa. This notion of equivalence is expressed formally by equivalence of theories. Two devices D_1 and D_2 are equivalent if a theory describing D_1 is an extension of a theory describing an appropriate implementation of D_1 constructed using instances of D_2 as primitive components, and if a similar proposition holds in which the roles of D_1 and D_2 reversed. This approach was used to demonstrate the equivalence of the

---

[6]Two first-order theories are *equivalent* if each one is an extension of the other.

four asynchronous devices mentioned above. An outline of the proof of equivalence for the inertial delay and the latch is given in [3] to illustrate the general approach.

Higher order logic: VERITAS, LAMBDA, and Nuprl

Higher order logic was first proposed as a formalism for hardware verification in the early account of the VERITAS project given by F. K. Hanna in [55]. The VERITAS approach to hardware verification is described in detail by Hanna and Daeche in [57], and a case study (the verification of a D-type flip-flop) can be found in [58]. The term 'VERITAS' is used to refer both to the general approach to hardware verification described in these papers and to the particular species of higher order logic used.

An implementation of the VERITAS logic in the purely functional programming language Miranda[7] is described by Hanna and Daeche in [56]. This logic is a version of polymorphic higher order logic based on the typed λ-calculus. The syntax of terms is similar to the syntax of terms described in chapter 2, but the type system of VERITAS includes elements of Martin-Löf's Intuitionistic Type Theory [86] and is therefore more flexible and expressive than the type system used here. For example, the type system of the VERITAS logic includes subtypes; these are not available in the formulation of higher order logic described in chapter 2.

A development of the VERITAS logic called VERITAS+ is described by Hanna, Daeche, and Longley in [60]. The VERITAS+ logic is a hybrid of higher order logic and Intuitionistic Type Theory; its type system includes subtypes and dependent types, as well as a mechanism for defining recursive data types similar to those discussed in this book in chapter 5. See [59] for a discussion of the use of these features for hardware verification. For an account of how VERITAS+ can be used for design synthesis, see [61].

Two other higher order logics which have been used for hardware verification are the Nuprl logic and the LAMBDA logic. The Nuprl proof development system has a very powerful higher order logic based on Martin-Löf's Intuitionistic Type Theory. Basin and Del Vecchio [5] explain how Nuprl can be used to verify combinational logic. Leeser [81] and Jackson [75] also discuss the use of the Nuprl system for hardware verification and synthesis. The LAMBDA logic is a (mechanized) classical higher order logic similar to the formulation introduced in chapter 2. See Fourman's tutorial [38] for an introduction to LAMBDA and its use in reasoning about hardware. The use of LAMBDA for the transformational design of systems is discussed by Busch in [19].

Temporal logic

In addition to work based on either first order or higher order predicate calculus, formal methods for specifying hardware behaviour and reasoning about hardware

---

[7]Miranda is a trade mark of Research Software Ltd. For an overview of the language, see [111].

correctness have also been based on *temporal logic.*

An early application of temporal logic to hardware verification is the correctness proof for the design of an arbiter given by Bochmann in [11]. Bochmann uses temporal operators such as □ ('henceforth') and ▽ ('eventually') to capture the time-dependent properties of hardware components. The arbiter correctness proof is done by proving that a collection of 'invariant assertions' hold for all states that can be reached from the initial state of the device. The correctness of the arbiter design then follows from these invariant assertions.

Moszkowski [100] defines a logical formalism for specifying hardware behaviour called ITL (Interval Temporal Logic). The truth of a formula in ITL is defined relative to a finite interval of discrete time. Modal operators are used to express temporal concepts in terms of these intervals. Moszkowski shows how this can be used to describe a wide variety of time-dependent aspects of hardware behaviour. In [99], Moszkowski describes a logic programming language called 'Tempura' which is based on a subset of ITL. Moszkowski shows how this language can be used to simulate specifications of hardware behaviour written in ITL. Some extensions to ITL and further applications of ITL to hardware verification are discussed by Leeser in [80]. Hale [54] gives a formal semantics for ITL in higher order logic and uses the HOL system to prove properties of Tempura programs.

Dill and Clarke [33] present a method for automatically verifying asynchronous circuits using temporal logic. Specifications are written in a version of propositional temporal logic called CTL. A circuit is shown to satisfy a CTL specification by first translating a gate-level description of the circuit into a state transition graph. The CTL specification for the circuit is then checked automatically against this state graph representation by a program called a *model checker.* This program checks that the paths, or sequences of states, in the state transition graph satisfy the given CTL specification. The automatic verification of an arbiter is given as an example to illustrate this approach. More recent work has shown that the model checking approach is capable of verifying circuits with a remarkable number of states [18, 17].

Chapter 4

Abstraction

The notion of abstraction plays a central role in making formal proof an effective method for dealing with the problem of hardware correctness. This chapter explains how two important types of abstraction—which will be referred to as abstraction *within* a model of hardware behaviour and abstraction *between* models of hardware behaviour—can be expressed in higher order logic.[1]

Abstraction within a model has to do with the way in which the correctness of individual designs is formulated. With the approach to hardware verification introduced in the previous chapter, correctness is stated by a proposition which asserts that some relationship of 'satisfaction' holds between the model of a circuit design and a specification of its intended behaviour. This relationship must, in general, be one of abstraction—it must relate a detailed model of an actual design to a more abstract specification of required behaviour. Sections 4.1–4.6 show how this notion of correctness as an abstraction relationship can be formalized in logic and incorporated into the method of hardware verification already introduced.

The second type of abstraction, called abstraction between models, is discussed in section 4.7. Here the concern is not with the correctness of individual designs, but with the relationship between two different collections of specifications for the primitive components used in all designs. One such collection can be an abstraction of another in the sense that it presents a more abstract view of the same primitive components. In this case, either set of specifications can be used to construct a design model for any particular device. Models built using the abstract primitives will generally be simpler—but also less accurate—than models built using the more detailed ones. But for certain kinds of devices, the alternative design models may be effectively equivalent. For this class of devices the more abstract primitives should be used, since they give models that are just as accurate as the ones constructed from the detailed primitives but are easier to use. Section 4.7 shows how this concept of an abstraction relationship between models can be expressed formally in logic.

This chapter is concerned only with the general ideas behind the formalization of these two kinds of abstraction. Only a very simplified account is given here, and some of the complexities that arise in practice are either ignored or mentioned only

---

[1] Here, a 'model' means a collection of formal specifications for the different kinds of primitive hardware components from which devices are built (cf. section 3.2.3).

briefly. The subsequent chapters, however, give concrete examples to show how the general principles introduced here are applied in practice.

4.1   Abstraction within a model

There are three important ways in which the specification of required behaviour for a device can be more abstract than a realistic model of its design.

First, the specification may be only a partial specification of required behaviour. Such a specification typically stipulates how a device is expected to behave only when it is used in certain environments; in all other environments, the behaviour of the device is not specified. The design model for a device generally gives more detail than this. It describes how the device behaves when it is placed in an arbitrary environment, not just in selected environments. In this case, a partial specification of required behaviour contains less information about the behaviour of the actual device than the model does—the formal relationship between the model and the specification of required behaviour is one of *behavioural abstraction*.

Second, the specification may be expressed in terms of a higher-level notion of data than is used in the model. The design model for a multiplier, for example, might describe its behaviour in terms of the individual binary values present on each of its input and output wires. An abstract specification for this device, however, is more likely to describe its functional behaviour in terms of the numbers being multiplied than in terms of individual bits. In this case, the formal relationship between the design model and the more abstract specification is one of *data abstraction*; the specification is written using a more abstract notion of data than the concrete binary representation used in the model.

Finally, the specification may be formulated in terms of a less detailed notion of time than is used in the model. The specification of required behaviour for a large device—a microprocessor, for example—is unlikely to include as much information about how it behaves over time as will be given by a detailed model of its design. A realistic model of a microprocessor might, for example, describe its behaviour at a level of temporal detail which includes information about system timing and propagation delay. But an abstract specification is more likely to describe it as a finite state machine, in which the emphasis is on the sequence of operations carried out rather than the exact times at which they occur. This specification would then represent a *temporal abstraction* of the more detailed behaviour given by the model.

The next three sections show how correctness statements can be formulated to express these three basic kinds of abstraction relationship. In the most general case a correctness statement may involve all three types of abstraction. The aim of the next three sections, however, is to provide a clear account of the motivation for each type of abstraction, and each one is therefore considered separately. Correctness statements in which all three types of abstraction are combined are considered later.

4.1.1 Behavioural abstraction

A specification of required behaviour is simply a boolean term which expresses a constraint on the values that can appear on the external wires of a device. As was discussed in chapter 3, a *partial* specification is one which imposes only a partial constraint on these values. This constraint will be satisfied by only very restricted combinations of values in the situations or contexts for which a specific behaviour is required of the device. But in the situations where the behaviour of the device is intended to be left unspecified, the specification will be satisfied by a relatively wide range of combinations of values.

A design model, however, generally describes the combinations of values that actually do appear on the external wires of a device—even when a wider range of values is allowed by a more abstract partial specification of expected behaviour. This means that there will be combinations of values allowed by the specification that do not satisfy the constraint imposed by the design model. A satisfaction relation based on behavioural abstraction must therefore express a relationship between a strong constraint (the model) and weaker one (the specification).

It is easy to formulate a correctness statement which expresses this relationship. Suppose that $M[v_1, \ldots, v_n]$ and $S[v_1, \ldots, v_n]$ are the design model for a device and a partial specification of its required behaviour respectively. The idea that the specification imposes a less restrictive constraint on the free variables $v_1, \ldots, v_n$ than the model is expressed by the correctness theorem shown below.

$$\vdash M[v_1, \ldots, v_n] \supset S[v_1, \ldots, v_n]$$

This theorem asserts that any combination of values that satisfies the constraint imposed by the model also satisfies the constraint imposed by the more abstract partial specification of required behaviour.

This is a weaker correctness statement than the one used in the inverter example in the previous chapter, where correctness was stated as a logical equivalence. Here the model is required only to imply the specification. Every combination of values that satisfies the model must also satisfy the specification. But there may also be combinations of values which are allowed by the specification, but which (according to the model) will never actually appear on the external wires of the device itself. This reflects the fact that the partial specification is a behavioural abstraction; it stipulates only selected aspects of the device's behaviour and therefore defines a *range* of allowable behaviour. The criterion of correctness expressed by logical implication is that the behaviour actually exhibited by the device must lie somewhere within this range.

Using logical implication to express correctness means that specifications can be simplified. Relaxing the criterion of correctness from equivalence to implication allows the specification to mention explicitly only those properties of the device

which are relevant to its functional correctness. The specification can therefore be
more succinct than is possible when it is required to be logically equivalent to a
detailed design model.

4.1.2   Data abstraction

Besides being only a partial specification, the specification of intended behaviour for
a device may also be written in terms of an abstract notion of the kinds of values it
operates on. The free variables in such a specification will not stand for the values
actually present on the external wires of a device, but for more abstract externally
observable quantities; and the specification will be expressed in terms of operations
appropriate to these abstract quantities, rather than the operations carried out by
the actual hardware on a more concrete representation of these values. The logical
types of the variables that represent these abstract values will therefore generally
differ from those of the variables in the design model. A satisfaction relation based
on data abstraction must therefore relate 'concrete' values of one type in the model
to more 'abstract' values of another type in the specification.

In the simplest case, both the model and the specification express a constraint
on free variables that directly correspond to physical wires, but use different logical
types to represent the range of values that can appear on them. The model and the
specification will then be terms of the forms

$$\underbrace{M[c_1, \ldots, c_n]}_{\text{type } \sigma_c} \qquad \text{and} \qquad \underbrace{S[a_1, \ldots, a_n]}_{\text{type } \sigma_a}$$

In this very simple case, each variable a_i in the specification represents the same
externally observable value as the corresponding variable c_i in the model. The
specification, however, is expressed as a constraint on abstract values of type σ_a,
instead of the concrete values of type σ_c that represent actual physical values in the
design model.

To formulate a correctness statement that relates these two specifications, we
must translate the constraint on values of type σ_c expressed by the model into
a constraint on more abstract values of type σ_a. This can be done by using an
appropriately-defined *data abstraction function* to map values of type σ_c to values
of type σ_a. Given such a function $f:\sigma_c \rightarrow \sigma_a$, a correctness statement which expresses
a relationship of data abstraction between the model and the specification can be
formulated as shown below.

$$\vdash M[c_1, \ldots, c_n] \supset S[f\ c_1, \ldots, f\ c_n]$$

This theorem states that every combination of values c_1, ..., c_n that, according
to the model, actually appears on the external wires of the device is a concrete

representation at a lower level of data abstraction for a combination of more abstract values $f\ c_1, \ldots, f\ c_n$ which is allowed by the specification.

As with behavioural abstraction, correctness is expressed in this theorem using logical implication—but here it is a translation of the values present in the model that must satisfy the specification, rather than the values themselves. The resulting correctness statement asserts that the operations on concrete values actually carried out by the device correctly implement the required operations on abstract values expressed by the specification.

In this very simple example there is a one-to-one correspondence between the free variables in the model and the free variables in the specification. But in general this may not be the case; an observable value represented in the abstract specification by a single variable may correspond to a collection of values in the design model. For example, the model of an 8-bit binary counter might contain eight boolean variables, one for each output wire, but an abstract specification for this device may simply represent its output by a single variable ranging over numbers.

A correctness statement based on data abstraction may therefore involve more complex functions of the variables in the model than was suggested above. An example is the correctness theorem shown below.

$$\vdash M[c_1, \ldots, c_n] \supset S[f_1(c_1, \ldots, c_i), f_2(c_{i+1}, \ldots, c_n)]$$

Here the specification is a constraint of the form '$S[a_1, a_2]$' on two abstract quantities a_1 and a_2. In the model these two abstract values are represented by a collection of n concrete values. Two data abstraction functions f_1 and f_2 are used to relate these concrete values to the abstract values which they represent. Of course, many other patterns of correspondence between the concrete values in a model and the abstract values in a specification are also possible.

The advantage of data abstraction is that it allows specifications of intended behaviour to be written in terms of abstract 'high-level' operations on data, without having to specify precisely how this data is represented. Abstraction functions are used to separate the details of data representation from specifications of required behaviour. This allows specifications to be expressed in terms of the mathematical entities and notation most appropriate to an intuitively clear and textually succinct statement of the computation a device is intended to carry out.

4.1.3 Temporal abstraction

An abstract specification may give less detail about how a device behaves over time than a realistic model of the device itself. It may, for example, constrain the device's behaviour only at certain significant or 'interesting' points of time, leaving unspecified the intermediate states through which it must pass to realize this behaviour. The specification may in fact employ a more abstract notion of time than

is used in a more detailed design model—a model which *does* describe the device's
behaviour at these intermediate states. In this case, a satisfaction relation must
establish a relationship between two different representations of time—an 'abstract'
representation of time in the specification, and a 'concrete' representation of time
in the model.

In the most common type of temporal abstraction, each unit of discrete time in
the specification corresponds to an interval of discrete time in the design model. Each
point of abstract time in the specification corresponds to a point of concrete time in
the model, and the model and the specification impose the same constraint at these
corresponding points of time. But the model also imposes a constraint at points of
concrete time that lie between what are considered to be adjacent points of time at
the more abstract level of the specification. A correctness statement that relates this
model to the more abstract specification must establish a correspondence between
two different time-scales—a fine-grained one in the model and a coarse-grained one
in the specification.

This correspondence can be described formally by a function that maps each
point of abstract time to a corresponding point of concrete time. Such a function is
a *time mapping* that describes the precise relationship between the time-scale used
in the specification and the time-scale used in the model. A simple example is shown
in figure 4.1. The solid lines represent continuous or real time. The dots represent
the points of real time which constitute the two discrete time-scales involved. The
function $f\!:\!num{\to}num$ describes the relationship between these two time-scales. To
every point of time t on the abstract time-scale, f assigns a corresponding point of
concrete time $f(t)$ such that the order of time is preserved:

$$\vdash \forall t_1\, t_2.\ (t_1 < t_2) \supset (f\, t_1 < f\, t_2)$$

This establishes a correspondence between units of time on the abstract time-scale
and intervals of time on the concrete time-scale by mapping successive points of
abstract time to selected points of concrete time.

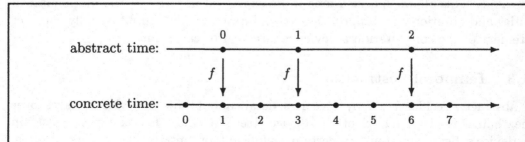

Figure 4.1: A mapping between time-scales.

Any correspondence between successive units of abstract time and contiguous intervals of concrete time can be described by a time mapping of this kind. The particular point of concrete time assigned to each point of abstract time will, of course, depend on the exact relationship between the model and the specification involved. For example, each unit of abstract time in the specification for a clocked synchronous device might correspond to an interval of concrete time between two rising edges of a clock signal in the design model. In this case, the time mapping would map points of abstract time to the points of concrete time at which these rising clock edges occur. A detailed account of how such a function can be defined is given in chapter 6.

Given an appropriate time mapping, a correctness statement that relates a design model to a specification at a higher level of temporal abstraction can be formulated as follows. Suppose that

$$M[c_1, \ldots, c_n] \quad \text{and} \quad S[a_1, \ldots, a_n]$$

are the design model and an abstract specification of required behaviour respectively. To simplify matters, assume that the free variables in both terms are functions of type $num \rightarrow bool$, and that c_i corresponds to a_i for $1 \leq i \leq n$. If the specification is a temporal abstraction of the model (in the sense discussed above) and if the device is correct, then each sequence of values a_i in the specification will be a subsequence of the values given by the corresponding variable c_i in the model. Each function a_i will be a sequence that could be obtained by sampling the values of c_i at only those points of concrete time that correspond to points of time on the abstract time-scale.

Using a time-mapping f to describe this correspondence, the required correctness statement can be formulated as shown below.

$$\vdash M[c_1, \ldots, c_n] \supset S[c_1 \circ f, \ldots, c_n \circ f]$$

This says that if the functions $c_1, \ldots, c_n$ satisfy the temporally detailed constraint imposed by the model, then the functions $c_1 \circ f, \ldots, c_n \circ f$ will satisfy the temporally abstract specification of required behaviour. The model describes the values that appear on each external wire c_i at all points of concrete time. The function f specifies which points of concrete time correspond to points of time on the more abstract time-scale. Composition on the right with f constructs an abstract sequence of values '$c_i \circ f$' from the sequence c_i by sampling it at these selected points of concrete time. The combination of abstract sequences obtained in this way must satisfy the temporally abstract specification. The resulting correctness statement says that the device satisfies the specification at each point in time that is regarded as significant or important at the abstract level of description.

The advantage of temporal abstraction is that it hides irrelevant details about intermediate state transitions. It is only at selected points of time that the device's behaviour is stipulated by the abstract specification. Furthermore, the use of an abstract time-scale not only allows the behaviour of the device at other points of time to be left unconstrained, but it also makes intermediate states transitions completely invisible to the specification. Intermediate states represented in the model by points of time on the concrete time-scale simply do not exist in the specification. This allows the specification to describe the required behaviour at only significant points of time, without also having to record precisely which points of time are of interest.

4.2   Two problems

The underlying satisfaction relation in all three forms of correctness discussed above is logical implication. In each case correctness is stated by an implication of the form

$$\vdash M[v_1, \ldots, v_n] \supset S[E[v_1], \ldots, E[v_n]],$$

in which the design model is the antecedent and an instance of the specification is the consequent. There are two problems that can arise when correctness is formulated this way. These are discussed briefly below.

4.2.1   Underspecification

Whenever the required behaviour of a device is stated by a partial specification, there is the possibility that it in fact *under*specifies the intended behaviour of the device. A partial specification may inadvertently fail to stipulate some important aspect of the intended behaviour, and therefore be satisfied by a wider range of values than is actually desired. In this case, the specification will be satisfied by some combinations of values which in fact ought *not* to appear on the external wires of the device. And when correctness is formulated as logical implication, a model that is satisfied by these undesirable combinations of values (and therefore represents an incorrect design) will, according to this formal notion of correctness, be considered correct with respect to this specification.

This is very much less likely to happen when correctness is formulated as logical equivalence. If the specification and the model are required to express the same constraint, then any weakness in the specification must either be matched exactly by a corresponding degree of 'nondeterminism' in the model or make it impossible to complete the correctness proof.

There is no complete solution to this problem—it is not possible to *prove* that a partial specification in fact covers all the essential aspects of a device's intended behaviour. And whenever it is possible to leave something unspecified, it is also possible to leave something essential unspecified.

4.2.2 Inconsistent models

A second problem with using logical implication to express correctness is that an inconsistent model then trivially satisfies any specification.[2] An inconsistent model is one which cannot be satisfied by any assignment of values to its free variables. A simple example is the term 'Pwr $x \wedge$ Gnd x', where Pwr x and Gnd x are instances of the specifications for power and ground defined in chapter 3. This term is logically equivalent to falsity, since no boolean value x can satisfy both Pwr x and Gnd x. If satisfaction is formulated as logical implication, then this inconsistent model satisfies (i.e. implies) any specification.

In general, if the model on the left hand side of an implication

$$M[v_1, \ldots, v_n] \supset S[v_1, \ldots, v_n]$$

is false for all values of the variables $v_1, \ldots, v_n$, then this implication is a theorem, no matter what constraint is imposed on these variables by specification on the right hand side of the implication. This is clearly unsatisfactory, since a theorem of this kind provides no meaningful assurance of functional correctness.

The ideal solution to this problem would be to have a collection of specifications for primitive components that always yields a consistent model, no matter how it is constructed from these primitives using the syntactic operations of composition ('$\wedge$') and hiding ('$\exists$'). This, however, may require the specifications for primitive components to be of considerable complexity. A more pragmatic solution is to check the consistency of the particular design model on which a proof of correctness is based. This can be done by proving a consistency theorem of the form

$$\vdash \exists v_1 \ldots v_n. \, M[v_1, \ldots, v_n]$$

in addition to proving an implicative correctness statement. Proving this extra theorem ensures that the model can be satisfied by at least one combination of values and therefore does not satisfy a specification merely because it is inconsistent. If none of the external wires of a device are bidirectional (i.e. every wire is either an input or an output), then a stronger consistency theorem can be formulated:

$$\vdash \forall i_1 \ldots i_n. \, \exists o_1 \ldots o_m. \, M[i_1, \ldots, i_n, o_1, \ldots, o_m]$$

This says that for any input values $i_1, \ldots, i_n$ there are output values $o_1, \ldots, o_m$ which, according to the model, are consistent with them. Again, this shows that the model does not satisfy a specification merely because it is inconsistent. An example of a consistency theorem of this second kind can be found in chapter 5.

---

[2]This is sometimes called the 'false implies anything problem' [21]. The pragmatic solution to this problem mentioned in this section is due to M. Fourman.

In general, one must prove a consistency theorem in addition to a correctness theorem whenever a satisfaction relation based on implication is used. Consistency theorems are, however, usually not proved in practice (e.g. in most of the examples presented in the literature) since the models which are used are generally simple enough to be easily seen to be consistent. But when formal verification is applied to much larger examples, it may be necessary to consider more explicitly the possibility that the models involved might be inconsistent.

4.3   Abstraction in practice

For clarity, only a highly simplified account was given above of the three most basic ways in which correctness can be expressed by a satisfaction relation based on abstraction. Some complexities which arise in practice are discussed below.

One aspect of data abstraction not discussed in the preceding sections is the mathematical task of defining logical types to provide representations of 'data'. To make effective use of data abstraction a variety of types is needed, both for writing abstract specifications of intended behaviour and for defining realistic design models. The free variables in both models and specifications stand for the values by which a device communicates with its environment. To provide a suitable representation of these values, it is generally necessary to introduce new logical types whose formal properties are appropriate to the kinds of values involved. As was discussed in chapter 2, this must be done by first defining these types and then proving that they have the desired properties. This aspect of the formalization of data abstraction is discussed in detail in chapter 5.

Another matter not discussed above is the task of defining the time mappings needed to relate abstract and concrete time-scales in temporal abstraction. The points of time at which values are of interest to an abstract specification usually depend on the operation of the device itself. For example, a specification may describe the values that must appear on the inputs and outputs of a device at points of abstract time that correspond to the rising edges of a clock. In this case, the correspondence between abstract and concrete time will depend on the behaviour of the clock, and a mapping between time-scales that describes this correspondence must be constructed from the clock signal itself. A general technique by which time mappings can be constructed in this way is discussed in detail in chapter 6.

In the correctness theorem given as an example of temporal abstraction,

$$ \vdash \mathrm{M}[c_1, \ldots, c_n] \supset \mathrm{S}[c_1 \circ f, \ldots, c_n \circ f] $$

a single time mapping f is used to construct a subsequence '$c_i \circ f$' from each sequence of values c_i in the model. In general, however, it may not be possible to use the same mapping of time-scales for every variable in the model. For example, the specification for a device driven by a two-phase clock might represent a temporal abstraction obtained by sampling the values present at certain points in the circuit on one phase of the clock and sampling the values present at other points on the other phase. A correctness statement in this case must employ two different time mappings, one for each clock phase. See chapter 6 for an example.

The difference between data and temporal abstraction is that one involves a translation of the values by which a device communicates with its environment, whereas the other involves a translation of the times at which these communications occur. When both types of abstraction are involved, the satisfaction relation used to formulate correctness can often be factored neatly into distinct data abstraction and temporal abstraction components. (See section 4.5 below.)

Although it is a generally useful principle of organization to distinguish between these two kinds of abstraction, some abstraction relationships do not fit neatly into one category or the other, but are best regarded as hybrid combinations of both. For example, the translation from a bit-serial representation of numeric data in a design model to a sequence of numbers in a specification is both a data abstraction (translating bits to numbers) and a temporal abstraction (relating several values spread out over points of concrete time to one value at a single point of abstract time). Abstractions of this kind are sometimes not easily split into distinct data and temporal components. However the formalization in logic of hybrid abstractions does not present any special problems.

The distinction between temporal/data abstraction and behavioural abstraction might seem—from a purely formal point of view—to be somewhat artificial. All the examples of data and temporal abstraction given above can also be seen as behavioural abstractions in which the specification is simply a weaker constraint than the model. Consider, for instance, the correctness theorem below.

$$\vdash M[c_1, \ldots, c_n] \supset S[f\ c_1, \ldots, f\ c_n]$$

This can be viewed as expressing a relationship of data abstraction between the model $M[c_1, \ldots, c_n]$ and an abstract specification $S[a_1, \ldots, a_n]$. But it can also be seen as expressing a relationship of behavioural abstraction in which the specification is the term '$S[f\ c_1, \ldots, f\ c_n]$'.

The distinction between these two views of the same correctness statement is a pragmatic distinction, rather than a strictly logical one. It is only when the specification for the correctness theorem shown above is taken to be the constraint on abstract values '$S[a_1, \ldots, a_n]$', where externally observable values are represented by abstract variables, that this theorem express a relationship of data abstraction. The distinction between the two possible views of this theorem is purely a matter of what is considered to be 'the specification' for the device in question.

In the preceding sections, correctness has been regarded as a relationship between a fully concrete design model and a 'top-level' abstract specification of intended behaviour. In general, however, the correctness proof for a large device must be structured hierarchically, so that a logical term which is considered to be the model of a component at one level in the hierarchy becomes the specification of required behaviour for a more concrete component at the next level down. A correctness proof therefore usually involves a hierarchy of nested abstractions. The notion of hierarchical proof is discussed in detail in section 4.6 below.

4.4   Validity conditions

One complexity not yet discussed is that a given specification may in fact present a valid abstract view of the actual behaviour of a device only under certain conditions. These are referred to as *validity conditions* on a correctness statement.

Suppose, for example, that the term $M[c_1, \ldots, c_n]$ is the model of a device and that $S[a_1, \ldots, a_n]$ is a specification expressed at a higher level of data abstraction. For a given design model and specification, it may not be possible to prove a correctness theorem of the simple form discussed above, namely

$$\vdash M[c_1, \ldots, c_n] \supset S[f\ c_1, \ldots, f\ c_n]$$

where f is an appropriate data abstraction function. The device modelled by $M[c_1, \ldots, c_n]$ may in fact behave as stipulated by the specification only for a restricted range of values on its input wires, or in only certain well-behaved environments.

In this case, one cannot prove a correctness statement of the unconditional kind shown above. Instead, the correctness statement must involve an extra constraint. This states the conditions under which the device in fact *does* behave as required by the specification, and it appears as the antecedent to an implication:

$$\vdash C[c_1, \ldots, c_n] \supset (M[c_1, \ldots, c_n] \supset S[f\ c_1, \ldots, f\ c_n])$$

The term '$C[c_1, \ldots, c_n]$' in this theorem is the validity condition on the abstraction relationship between the model and the specification. By imposing a constraint on the variables c_1, ..., c_n this term describes the environments in which the device modelled by $M[c_1, \ldots, c_n]$ does behave as required by the abstract specification. The specification presents a valid abstract view of the device's behaviour only when it is placed in an environment that satisfies this constraint.

Validity conditions can arise whenever correctness is formulated using any of the three types of abstraction discussed in the preceding sections. In each case, a validity condition expresses a constraint that must be satisfied by the environment in which a device is operating in order to ensure that it will behave as required by the specification. Particular examples of the sorts of validity conditions that arise in practice can be found in chapters 5 and 6.

4.5 A notation for correctness

In the most general case, a correctness statement can involve a combination of all three types of abstraction—data, temporal, and behavioural. Furthermore, it may employ several different time mappings, as well as data abstraction functions that map the values of several free variables in the model to a single abstract value in the specification.

For notational clarity, however, the discussion of abstraction in the remaining sections of this chapter will be restricted to correctness statements expressible by theorems of the form shown below.

$$\vdash C[c_1, \ldots, c_n] \supset (M[c_1, \ldots, c_n] \supset S[f \circ c_1 \circ g, \ldots, f \circ c_n \circ g]) \tag{4.1}$$

This is a simple combination of behavioural, temporal, and data abstraction. The term $M[c_1, \ldots, c_n]$ is the design model, and the specification is a term of the form $S[a_1, \ldots, a_n]$. The term $C[c_1, \ldots, c_n]$ is a validity condition. We assume that each concrete variable c_i has a logical type of the form $num \rightarrow \sigma_c$ and represents a sequence of externally observable concrete values of type σ_c at points of time on a concrete time-scale. The function $f : \sigma_c \rightarrow \sigma_a$ is a data abstraction function that maps concrete values of type σ_c to abstract values of type σ_a. Finally, the function $g : num \rightarrow num$ is a time mapping from the abstract time-scale used in the specification to the concrete time-scale used in the model.

Various special cases of this general form of correctness are possible. For example, the data abstraction function f can be the identity function—in which case there is no data abstraction. Likewise, the time mapping g may be the identity. Furthermore, there may be no validity condition, in which case we have a correctness statement of the unconditional form

$$\vdash M[c_1, \ldots, c_n] \supset S[f \circ c_1 \circ g, \ldots, f \circ c_n \circ g].$$

To simplify the subsequent discussion of abstraction, the following abbreviations are used. Any correctness statement of the general form given by theorem-scheme 4.1 can be written

$$\vdash C[c_1, \ldots, c_n] \supset (M[c_1, \ldots, c_n] \supset S[F\ c_1, \ldots, F\ c_n])$$

where F is the higher order *abstraction function* $\lambda c. f \circ c \circ g$. A correctness theorem of this form will therefore be abbreviated by writing

$$\vdash C[c_1, \ldots, c_n] \supset M[c_1, \ldots, c_n] \underset{F}{\text{sat}} S[a_1, \ldots, a_n]$$

where it is assumed that F stands for a function of the form $\lambda c. f \circ c \circ g$, and where the function f is a data abstraction function and the function g is a time mapping.[3] This notation will also be used for correctness theorems not qualified by a validity condition.

When it is not necessary to mention the names of externally observable values, the free variables in a correctness statement will simply be omitted. Correctness will be abbreviated by writing

$$\vdash C \supset M \underset{F}{\text{sat}} S \quad \text{and} \quad \vdash M \underset{F}{\text{sat}} S$$

where the terms C and M are a validity condition and a design model respectively, and where S is an abstract specification of required behaviour. Again, the abstraction function F is assumed to have the form $\lambda c.\, f \circ c \circ g$. Finally, when only behavioural abstraction is involved, correctness statements will be written

$$\vdash C \supset M \underset{I}{\text{sat}} S \quad \text{and} \quad \vdash M \underset{I}{\text{sat}} S$$

where I stands for the identity abstraction function $\lambda c.\, c$ (i.e. the relation $\underset{I}{\text{sat}}$ can just be read as logical implication).

4.6   Abstraction and hierarchical verification

The simple inverter proof in chapter 3 was based on a single model of the entire circuit, constructed from the specifications of all the primitive components used in its design. For devices of any considerable size, however, this direct approach is usually impractical. Instead the design must be structured into a hierarchy of models, and its correctness demonstrated by *hierarchical verification.*

Figure 4.2 shows a simple example of hierarchical verification. The design to be verified is structured into a two-level hierarchy of components. At the top level, there are two components S_1 and S_2, connected together by the internal wire z. At this level these components are considered to be primitive devices. The term M models the behaviour of the entire device at this level. It is constructed by composing the terms S_1 and S_2 and hiding the internal wire z. The correctness statement at this level of the proof asserts that the model M satisfies the specification S, which describes the intended behaviour of the entire design.

At the next level down, S_1 and S_2 become specifications of required behaviour for the two devices modelled by M_1 and M_2. These models are constructed from the specifications of the primitive components P_1, P_2, P_3, and P_4. At this level there are two separate correctness theorems to be proved. These assert that the devices modelled by M_1 and M_2 correctly implement the abstract behaviours given by the

---

[3]This notation expresses a concept of satisfaction which is similar to that formalized by the sat relation in CSP [68]. The 'sat' notation used here, however, is not the same as 'sat' in CSP.

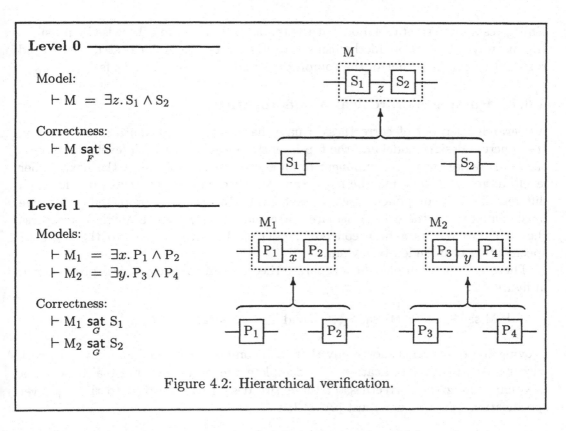

Figure 4.2: Hierarchical verification.

specifications S_1 and S_2 respectively. It follows from this, and from the correctness result for M proved at the top level, that wiring together the two devices modelled by M_1 and M_2 gives a concrete implementation of the entire design which is correct with respect to the top-level specification S.

This hierarchical approach to hardware verification is possible in logic because design models and specifications have the same syntactic status. Both are simply boolean terms, and the model-building operations of composition ('$\wedge$') and hiding ('$\exists$') can be applied to both. Terms used as abstract specifications at one level in a hierarchical proof can therefore be treated as models at the next higher level. In a formalism in which specifications and models are syntactic entities of two distinct kinds, this direct approach to hierarchical verification is not possible.

An important advantage of hierarchical verification, of course, is that even if several instances of the same kind of component are used at one level of the hierarchy, a design for that component has to be verified only once at the next level down. Furthermore, if a component is proved correct with respect to a concise, abstract specification of required behaviour, then this can be used in place of a more detailed design model at the next higher level. In the hierarchical proof shown in figure 4.2, for example, the design model M at the top level is constructed from the abstract specifications S_1 and S_2, rather than the more detailed concrete models M_1 and M_2.

This gives a more tractable model at the top level than would otherwise be possible. In this way, abstraction mechanisms—together with hierarchical structuring and regularity—can help control the complexity of large correctness proofs.

4.6.1   Putting hierarchical proofs together

A hierarchical proof of correctness usually has many intermediate levels between the concrete design model and the top-level specification. At each level, correctness theorems relate each subcomponent to an abstract specification at the next higher level. In general, there may be many separate theorems at each level, one for each different kind of component used at that level. To obtain a completed proof, one must combine all these intermediate correctness results into a single correctness theorem that relates a fully concrete model of the entire design to the top-level specification of intended behaviour.

There are, for example, three separate theorems in the hierarchical proof shown in figure 4.2:

$$\vdash M \underset{F}{\text{sat}} S, \qquad \vdash M_1 \underset{G}{\text{sat}} S_1, \qquad \text{and} \qquad \vdash M_2 \underset{G}{\text{sat}} S_2.$$

Proving these theorems shows only that each component in the hierarchy is correct with respect to its specification. To complete the proof, one must also derive a theorem stating the correctness of the entire design with respect to the top-level specification. That is, one must prove that

$$\vdash (\exists z. (\exists x. P_1 \wedge P_2) \wedge (\exists y. P_3 \wedge P_4)) \underset{H}{\text{sat}} S \qquad \text{where } H = F \circ G.$$

This theorem states that a complete and fully detailed design model constructed from the primitives P_1, P_2, P_3, and P_4 satisfies the top-level abstract specification S. The abstraction function H in this theorem is simply the composition of the abstraction functions F and G.

The aim, as illustrated by this example, is to infer the correctness of entire designs from the separate correctness results proved for each level in a hierarchical proof. For this to be possible in general, the satisfaction relation that is used must have certain special properties. These are summarized by the three rules shown in figure 4.3.

The sat-TRANS rule requires the satisfaction relation to be transitive. This allows any two correctness theorems derived for adjacent levels in a hierarchical proof to be composed to obtain a theorem that spans both levels. The resulting correctness theorem relates the model of the lower level to the abstract specification of the upper level. The abstraction function for this theorem is simply the composition of the abstraction functions for the two separate levels.

The $\wedge$-MONO rule states that composition of models must be monotonic with respect to satisfaction. This allows a correctness theorem for a composite device to be derived from separate correctness theorems for each of its subcomponents. The

- **sat-TRANS:**
$$\frac{\vdash M_1 \underset{F}{\text{sat}} M_2 \quad \vdash M_2 \underset{G}{\text{sat}} S}{\vdash M_1 \underset{G \circ F}{\text{sat}} S}$$

- **∧-MONO:**
$$\frac{\vdash M_1 \underset{F}{\text{sat}} S_1 \quad \vdash M_2 \underset{F}{\text{sat}} S_2}{\vdash (M_1 \wedge M_2) \underset{F}{\text{sat}} (S_1 \wedge S_2)}$$

- **∃-EXT:**
$$\frac{\vdash M \underset{F}{\text{sat}} S}{\vdash (\exists c.\, M) \underset{F}{\text{sat}} (\exists a.\, S)}$$

Figure 4.3: Three meta-theorems about satisfaction.

rule states that if the models M_1 and M_2 satisfy the abstract specifications S_1 and S_2 respectively, then the composition of the models will satisfy the conjunction of these specifications. It is assumed that the same abstraction function is used for both models, and this is also the abstraction function in the derived correctness result.

The ∃-EXT rule states that satisfaction must be preserved when internal wires are hidden using existential quantification. The variables c and a are corresponding concrete and abstract values in the model and the specification, respectively. The rule states that if the design model M satisfies the specification S, then the model '$\exists c.\, M$' obtained by hiding the value c will satisfy the abstract specification '$\exists a.\, S$' obtained by existentially quantifying the corresponding abstract variable a. The abstraction function in the derived correctness result is the same as the abstraction function in the original theorem.

For hierarchical verification to work, meta-theorems similar to the rules shown in figure 4.3 must hold of the satisfaction relation used in the proof. It is easy to prove that these rules hold for the class of correctness theorems introduced in section 4.5. Similar rules can also be proved for more complex satisfaction relations—for example ones in which several abstraction functions are used or several concrete values in the model are mapped to a single abstract value in the specification.

Using these rules about satisfaction, the separate theorems derived for each level of a hierarchically-structured proof can always be combined to obtain a correctness statement for the entire design. Indeed, there is a systematic procedure for proving this correctness statement.[4] A correctness theorem is obtained for each level in the hierarchy by combining the correctness results for the components at each level

---

[4]The proof may therefore never actually need to be carried out; it may be enough to know that it *could* be done. This is important when very large designs are considered.

using the rules $\wedge$-MONO and $\exists$-EXT. The rule sat-TRANS is then used to compose the correctness theorems that link adjacent levels in the hierarchy to obtain a correctness theorem that relates the most concrete design model to the top-level specification. For the simple example shown in figure 4.2, this process consists of the derivation shown below.

1. $\vdash M_1 \underset{G}{\text{sat}} S_1$ [correctness of M_1]

2. $\vdash M_2 \underset{G}{\text{sat}} S_2$ [correctness of M_2]

3. $\vdash (M_1 \wedge M_2) \underset{G}{\text{sat}} (S_1 \wedge S_2)$ [$\wedge$-MONO: 1, 2]

4. $\vdash (\exists z.\, M_1 \wedge M_2) \underset{G}{\text{sat}} (\exists z.\, S_1 \wedge S_2)$ [$\exists$-EXT: 3]

5. $\vdash (\exists z.\, S_1 \wedge S_2) \underset{F}{\text{sat}} S$ [correctness of M]

6. $\vdash (\exists z.\, M_1 \wedge M_2) \underset{FoG}{\text{sat}} S$ [sat-TRANS: 4, 5]

7. $\vdash (\exists z.\, (\exists x.\, P_1 \wedge P_2) \wedge (\exists y.\, P_3 \wedge P_4)) \underset{FoG}{\text{sat}} S$ [6, and definitions of M_1, M_2]

In the first four steps of this proof, the two correctness theorems for each of the two components at level 1 are combined using the rules $\wedge$-MONO and $\exists$-EXT. The specification '$\exists z.\, S_1 \wedge S_2$' in the resulting theorem is just the design model for level 0, and the desired correctness theorem therefore follows immediately by the transitivity of satisfaction. For a hierarchical design of more than two levels, the sequence of deductions illustrated by this example is applied recursively.

4.6.2   Hierarchical verification and validity conditions

The rules given in the previous section are somewhat over-simplified in that they do not take validity conditions into account. Where validity conditions are involved, a more complex process of reasoning is required to combine the correctness theorems obtained at each level in a hierarchical proof. In particular, one must show that any validity conditions which arise at intermediate levels in the hierarchy are in fact satisfied.[5] This may involve strengthening intermediate specifications in the hierarchy, which in turn may entail strengthening validity conditions at lower levels.

Rules for combining correctness results that include validity conditions can be formulated in several different ways. One possible formulation consists of the three extended meta-theorems about satisfaction shown in figure 4.4.

The most straightforward of these meta-theorems is the extended $\wedge$-MONO rule. This states that the validity condition for a composite design is just the conjunction of the validity conditions for its components. The extended sat-TRANS rule reflects

---

[5]See also Eveking's paper [35] for a discussion of the problem of re-analysis of correct subsystems.

- **sat-TRANS:**

$$\frac{\vdash C_1 \supset M_1 \underset{F}{\text{sat}} (C_2 \wedge M_2) \quad \vdash C_2 \supset M_2 \underset{G}{\text{sat}} S}{\vdash C_1 \supset M_2 \underset{G \circ F}{\text{sat}} S}$$

- **∧-MONO:**

$$\frac{\vdash C_1 \supset M_1 \underset{F}{\text{sat}} S_1 \quad \vdash C_2 \supset M_2 \underset{F}{\text{sat}} S_2}{\vdash (C_1 \wedge C_2) \supset (M_1 \wedge M_2) \underset{F}{\text{sat}} (S_1 \wedge S_2)}$$

- **∃-EXT:**

$$\frac{\vdash C \supset M \underset{F}{\text{sat}} S}{\vdash C \supset (\exists c. M) \underset{F}{\text{sat}} (\exists a. S)} \qquad [c \text{ not free in } C]$$

Figure 4.4: Extended meta-theorems about satisfaction.

the fact that intermediate validity conditions must be satisfied in order to compose the correctness results for two adjacent levels of a hierarchical proof. Here, the abstract specification at the lower level consists of both the model and the validity condition for the higher level. In the extended ∃-EXT rule, the validity condition on the derived correctness theorem is the same as the validity condition for the given correctness theorem. But the rule can be applied only when the existentially quantified variable c does not occur in the condition. That is, the validity condition may not *directly* constrain the value which is to be hidden.

In addition to these three extended meta-theorems, the following VCOND rule is sometimes needed.

- **VCOND:**

$$\frac{\vdash (C_1 \wedge M) \supset C_2 \quad \vdash C_2 \supset M \underset{F}{\text{sat}} S}{\vdash C_1 \supset M \underset{F}{\text{sat}} S}$$

This rule allows a strong validity condition C_2 to be replaced by a weaker validity condition C_1 when it is known that the constraint imposed by C_1 and the model M is sufficient to ensure that C_2 is satisfied. This inference is needed in order to simplify validity conditions that arise in connection with the three rules in figure 4.4. For example, the VCOND rule may be needed to eliminate a free variable c in the validity condition of a correctness theorem obtained using the ∧-MONO rule, so that the ∃-EXT rule can subsequently be applied.

An example proof which illustrates the process of reasoning represented by these rules is given in the case study discussed in chapter 6.

4.7   Abstraction between models

The type of abstraction discussed in preceding sections is called abstraction 'within' a model because it takes place within the context of a fixed choice of specifications for the primitive components of a device. In this section, an overview is given of the formalization in logic of a different type of abstraction relationship—abstraction *between* models. Here the concern is not with expressing the correctness of an individual design, but with the relationship between two formal models of a single technology. Only a brief sketch of the basic idea of abstraction between hardware models is given here, but chapter 7 contains a detailed example.

In logic, a hardware model is just a collection of terms that describe the primitive components from which devices are built. An example is the simple CMOS transistor model consisting of the specifications for power, ground, and N-type and P-type transistors defined in chapter 3. The idea of a relationship of abstraction between two such models, both of which describe the same collection of primitives, can be expressed formally as an assertion about the correctness results that can be proved about individual design descriptions using the two models.

Suppose, for example, that $\mathcal{M}_c = \{P_{c1}, \ldots, P_{cn}\}$ and $\mathcal{M}_a = \{P_{a1}, \ldots, P_{an}\}$ are two sets of specifications for the primitive components used in a particular hardware technology. Informally, the hardware model $\mathcal{M}_a$ is an abstraction of the hardware model $\mathcal{M}_c$ if the specifications that constitute $\mathcal{M}_a$ are in some sense abstractions or simplifications of the specifications that constitute $\mathcal{M}_c$. In this case, the abstract model $\mathcal{M}_a$ will capture only part of the hardware behaviour described by the more detailed model $\mathcal{M}_c$. This means that there will be correctness statements that can be formulated using the detailed primitives, but which cannot be expressed using the more abstract ones. A formalization of the abstraction relationship between the two hardware models must therefore be based on correctness statements expressible in both models.

Because the abstract primitives $\mathcal{M}_a$ are simpler than the detailed primitives $\mathcal{M}_c$, they are also likely to be less accurate. In general, inaccuracy in a hardware model is manifested by the ability to prove correctness with respect to specifications that do not reflect the actual behaviour of the physical hardware. There will therefore be correctness theorems which can be proved in the abstract hardware model $\mathcal{M}_a$, but which cannot be proved using the more detailed hardware model $\mathcal{M}_c$. A formal characterization of the abstraction relationship between these two models can be based on this difference in their accuracy.

These ideas can be expressed formally in higher order logic as follows. Let the term $M_a[a_1, \ldots, a_n]$ be an arbitrary design model constructed from the abstract primitive specifications in the set $\mathcal{M}_a$. The most general form of a correctness theorem for such a model is a behavioural abstraction of the following form.

$$\vdash M_a[a_1, \ldots, a_n] \underset{I}{\text{ sat }} S[a_1, \ldots, a_n] \tag{4.2}$$

This is the most general form, since any correctness statement that employs data or temporal abstraction is just a logical implication.[6] Suppose that $M_c[c_1, \ldots, c_n]$ is a model of the same design constructed using the detailed primitive specifications in the set $\mathcal{M}_c$. A proposition which asserts the correctness of this more detailed design model with respect to the same specification used above will have the general form

$$\vdash C[c_1, \ldots, c_n] \supset M_c[c_1, \ldots, c_n] \underset{F}{\text{ sat }} S[a_1, \ldots, a_n] \tag{4.3}$$

where F is an abstraction function and $C[c_1, \ldots, c_n]$ is a validity condition. An abstraction function will be needed here because the design model in this correctness statement is more detailed than the model in the previous one. A validity condition may be necessary for the same reason.

These two propositions express equivalent correctness assertions about the design of a particular device described using the two hardware models. Proposition 4.2 asserts the correctness of the design modelled using the abstract primitives $\mathcal{M}_a$ with respect to the specification $S[a_1, \ldots, a_n]$. Proposition 4.3 is a translation of this correctness assertion into the language of the more detailed hardware model given by the primitives $\mathcal{M}_c$. For clarity, the two correctness statements can be abbreviated by

$$M_a \underset{I}{\text{ sat }} S \qquad \text{and} \qquad C \supset M_c \underset{F}{\text{ sat }} S.$$

Given this translation from an arbitrary correctness statement in the abstract hardware model $\mathcal{M}_a$ into an equivalent correctness assertion expressed in the more detailed hardware model $\mathcal{M}_c$, the abstraction relationship *between* these two models can be characterized formally as follows. The idea that $\mathcal{M}_a$ is an abstraction of $\mathcal{M}_c$ is expressed by the assertion that any correctness statement expressible in both models which is provable in the detailed model $\mathcal{M}_c$, is also provable in the more abstract model $\mathcal{M}_a$. That is, for an arbitrary design modelled by M_c and M_a

$$\vdash C \supset M_c \underset{F}{\text{ sat }} S \quad \text{implies} \quad \vdash M_a \underset{I}{\text{ sat }} S \quad \text{for all specifications } S.$$

The idea that the abstract model $\mathcal{M}_a$ may be less accurate than the detailed model $\mathcal{M}_c$ is expressed by the assertion that the converse implication holds for only *some*

---

[6]See the discussion of this point in section 4.3.

designs. That is, for only some design models M_c and M_a will the implication

$$\vdash M_a \underset{I}{\mathsf{sat}} S \quad \text{implies} \quad \vdash C \supset M_c \underset{F}{\mathsf{sat}} S$$

hold for all specifications S. For these designs, every correctness result obtained using the abstract (i.e. simple) hardware model is also provable using the more detailed (but also more complex) model. Proving this converse implication shows that if only certain correctness assertions are of interest, then the abstract model of hardware behaviour given by the abstract primitives $\mathcal{M}_a$ is a sound basis for reasoning about the class of designs for which this implication holds.

4.8   Other approaches

The idea of abstraction is well known in software verification, and many of the ideas discussed in this chapter have analogues in methods for reasoning about program correctness. For example, the use of abstraction functions to relate specifications at two different levels of data abstraction is just the approach to reasoning about the correctness of software data representations originally proposed by Hoare in [69]. Another approach to abstraction for hardware verification is sketched below.

Interpretation of theories in first order logic

One researcher who has concentrated on the use of abstraction mechanisms in hardware verification is Hans Eveking, whose basic approach to verification was described in chapter 3. In an early work on the subject, Eveking discusses three abstraction mechanisms for suppressing detail in formal descriptions of hardware behaviour [34]. The first is a form of 'structural' abstraction, in which the values on internal wires are hidden from abstract specifications. The second abstraction mechanism uses Conlan assertions (assumptions on which proofs are based) to express behavioural abstraction. A form of temporal abstraction is provided by the third abstraction mechanism. Eveking calls this 'partially defined behaviour in the time-dimension' and gives an example in which he abstracts from a timing level flip-flop description to a register transfer level description of a conditional transfer device.

In [37] Eveking shows how abstraction can be expressed in first order logic by interpreting one theory in another. An interpretation of a theory T_2 in a theory T_1 is a syntactic translation of the axioms of T_2 such that each translated axiom is a provable theorem of T_1. Eveking shows how this concept can be used to express the correctness of a simple clocked synchronous device with respect to a temporally abstract specification.

Chapter 5 ————————————————

Data Abstraction

Data abstraction is based formally on the use of logical types to model data. To make effective use of data abstraction, it is generally necessary to define special-purpose types for both design models and specifications of required behaviour. The formal properties these types are required to have will depend on the kind of behaviour being specified, on the level of abstraction at which the devices are described, and on how accurate the specifications are intended to be.

This means that no fixed collection of logical types can be an adequate basis for specifying all devices. The types *bool* and *num→bool*, for example, are sufficient for specifying hardware behaviour at the level of abstraction where the devices used are flip-flops and combinational logic gates. But at the level of abstraction where the primitive components are transistors, an accurate model of behaviour has to account for more kinds of values than can be represented by the two truth-values T and F. It may be necessary to represent electrical signals of several different strengths, or to represent 'undefined' or 'floating' values. The types *bool* and *num→bool* are also insufficient for specifications at the register-transfer level of abstraction, where it is often necessary to specify behaviour not in terms of the values on single wires but in terms of vectors of bits and arithmetical operations on fixed-width binary words. At the architecture level, concise specifications may require comparatively complex abstract data types, such as stacks and queues.

In higher order logic, a new type can be introduced only by defining it using the type definition mechanism described in chapter 2. An appropriate representation must be found for the values of the new type, and an abstract characterization for the new type must be derived from its definition. This can involve a significant amount of formal proof. There is, however, a systematic method for defining a certain class of types in higher order logic. This chapter provides an overview of these types and gives examples to show how they can be used to support reasoning about hardware using data abstraction.

5.1 Defining concrete types in logic

Many of the sorts of values which arise naturally in specifications—especially at lower levels of abstraction—can be represented by the values of what are called 'concrete data types'. These are types whose values are generated by a set of *constructors* which yield concrete representations for these values. Examples include types that denote finite sets of atomic values (enumerated types), types that denote sets of structured values (record types) or finite disjoint unions of structured values (variant records), and types that denote sets of recursive data structures (recursive types).

There is a systematic method by which an arbitrary concrete type can be defined formally in higher order logic. This is based on the two-step process for introducing a new type explained in section 2.7.2. The required type is defined using the primitive rule of type definition, and an abstract characterization of the newly-defined type is then derived from its definition. The resulting characterization consists of a single theorem of higher order logic and forms the basis for all further proofs about the new type.

The details of the logical basis for this method of defining concrete types are beyond the scope of this book—for a full discussion, see the paper [88]. The sections that follow, however, provide an overview of the class of types definable by the method, the form of the theorems used to characterize these types in logic, and some fundamental properties which follow from these theorems.

5.1.1   An example: the type of lists

A simple example of a recursive concrete type is the type of finite, homogeneous lists. This type can be described informally[1] by the equation shown below.

$$(\alpha)\mathit{list} \; ::= \quad \mathsf{Nil} \quad | \quad \mathsf{Cons}\; \alpha\; (\alpha)\mathit{list} \qquad\qquad (5.1)$$

This equation is an informal recursive definition of the type of finite lists of values of type α. The symbols Nil and Cons are the usual constructors by which list values are formed. The symbol Nil stands for the empty list, and the symbol Cons stands for the operation which constructs a list of length $n+1$ by adding a value of type α onto the front of a list of length n. The set of values defined informally by this recursive equation consists of the smallest set that contains Nil and is closed under the list-forming operation denoted by Cons.

To make the set of values described by this equation into a logical type, a formal definition must be made using the rule for type definitions explained in chapter 2. The details will not be given here (they can be found in [88]), but once the type $(\alpha)\mathit{list}$ has been defined, its definition can be used to prove the abstract characterization of lists consisting of the single theorem shown below.

$$\vdash \forall e\, f.\, \exists!\mathit{fn}.\, (\mathit{fn}\; \mathsf{Nil} = e) \wedge (\forall h\, t.\, \mathit{fn}(\mathsf{Cons}\; h\; t) = f\; (\mathit{fn}\; t)\; h\; t) \qquad\qquad (5.2)$$

This theorem captures the essential properties of the type $(\alpha)\mathit{list}$. It is analogous to the primitive recursion theorem for natural numbers discussed in section 2.6; it

---

[1]Here, and in what follows, *informally* just means not in the language of higher order logic.

asserts that a function $fn:(\alpha)list \rightarrow \beta$ can be defined uniquely by 'primitive recursion' on lists—that is, by giving a value e to define $fn(\text{Nil})$ and a function f to define $fn(\text{Cons } h \ t)$ in terms of $(fn \ t)$, h, and t.

All the usual properties of lists follow from theorem 5.2. In particular, it is possible to derive from this abstract characterization of lists the three fundamental properties shown below.

$$\vdash \forall h \ t. \ \neg(\text{Nil} = \text{Cons } h \ t)$$

$$\vdash \forall h_1 \ h_2 \ t_1 \ t_2. \ (\text{Cons } h_1 \ t_1 = \text{Cons } h_2 \ t_2) \supset ((h_1 = h_2) \wedge (t_1 = t_2))$$

$$\vdash \forall P. \ (P \ \text{Nil} \wedge \forall t. \ P \ t \supset \forall h. \ P(\text{Cons } h \ t)) \supset \forall l. \ P \ l$$

These three theorems are analogous to Peano's Postulates for the natural numbers. The first two state that Nil and Cons yield distinct values of type $(\alpha)list$ and that Cons is injective. The third theorem states the validity of structural induction on lists and provides the formal means for proving properties of lists by structural induction. It also follows from this induction theorem that every value of type $(\alpha)list$ is either equal to Nil, or is constructed from Nil by finitely many applications of Cons.

Defining equations for primitive recursive functions on lists can also be derived from theorem 5.2. As was explained in chapter 2, function constants that satisfy recursive equations are not directly definable using the rule for constant definitions; to define such a constant, one must first prove that the proposed recursive defining equation is in fact satisfiable. It follows immediately from theorem 5.2, however, that any primitive recursive definition on lists can be satisfied by a (unique) total function. This provides a direct means for constructing such functions in logic and for justifying the introduction of constants that denote them.

For example, given theorem 5.2 it is straightforward to define a constant that denotes a primitive recursive *length* function on lists. Specializing the variables e and f in a suitably type-instantiated version of theorem 5.2 to 0 and $\lambda x \ y \ z. \ x+1$ respectively yields (after some simplification) the theorem shown below.

$$\vdash \exists! fn. \ (fn \ \text{Nil} = 0) \wedge (\forall h \ t. \ fn(\text{Cons } h \ t) = (fn \ t) + 1)$$

This asserts the (unique) existence of a function which satisfies the usual recursive definition of the length of a list. Given this theorem, a constant 'Length' can then be introduced to denote the function whose existence it asserts. This can be done formally by an appropriate non-recursive definition involving the constant ε, as was explained in section 2.6. The result is the following pair of defining equations for the length of a list:

$$\vdash \text{Length Nil} = 0$$

$$\vdash \text{Length (Cons } h \ t) = (\text{Length } t) + 1$$

Any function constant that satisfies a primitive recursive definition on lists can be defined in a similar way—i.e. by first specializing the variables e and f in theorem 5.2 to obtain a theorem which asserts the existence of the desired function, and then introducing a constant to name this function by a non-recursive definition using ε. This method for defining functions on lists is completely analogous to the method for justifying primitive recursive definitions on the natural numbers discussed in chapter 2.

5.1.2   Concrete types in general

The type of lists is a simple instance of the general class of concrete types which can be defined using the method explained in detail in [88]. Every such type can be described informally by an equation similar in form to the equation for lists shown above. The general form of such an equation is

$$(\alpha_1,\ldots,\alpha_n)op \ ::= \ \ \mathsf{C}_1\,\sigma_1^1 \ \ldots \ \sigma_1^{k_1} \ \mid \ \cdots \ \mid \ \mathsf{C}_m\,\sigma_m^1 \ \ldots \ \sigma_m^{k_m} \qquad (5.3)$$

where each type on the right-hand side of the equation is either a type expression already present in the logic or just the type expression '$(\alpha_1,\ldots,\alpha_n)op$' itself. This specifies a compound type $(\alpha_1,\ldots,\alpha_n)op$ with n type variables $\alpha_1 \ldots$, α_n where $n \geq 0$. If $n = 0$ then op is a type constant; otherwise op is an n-ary type operator. The concrete data type specified by the equation has m constructors C_1, $\ldots$, C_m where $m \geq 1$. Each constructor C_i takes k_i arguments, where $k_i \geq 0$; and the types of these arguments are given by the type expressions σ_i^j for $1 \leq j \leq k_i$. If one or more of these type expressions is the type $(\alpha_1,\ldots,\alpha_n)op$ itself, then the equation specifies a recursive type. In any specification of a recursive type, at least one constructor must be non-recursive—i.e. all its arguments must have types that already exist in the logic.

The above equation is similar to a 'datatype' declaration in Standard ML [116]; it simply states the names of the constructors for a type and the types of their arguments. The type described by the equation denotes the set of all values that can be finitely generated using the constructors C_1, $\ldots$, C_m, where each constructor is injective and any two different constructors yield different values. Every such value is denoted by a term of the form

$$\mathsf{C}_i\,x_i^1 \ \ldots \ x_i^{k_i}$$

where x_i^j is a term of type σ_i^j for $1 \leq j \leq k_i$. In addition, any two terms

$$\mathsf{C}_i\,x_i^1 \ \ldots \ x_i^{k_i} \qquad \text{and} \qquad \mathsf{C}_j\,x_j^1 \ \ldots \ x_j^{k_j}$$

denote equal values exactly when their constructors are the same (i.e. $i = j$) and these constructors are applied to equal arguments (i.e. $x_i^l = x_j^l$ for $1 \leq l \leq k_i$).

Any type described informally by an equation of the form shown above can be characterized formally in logic by a single theorem of the form

$$\vdash \forall f_1\ f_2\ \cdots\ f_m.\ \exists!\,fn\!:\!(\alpha_1,\ldots,\alpha_n)op\!\to\!\beta.$$
$$\forall x_1^1\ \cdots\ x_1^{k_1}.\ fn(\mathsf{C}_1\ x_1^1\ \ldots\ x_1^{k_1}) = f_1\ (fn\ x_1^1)\ \ldots\ (fn\ x_1^{k_1})\ x_1^1\ \ldots\ x_1^{k_1}\ \wedge$$
$$\forall x_2^1\ \cdots\ x_2^{k_2}.\ fn(\mathsf{C}_2\ x_2^1\ \ldots\ x_2^{k_2}) = f_2\ (fn\ x_2^1)\ \ldots\ (fn\ x_2^{k_2})\ x_2^1\ \ldots\ x_2^{k_2}\ \wedge$$
$$\vdots \tag{5.4}$$
$$\forall x_m^1\ \cdots\ x_m^{k_m}.\ fn(\mathsf{C}_m\ x_m^1\ \ldots\ x_m^{k_m}) = f_m\ (fn\ x_m^1)\ \ldots\ (fn\ x_m^{k_m})\ x_m^1\ \ldots\ x_m^{k_m}$$

where the right hand sides of the equations include recursive applications ($fn\ x_i^j$) of the function fn only for variables x_i^j of type $(\alpha_1,\ldots,\alpha_n)op$. (See, for example, theorem 5.2 above.) This asserts the unique existence of primitive recursive functions defined by cases on the constructors C_1, C_2, ..., C_m. This is a slight extension of the *initiality* property by which structures of this kind are characterized in the 'initial algebra' approach to specifying abstract data types [40]. This property provides an abstract characterization of the type $(\alpha_1,\ldots,\alpha_n)op$ which is both succinct and complete, in the sense that it completely determines the structure of the values of the type up to isomorphism.

A major practical advantage of this characterization is its uniform treatment of all concrete types. Every type which can be described informally by an equation of the kind shown above is characterized by a single theorem of the same general form.[2] A further advantage is that many useful standard properties follow from these theorems in a uniform way, with relatively short formal proofs.

For example, from theorem 5.4 it is easy to prove an alternative characterization of the type $(\alpha_1,\ldots,\alpha_n)op$ which is analogous to the conventional axiomatization of the natural numbers given by Peano's Postulates. This characterization consists of the following fundamental properties: the constructors C_1, C_2, ..., C_m yield distinct values; each constructor which is not a constant is injective; and the principle of structural induction holds for the type $(\alpha_1,\ldots,\alpha_n)op$. The three theorems about lists in the preceding section show how these properties are stated formally for the type $(\alpha)list$. Similar theorems hold for any concrete type which can be described by an equation of the form given by equation 5.3.

Another important property of the characterization of the type $(\alpha_1,\ldots,\alpha_n)op$ given by theorem 5.4 is that it provides a formal means for defining a wide class of useful functions on this type. For recursive types, theorem 5.4 allows one to prove the existence of primitive recursive functions on the type. This is illustrated by the method for defining primitive recursive functions on lists explained in the previous section. For non-recursive types, the characterization given by theorem 5.4

---

[2]This uniformity is the basis for the *efficient* automation in the HOL system of the process of defining these types and proving characterizing theorems for them. See [88] for the details.

also provides a means for defining functions. In this case, the theorem states the unique existence of functions defined by cases on the constructors, and this provides a simple and direct way of constructing particular instances of these functions. This is illustrated by an example given later in this chapter.

5.1.3   Mechanization in HOL

There is a set of automatic theorem-proving tools implemented in the HOL system to provide mechanized support for reasoning about concrete types of the kind discussed above. The main component is an ML procedure which carries out all the logical inferences necessary to define an arbitrary concrete type in higher order logic and to prove an abstract characterization for it. The user input to this programmed proof rule is an informal specification of the type to be defined, in the form of an equation of the kind discussed above. The output is an abstract characterization of the required logical type, in the form of an instance of theorem-scheme 5.4. This theorem is proved automatically, by purely logical inference, from an automatically-constructed formal definition of the particular concrete type requested by the user.

Also implemented in HOL are procedures for proving the standard properties of concrete types discussed in the preceding section. A procedure is provided, for example, for proving a structural induction theorem for any concrete type. The justification of primitive recursive definitions on concrete recursive types is also automated. A full description of all these tools can be found in the HOL manual [47]. The underlying theory is explained in [88].

5.2   An example: a transistor model

This section shows how an instance of the class of concrete types just introduced can be used to formulate a CMOS transistor model which is more realistic than the one in chapter 3. An example is also given of a correctness proof involving data abstraction based on a design model defined using this concrete type. The section begins with a discussion of the inadequacies of the simple transistor model defined in chapter 3.

5.2.1   Inadequacies of the switch model

In the transistor model defined in chapter 3, transistors are regarded as ideal switches controlled by the boolean value present on their gates. For example, the specification for an N-type transistor describes this device as an ideal switch which is closed when its gate has the value T and open when its gate has the value F. Although this very simple *switch model* of transistor behaviour can be useful for some purposes, it clearly fails to capture many important aspects of the way real CMOS devices behave.

One of these aspects is the fact that the switching behaviour of a real CMOS transistor does not depend simply on the 'logic level' present on its gate, but on the magnitude of the gate-to-source voltage V_{gs} compared to some non-zero threshold voltage V_t. This means that a transistor does not transmit both logic levels equally well. An N-type transistor, for example, transmits logic low well but logic high poorly. In the switch model the specifications for N-type and P-type transistors do not reflect this important aspect of transistor behaviour.

This simplification makes it possible to prove in the switch model the 'correctness' of certain CMOS circuits which do not work in practice. A trivial example is the device shown below, in which the value on the input *in* is transmitted through an N-type transistor to drive a capacitative load at the output *out*.

$$\vdash (\exists p.\, \mathsf{Pwr}\, p \wedge \mathsf{Ntran}(p, in, out)) = (out = in)$$

This is just an N-type transistor with its gate connected directly to power. In the switch model, this is equivalent to a wire that connects the output directly to the input. This is reflected in the correctness theorem on the right, which asserts that a model of this circuit constructed using the switch model primitives defined in chapter 3 is logically equivalent to the specification '$out = in$'.

In reality, of course, the above circuit does not behave like a direct connection between *out* and *in*. If the output drives a capacitative load, and the input is at logic level high, then the voltage at *out* will only reach a level which is the threshold voltage V_t less than V_{DD}. This voltage may be too low to drive the gate of another transistor, so it must be treated as distinct from the logic level high. The switch model correctness statement shown above is therefore misleading, for it asserts that the device provides a completely transparent connection between *out* and *in*.

5.2.2 A three-valued logical type

The fundamental problem with the switch model is that it specifies the behaviour of transistors using a logical type with only two values. Each wire in a circuit must have either the value high (modelled by T) or the value low (modelled by F). The physical phenomenon of a 'degraded' logic level—one which is distinct from both these values, and which cannot be used to drive the gate of a transistor—is not even a possibility in this model.

To overcome this problem, a type with more than two values is needed. The simplest solution is a defined type with exactly three distinct values. Using the informal notation introduced in section 5.1.2, an appropriate type *tri* is defined by the equation shown below.

$$tri ::= \text{Hi} \mid \text{Lo} \mid \text{X}$$

This informal definition states that tri denotes a set containing exactly three distinct values—namely Hi, Lo, and X. The corresponding abstract characterization consists of the following single theorem.

$$\vdash \forall a\,b\,c.\,\exists!\,fn{:}tri{\rightarrow}\alpha.\,(fn\ \text{Hi} = a) \wedge (fn\ \text{Lo} = b) \wedge (fn\ \text{X} = c) \tag{5.5}$$

This theorem provides a complete and abstract characterization of the defined type tri. It takes the form of a degenerate 'primitive recursion' theorem; since tri is an enumerated type with no recursive constructors, it simply states that any function defined by cases on Hi, Lo, and X exists and is uniquely defined.

It follows immediately from this theorem that the type constant tri denotes a set containing exactly three values. The fact that fn always exists implies that Hi, Lo, and X are distinct, and the fact that fn is uniquely determined by its values for Hi, Lo, and X implies that these are the only values of type tri. These two properties are stated formally by the theorems shown below.

$$\vdash \neg(\text{Hi} = \text{X}) \wedge \neg(\text{Lo} = \text{X}) \wedge \neg(\text{Hi} = \text{Lo}) \tag{5.6}$$

$$\vdash \forall P.\,(P\ \text{Hi} \wedge P\ \text{Lo} \wedge P\ \text{X}) \supset \forall t{:}tri.\,P\ t \tag{5.7}$$

These theorems correspond to two of the 'standard' properties of concrete types discussed on page 73. The first is the statement for the particular type tri of the general property that the constructors of a concrete type yield distinct values. The second theorem is a degenerate example of the structural induction theorem which holds of every concrete type.

5.2.3   A threshold switching model[3]

Once the type tri has been defined, it can be used as the basis for a hardware model which at least partly captures the threshold switching behaviour of real CMOS devices. The idea is to represent the strongly-driven logic levels high and low by the values Hi and Lo, and to represent all degraded logic levels that cannot reliably drive the gates of transistors by the value X.

The specifications in figure 5.1 constitute a *threshold switching* model of CMOS transistor behaviour based on this representation of logic levels. The terms Pwr p and Gnd g model VDD and VSS as constant sources of Hi and Lo respectively. The specifications for N-type and P-type transistors are intended to reflect the fact that

---

[3]The transistor model defined in this section is based on a suggestion made by M. Fourman at the workshop on *Theoretical Aspects of VLSI Architectures* at the University of Leeds in 1986.

$$\vdash \mathsf{Gnd}\; g = (g = \mathsf{Lo})$$

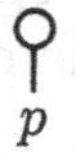

$$\vdash \mathsf{Pwr}\; p = (p = \mathsf{Hi})$$

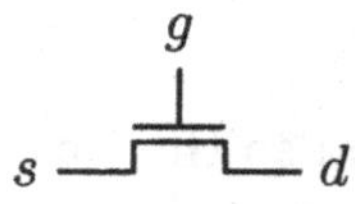

$$\vdash \mathsf{Ntran}(g, s, d) = ((g = \mathsf{Hi}) \supset ((d = \mathsf{Lo}) = (s = \mathsf{Lo})))$$

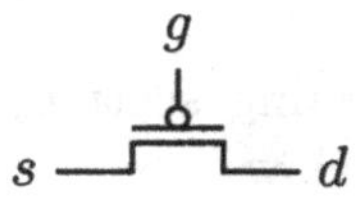

$$\vdash \mathsf{Ptran}(g, s, d) = ((g = \mathsf{Lo}) \supset ((d = \mathsf{Hi}) = (s = \mathsf{Hi})))$$

Figure 5.1: A threshold switching model.

these devices do not transmit both logic levels equally well. For example, it follows from the specification for an N-type transistor that when the gate g has the value Hi and the source s has the value Lo (i.e. when the gate-to-source voltage is large) then the drain d must also have value Lo. This reflects the fact that the logic level modelled by Lo is transmitted unchanged through an N-type transistor. But when both g and s have the value Hi, then the value of d may be either Hi or X. The specification 'Ntran(g, s, d)' is satisfied in both cases. This reflects the fact that the value Hi can be degraded to X when it is transmitted through an N-type transistor. The specification for a P-type transistor is similar.

By modelling the range of values which can appear on the wires of a circuit using the special-purpose concrete type *tri*, instead of the primitive type *bool*, the threshold switching model captures the actual behaviour of CMOS transistors more accurately than the simpler switch model. Design errors are therefore less likely to escape discovery if correctness proofs are based on the threshold switching model instead of the switch model. The formal relationship between these two models is examined in more detail in chapter 7.

5.3   An example of data abstraction

In this section the CMOS inverter proof done in chapter 3 using the switch model of transistors is redone using the more accurate threshold switching model just defined. The aim is to provide an example to illustrate the approach to data abstraction introduced in chapter 4. Data abstraction is used to relate a model defined in terms of the three-valued type *tri* to a specification written in terms of the primitive type *bool*. Although this is an extremely simple example, it does illustrate some important aspects of the general approach.

One of the simplest possible specifications for an inverter is the one already used in the correctness proof given in chapter 3:

$$i \longrightarrow\!\!\!\triangleright\!\!\circ\!\!\longrightarrow o \qquad\qquad \vdash \mathsf{Not}(i{:}bool, o{:}bool) = (o = \neg i)$$

The values on the input and output are modelled by booleans, and so the variables i and o have logical type *bool*. This simple and direct specification will also be used in the threshold model proof that follows.

Using the threshold switching primitives defined in the preceding section, the design model for a standard CMOS inverter is defined as shown below.

$$\vdash \mathsf{Inv}(i{:}tri, o{:}tri) = \exists g\, p.\, \mathsf{Pwr}\, p \wedge \mathsf{Gnd}\, g \wedge \mathsf{Ntran}(i, g, o) \wedge \mathsf{Ptran}(i, p, o)$$

The structure of this definition is identical to the one given in chapter 3, where the switch model primitives are used. In this model, however, the terms $\mathsf{Pwr}\, p$, $\mathsf{Gnd}\, g$, $\mathsf{Ntran}(i, g, o)$ and $\mathsf{Ptran}(i, p, o)$ are instances of the threshold switching primitives shown in figure 5.1.

5.3.1   The data abstraction function

To formulate a correctness statement for the inverter, a data abstraction function is needed to relate values of type *tri* in the model to values of type *bool* in the specification. In the model, the two strongly-driven logic levels high and low are represented by Hi and Lo; in the specification, they are represented by T and F. The required data abstraction function must therefore map Hi to T and Lo to F.

Given theorem 5.5, which characterizes the defined type *tri*, it is trivial to define a constant **abs**:*tri*→*bool* which denotes the required function. Taking an instance of this theorem in which the type *bool* is substituted for the type variable α, and specializing the universally-quantified variables a and b to T and F respectively, yields the following theorem.

$$\vdash \forall c.\, \exists!\mathit{fn}.\, (\mathit{fn}\ \mathsf{Hi} = \mathsf{T}) \wedge (\mathit{fn}\ \mathsf{Lo} = \mathsf{F}) \wedge (\mathit{fn}\ \mathsf{X} = c)$$

From this, one can immediately infer the existence of a function which has precisely the desired property:

$$\vdash \exists \mathit{fn}.\, (\mathit{fn}\ \mathsf{Hi} = \mathsf{T}) \wedge (\mathit{fn}\ \mathsf{Lo} = \mathsf{F})$$

Using the technique for defining constants explained in section 2.5, a constant **abs** can be introduced to denote the function whose existence is guaranteed by this theorem. The result is the theorem shown below.

$$\vdash (\text{abs Hi} = \text{T}) \wedge (\text{abs Lo} = \text{F}) \tag{5.8}$$

This states that the data abstraction function **abs** maps the value Hi to T and the value Lo to F, as required.

There is one important consequence of the above definition of **abs** which may not be immediately obvious. In higher order logic, all functions of type $tri{\rightarrow}bool$ are total functions, and the data abstraction function **abs**:$tri{\rightarrow}bool$ therefore must yield *some* boolean value when applied to X. But the constant **abs** is defined so that it is impossible to prove *which* boolean value is denoted by the application 'abs X'. That is, neither $\vdash$ abs X = T nor $\vdash$ abs X = F is a theorem of the logic. One of these two equations must be 'true', but neither of them can be proved.

This is a consequence of the way in which the constant **abs** is defined using the primitive constant ε. The underlying definition of **abs** (which was not actually shown above) is the following equation.

$$\vdash \text{abs} = \varepsilon fn. (fn \text{ Hi} = \text{T}) \wedge (fn \text{ Lo} = \text{F})$$

All that can be proved from this definition is that the function **abs** has the property stated by the predicate '$\lambda fn. (fn \text{ Hi} = \text{T}) \wedge (fn \text{ Lo} = \text{F})$'. That there *is* a function with this property was proved above. It follows from this, and from the axiom for ε discussed in section 2.5, that **abs** in fact has this property. But this is the only significant fact that can be proved about **abs**, since the axiom shown in section 2.5 is the only property of ε made available by the primitive basis of the logic. (See section 2.5 for further discussion of this point.)

The function **abs** is defined in this way because this makes it impossible to prove certain theorems which would give a false assurance of correctness. Suppose, for example, that instead of being defined as shown above, the constant **abs** is defined such that the following theorem holds.

$$\vdash (\text{abs Hi} = \text{T}) \wedge (\text{abs Lo} = \text{F}) \wedge (\text{abs X} = \text{T})$$

If **abs** is defined in this way, then it is also possible to prove the theorem

$$\vdash (\exists p. \text{Pwr } p \wedge \text{Ntran}(p, in, out)) \supset (\text{abs } out = \text{abs } in)$$

But this is a correctness statement for the CMOS device shown on page 75. It asserts that an N-type transistor with its gate connected directly to power can be viewed, at a higher level of data abstraction, as a direct connection between *in* and *out*. This is exactly the sort of correctness statement that the threshold model is designed to eliminate. It can, however, be proved only if $\vdash$ abs X = T can be derived from the definition of **abs**. So when **abs** is defined formally as discussed above, this fallacious correctness theorem in fact *cannot* be proved.

The method used to define abs also illustrates one of the pragmatic advantages of the approach taken here to characterizing concrete types in logic. For every concrete type there is a theorem which asserts the existence of a wide class of functions from the type itself to any other type. This provides a direct means for defining data abstraction functions from the values used in design models to the values used in specifications.

The abs example is, of course, very simple—the function abs is just defined by cases on the values of an enumerated type. But when recursive types are used in design models, the way in which they are characterized provides a direct and powerful means for defining data abstraction functions by primitive recursion. One application in which such functions arise naturally is in reasoning about hardware devices that operate on vectors of bits—i.e. finite sequences of binary digits. This application is considered in detail in section 5.4.

5.3.2   The correctness proof

Once abs has been defined, it is straightforward to formulate a correctness statement for the inverter which uses data abstraction to relate the model $\mathsf{Inv}(i, o)$ to the more abstract specification $\mathsf{Not}(i, o)$. The correctness statement must be qualified by a validity condition which restricts the range of values on the input to the strongly-driven logic levels Hi and Lo. This is necessary because the specification represents a valid abstract view of an inverter only when the device is used in an environment in which the input is always strongly driven.

A correctness statement with the required validity condition can be formulated as shown below.

$$\vdash \neg(i = \mathsf{X}) \supset \mathsf{Inv}(i, o) \supset \mathsf{Not}(\mathsf{abs}\ i,\ \mathsf{abs}\ o)$$

This says that if the circuit modelled by $\mathsf{Inv}(i, o)$ is used in an environment in which its input is always strongly driven, then it will behave as required by the abstract specification $\mathsf{Not}(i, o)$. Expressed in the notation of chapter 4, we have

$$\vdash \neg(i = \mathsf{X}) \supset \mathsf{Inv}(i, o) \underset{\mathsf{abs}}{\mathsf{sat}} \mathsf{Not}(i, o)$$

The data abstraction function abs translates values of type *tri* in the model to the corresponding values of type *bool* in the specification. The term '$\neg(i = \mathsf{X})$' is a validity condition on the abstraction relationship between the model and the specification. This condition limits correctness to the assertion that the inverter will behave as required only if the value on its input is not X.

The proof of this correctness theorem is simple. The 'induction' theorem for *tri* shown on page 76 (i.e. theorem 5.7) allows the proof to be done by case analysis on the value of i. When $i = \mathsf{X}$ the validity condition is false, and the implication is therefore vacuously true. When $i = \mathsf{Hi}$ or $i = \mathsf{Lo}$, it follows from theorem 5.6

that the validity condition is true. The proof therefore reduces to showing that the implication

$$\text{Inv}(i, o) \supset \text{Not}(\text{abs } i, \text{abs } o) \tag{5.9}$$

holds for $i = \text{Hi}$ and $i = \text{Lo}$. By a simple derivation which is similar to the first few steps in the switch model proof on page 41, it follows that

$$\vdash \text{Inv}(i, o) \ = \ ((i = \text{Hi}) \supset (o = \text{Lo})) \wedge ((i = \text{Lo}) \supset (o = \text{Hi})).$$

So proving that implication 5.9 holds for $i = \text{Hi}$ and $i = \text{Lo}$ reduces to proving

$$\vdash \text{Not}(\text{abs Hi}, \text{abs Lo}) \qquad \text{and} \qquad \vdash \text{Not}(\text{abs Lo}, \text{abs Hi}).$$

These two theorems follow immediately from the definition of Not and the defining equations for abs given by theorem 5.8.

5.3.3   Data abstraction and partial functions

One general point illustrated by the inverter example is that it is possible to avoid dealing explicitly with data abstraction functions which are *partial* functions.

Why such functions might seem to be appropriate, or even necessary, can be explained by considering how 'data' is represented in this example. Two logical types are used—the three-valued type *tri* and the two-valued type *bool*. In addition to the values Hi and Lo, which correspond to the two boolean values T and F, the type *tri* also has the third value X. This represents the physical phenomenon of a degenerate logic level in design models based on the threshold switching primitives. This kind of logic level, however, is simply not represented in a specification of required behaviour based on the two-valued type *bool*. It is therefore undesirable for a data abstraction function from *tri* to *bool* to assign a particular boolean value to X, since the physical phenomenon modelled by X is not even represented in the specification. It might seem natural, then, to make the data abstraction function from *tri* to *bool* a partial function—one which is *undefined* when applied to X.

The method used in this example to define the function abs, however, avoids the need to develop a theory of partial functions in higher order logic. Instead, abs is a total function, but is defined so that nothing definite can be proved about the boolean value denoted by 'abs X'. This avoids the possibility of proving misleading correctness theorems (like the one on page 79) which might otherwise be provable if abs X just happens to satisfy the specification of required behaviour.

Although abs is a total function, the validity condition used in the correctness statement for the inverter effectively restricts its domain to only those values of type *tri* for which a partial function would in fact be defined. The net effect is to 'simulate' a partial data abstraction function by a total function (abs) together with a predicate which restricts the range of this total function (the validity condition). This is a natural general technique for representing partial functions by total functions. The same method can be used whenever the representation of data in a model is richer than the representation of data in a specification, and it is therefore necessary to restrict the range of a data abstraction function to only a subset of the values that can arise in the model.

5.4   Reasoning about hardware using bit-vectors

A commonly used technique for reasoning about devices that operate on vectors of bits is to prove a single correctness theorem for an entire class of n-bit wide implementations [21, 45, 73]. An example is the class of all n-bit ripple-carry binary adders. The recursive structure of this class of devices (an $n+1$ bit adder is just a 1-bit adder connected to an n-bit adder) makes it straightforward to formulate and prove a single correctness theorem which states the correctness of every n-bit adder. The correctness of a 16-bit adder, or an adder of any other particular size, can then be inferred directly from this more general result.

An important advantage of this approach is that it often makes proofs simpler than would otherwise be possible. For example, a direct proof of correctness for a 16-bit adder is likely to involve the manipulation of large algebraic expressions which define the relationships that hold among the individual binary digits in the design.[4] But a correctness theorem for the class of all n-bit adders is much simpler to prove, since it can be proved by induction on the size of the device.

To use this approach in higher order logic, a logical type is needed to represent the set of all bit-vectors, or n-bit binary words. Gordon [45] uses a representation based on $num \rightarrow bool$, the type of total functions from the natural numbers to the booleans. Adopting this representation has the advantage of making it unnecessary to define a special-purpose type to model bit-vectors.[5] There is, however, a problem with this representation which leads to unnecessary complexity in specifying and reasoning about a class of n-bit devices. This problem and an alternative representation of bit-vectors which avoids it are discussed in the sections that follow.

In addition to a representation for n-bit words, two other things are needed for reasoning about a class of n-bit devices in logic. The first is a method for constructing a design model for an entire class of circuits, and the second is a method for defining data abstraction functions on n-bit words. These two requirements are also discussed in the sections that follow.

---

[4] In fact, this is how the correctness of a 16-bit adder would be proved automatically by Barrow's VERIFY system [4], which does not support reasoning about a class of n-bit devices.

[5] Of course num is not a primitive type of the logic, but it is so fundamental that it can hardly be considered 'special-purpose'.

5.4.1 Representing bit-vectors by functions

The type *num→bool* is commonly used to represent bit-vectors in higher order logic. The idea of this representation is that each bit-vector is modelled by a function of type *num→bool* which maps bit positions (represented by natural numbers) to bits (represented by booleans). The n bit-positions in a bit-vector of length n are numbered from 0 to $n-1$. When a bit-vector is interpreted as an n-bit binary number, the least significant bit occurs at position 0, and the most significant bit occurs at position $n-1$. For example, the sequence of booleans 'TFTT', which represents to the 4-bit binary number 1101, would be modelled by a function f, where $f(0) = \mathsf{T}$, $f(1) = \mathsf{F}$, $f(2) = \mathsf{T}$, and $f(3) = \mathsf{T}$.

Associated with this representation is a method for defining a parameterized design model to represent a class of n-bit devices. This is based formally on primitive recursion on the natural numbers, and is best explained by considering an example. A one-bit multiplexer, which selects one of two inputs a or b depending on the value of a control input c, can be modelled in logic by the term $\mathsf{Mux1}(c, a, b, out)$ defined below.

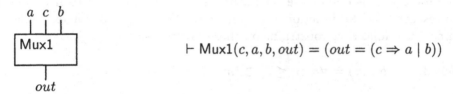

$$\vdash \mathsf{Mux1}(c, a, b, out) = (out = (c \Rightarrow a \mid b))$$

Each of the free variables a, b, c, and *out* in this definition has type *bool* and corresponds to a single one-bit input or output.

An multiplexer $n+1$ bits wide can be built by placing $n+1$ instances of a one-bit multiplexer in parallel, as shown in figure 5.2. To describe the behaviour of the class of devices represented by this diagram, it is necessary to define a model in which composition ('∧') is applied to $n+1$ instances of the specification for a one-bit multiplexer. This is done by using primitive recursion on the natural numbers to

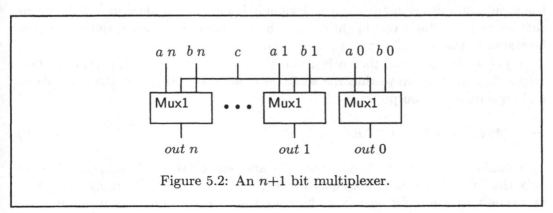

Figure 5.2: An $n+1$ bit multiplexer.

define a model which is parameterized by the size n. The defining equations for this model are as follows.

$$\vdash \text{Mux } 0 \ (c, a, b, out) = \text{Mux1}(c, a\, 0, b\, 0, out\, 0)$$

$$\vdash \text{Mux } (n{+}1) \ (c, a, b, out) = $$
$$\text{Mux1}(c, a(n{+}1), b(n{+}1), out(n{+}1)) \wedge \text{Mux } n \ (c, a, b, out)$$

These equations define a term Mux n (c, a, b, out) to model the structure shown in figure 5.2. The variable n in this term stands for the size of the multiplexer whose behaviour it models. When n is 0, the device is a single one-bit multiplexer; when n is greater than 0, the device consists of a one-bit multiplexer connected in parallel to an $n{-}1$ bit multiplexer.

The variables a, b, and out in this design model range over functions of type $num{\rightarrow}bool$ and represent the $n{+}1$ bit words that appear on the inputs and output of the multiplexer. The primitive recursive definition of the model simply applies the composition operation to $n{+}1$ instances of the specification for a one-bit multiplexer. Each of these constrains one of the bit-positions numbered from 0 to n in the bit-vectors represented by the functions a, b and out. When n is 3, for example, the model imposes the following constraint on these functions.

$$\vdash \text{Mux } 3 \ (c, a, b, out) = \forall n.\, (n \leq 3) \supset \text{Mux1}(c, a\, n, b\, n, out\, n)$$

This represents the effect of placing four instances of a one-bit multiplexer in parallel to obtain a multiplexer that operates on 4-bit words.

5.4.2   The problem

The problem with using $num{\rightarrow}bool$ to represent bit-vectors can be illustrated by considering the parameterized model just defined. The trouble is that the model does not determine a unique representation for the combinations of bit-vectors on the input and output of the class of devices it is intended to describe. This means that certain assertions one might want to prove about this class of devices cannot be stated in the most direct and natural way.

Suppose, for example, that n is 3 and the control wire c has the value T. One might then want to prove that the value on input a is selected by the multiplexer and appears on the output out:

$$\text{Mux } 3 \ (\text{T}, a, b, out) \supset (out = a) \tag{5.10}$$

This implication, however, is not true. The antecedent 'Mux 3 (T, a, b, out)' implies only that $out(n)$ and $a(n)$ are equal for $0 \leq n \leq 3$. It does not imply that these two values are equal for all n and therefore that the two functions out and a are themselves equal. Similarly, the model does not satisfy the natural formulation of correctness shown below.

$$\forall n. \text{ Mux } n \ (c, a, b, out) \supset (out = (c \Rightarrow a \mid b))$$

This correctness statement is false, since there are functions a, b, and out that satisfy the model but not the specification.

The essence of the problem is that each bit-vector is not uniquely represented by a single function of type $num{\rightarrow}bool$. For example, the functions a and out in implication 5.10 are intended to model 4-bit words, and the term Mux 3 (T, a, b, out) is expected to imply that these 4-bit words are equal. But there are an infinite number of different representations in $num{\rightarrow}bool$ for any particular 4-bit word, and the constraint imposed by this term on the functions a and out does not ensure that they are equal representations for the same 4-bit word.

There are various *ad hoc* solutions to this problem. One solution is to include the size parameter in any assertions to be proved about the behaviour of a class of devices. For example, one could prove (by induction on n) the following correctness theorem for the class of all multiplexer designs.

$$\vdash \forall n. \text{ Mux } n \ (c, a, b, out) = \forall i. \ i \le n \supset (out \ i = (c \Rightarrow a \ i \mid b \ i))$$

But this means having to retain the size parameter n in future reasoning based on this correctness statement—for example, in a hierarchical proof in which the specification on the right-hand side is used as a model at a higher level in the hierarchy. Furthermore, the specification used here is not abstract; it makes explicit reference to the details of the representation of n-bit words. Another solution is to strengthen the constraint imposed by the model on the functions a, b, and out so that each bit-vector is represented by a unique function. A better solution, however, is to model bit-vectors by a more appropriate type, one in which each n-bit word already has a unique representation.

5.4.3 A better representation

The recursive type of lists discussed earlier in this chapter provides a representation for bit-vectors in which each finite sequence of bits is modelled by exactly one value. This type was defined informally by the following equation:

$$(\alpha)list \quad ::= \quad \text{Nil} \quad | \quad \text{Cons } \alpha \ (\alpha)list$$

A substitution instance of the polymorphic type defined by this equation is the type $(bool)list$, the type of finite-length lists of booleans. Each bit-vector can be represented by a value of this type built up using the constructors Nil and Cons. For example, the 4-bit word corresponding to the sequence of boolean values 'TTFT' can be represented by the term shown below.

Cons T (Cons T (Cons F (Cons T Nil))) : $(bool)$ $list$

Any finite sequence of bits can be represented by a value of type $(bool)$ $list$ in a similar way. The empty bit-vector is represented by the empty list Nil, and a non-empty vector of n boolean values b_1, ..., b_n is represented by the list denoted by 'Cons b_1 (Cons b_2 ... (Cons b_n Nil)...))'.

The advantage of using lists to model bit-vectors is that they give a unique representation in logic for each possible finite sequence of bits. Each bit-vector corresponds to precisely one list, and every list corresponds to a vector of bits. This follows from the properties of the defined type $(bool)$ $list$ stated formally by the three theorems about lists discussed in section 5.1.1:

$$\vdash \forall h\, t.\, \neg(\text{Nil} = \text{Cons } h\ t)$$

$$\vdash \forall h_1\, h_2\, t_1\, t_2.\, (\text{Cons } h_1\ t_1 = \text{Cons } h_2\ t_2) \supset ((h_1 = h_2) \wedge (t_1 = t_2))$$

$$\vdash \forall P.\, (P\ \text{Nil} \wedge \forall t.\, P\ t \supset \forall h.\, P(\text{Cons } h\ t)) \supset \forall l.\, P\ l$$

The first two theorems imply that two lists constructed using Nil and Cons are equal if and only if they represent exactly the same sequence of values. In other words, two lists are equal if and only if they model the same bit-vector. The third theorem (induction) implies that every value of type $(bool)$ $list$ is either equal to Nil or is constructed from Nil by finitely many applications of Cons. This means that the set denoted by $(bool)$ $list$ contains only values that represent vectors of bits. There are no 'extra' values.

The metalinguistic abbreviations shown in the following table are used to make list expressions more readable.

Abbreviations for Lists	
Term	*Abbreviation*
Nil	[]
Cons b t	$[b \mid t]$
Cons b_1 (Cons b_2 ... (Cons b_n Nil)...))	$[b_1;\ b_2;\ ...\ ;b_n]$

These abbreviations introduce a notation for lists which is similar to the syntax for lists in Prolog [26]. The notation introduced here, however, does not include 'nested' list expressions like $[x; [b; c]]$. These are allowed in Prolog, but they cannot be represented in higher order logic by well-typed terms built up with Nil and Cons.

When bit-vectors are represented by lists, an explicitly-stated size parameter is not needed to define a design model for a class of n-bit devices. Models can instead be defined by primitive recursion on the lists which represent bit-vectors in the design itself. The size of the device represented by the model is then implicitly determined by the values of the variables that represent bit-vectors.

Consider, for example, the multiplexer design in figure 5.2 on page 83. The class of circuit designs represented by this diagram can be modelled in logic by the term $\mathsf{Mux}(c, a, b, out)$ defined by primitive recursion as follows:

$$\vdash \mathsf{Mux}(c, a, b, [\,]) = (a = [\,]) \wedge (b = [\,])$$

$$\vdash \mathsf{Mux}(c, a, b, [h_o \,|\, t_o]) =$$
$$\exists h_a\, h_b\, t_a\, t_b.$$
$$(a = [h_a \,|\, t_a]) \wedge (b = [h_b \,|\, t_b]) \wedge \mathsf{Mux1}(c, h_a, h_b, h_o) \wedge \mathsf{Mux}(c, t_a, t_b, t_o)$$

These two equations define a model $\mathsf{Mux}(c, a, b, out)$ in which the variables a, b, and out represent bit-vectors by values of type $(bool)list$. The definition is done by primitive recursion on the output list out, and simply applies the constraint imposed by the specification of a one-bit multiplexer to the appropriate triples of bits taken from the three lists a, b, and out. As was discussed in section 5.1.1, the validity of this primitive recursive definition follows directly from the abstract characterization of lists given by theorem 5.2.

The defining equations shown above are slightly complicated by the fact that it is necessary to ensure that the resulting model $\mathsf{Mux}(c, a, b, out)$ is satisfied only if the three lists a, b, and out represent bit-vectors of the same length. A less cluttered picture of the essence of this definition is given by the two theorems below.

$$\vdash \mathsf{Mux}(c, [\,], [\,], [\,]) = \mathsf{T}$$

$$\vdash \mathsf{Mux}(c, [h_a \,|\, t_a], [h_b \,|\, t_b], [h_o \,|\, t_o]) = \mathsf{Mux1}(c, h_a, h_b, h_o) \wedge \mathsf{Mux}(c, t_a, t_b, t_o)$$

These two equations follow immediately from the more complex primitive recursive definition given above. They define the model $\mathsf{Mux}(c, a, b, out)$ for lists a, b, and out of equal length. The first equation defines a 'zero-bit' multiplexer. This does not correspond, of course, to any real physical device; it merely provides a zero (namely T) for the binary operation on models of composition ('$\wedge$'). The second equation is recursive; it defines a multiplexer of size $n+1$ to be a one-bit multiplexer connected in parallel to an n-bit multiplexer.

The correctness of the class of multiplexers modelled by $\mathsf{Mux}(c, a, b, out)$ can be stated with respect to a very simple and clear specification of required behaviour. An explicit size parameter is not needed in the specification, and correctness can be stated simply by the following equivalence:

$$\vdash \mathsf{Mux}(c, a, b, out) = (out = (c \Rightarrow a \,|\, b))$$

This theorem is straightforward to prove by structural induction on the list out, using the induction theorem for the defined concrete type of lists.

The main advantage of using lists to represent bit-vectors is that it provides a direct and unambiguous representation for each finite sequence of bits. When bit-vectors are represented by functions, there are many different representations for each bit-vector. This means that either the lengths of bit-vectors must be mentioned explicitly by including a size parameter in both models and specifications, or a standard representation must somehow be chosen for each bit-vector, perhaps by strengthening the constraint imposed by a model. But when bit-vectors are modelled by lists, none of this is necessary.

The concrete type of lists also provides a *structured* representation of bit-vectors. This allows the design model for a regular class of devices to be defined recursively on the structure of the lists which represent data in the design itself. Such a model is implicitly parameterized by size, in the sense that the model for a device of any fixed size n can be obtained from it by instantiating its free variables to particular lists of length n.[6]

This implicit form of parameterization helps to keep specifications of required behaviour clear and simple, as was illustrated by the example given above. It also, however, tends to make the definitions of models more complex than the definitions of explicitly-parameterized models. The definitions of models based on lists must include what is essentially explicit wiring information. One approach to this problem would be to develop a collection of higher order 'combining forms' in logic, such as the ones used for building models in Sheeran's design language Ruby [104].

The implicitly parameterized approach to design models is possible only when there is a correspondence between the structure of the lists in the model and the structure (usually linear) of the class of circuit designs it represents. This is *not* the case in the example considered in the next section, where a different technique is used to model a certain class of tree-shaped circuit designs. In this example, the design cannot be indexed by the size of the bit-vector on its input, since the class of devices to be modelled includes many alternative designs for each possible size of input vector.

5.5   Reasoning about tree-shaped circuits

Many important devices are implemented in hardware by tree-shaped structures. The example given in this section shows how concrete recursive types can be used to reason about devices of this kind. The idea is to construct a design model for a class of tree-structured circuits using a type whose values have the same sort of structure as the devices themselves. In the very simple example given here, a recursive type of binary trees is used to define a model of the class of all n-bit test-for-zero devices constructed using a tree of two-input OR-gates.

---

[6] For some much more complex examples of this approach, see Chin's paper on verifying hardware for signed-binary arithmetic [23].

This example also shows how data abstraction can be used to formulate the correctness of a class of n-bit circuit designs. The inputs to the devices considered in this section are n-bit binary words, and these are represented in the model using the list type discussed above. A recursively-defined data abstraction function is used to relate this model to a more abstract specification in which the value on the input of the device is represented by a natural number.

5.5.1 The class of devices to be modelled

An n-bit test-for-zero device can be implemented in hardware by a tree of two-input OR-gates connected to an inverter. Figure 5.3 shows two correct implementations of this kind for a six-bit device. Each of these circuits takes a six-bit binary word on its input wires. The output of each device is a boolean value which is true if the binary number represented by its input is zero, and false otherwise.

Both of the circuits shown in figure 5.3 are functionally correct. The circuit on the right, however, is an optimal tree-shaped implementation for a six-bit device, in the sense that the length of the path from inputs to output is the shortest possible and the gate delay through the device is therefore minimal. By contrast, the structure of the circuit on the left is that of a 'degenerate' binary tree; its structure is essentially linear. If the criterion by which circuits are judged is that of minimising delay, then this is the worst implementation of a six-bit test-for-zero device.

In general, the best implementation of a test-for-zero device built using two-input OR-gates will be a binary tree of height $\lceil \log_2 n \rceil$, and the worst implementation will be a degenerate tree of height $n-1$. The class of all devices of the latter kind (i.e. the set containing only the degenerate tree-shaped circuits) is easy to model using the techniques explained in the previous sections; a design model can be constructed by primitive recursion on the list which represents the n-bit input of the device. But

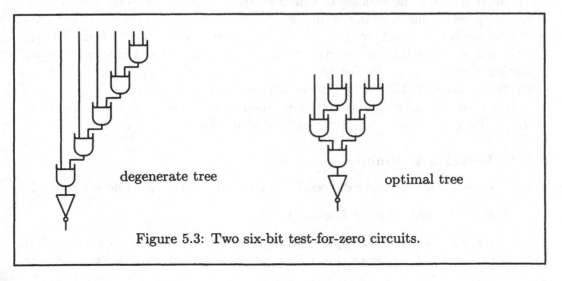

degenerate tree   optimal tree

Figure 5.3: Two six-bit test-for-zero circuits.

a model for the class of *all* n-bit test-for-zero devices cannot be constructed this
way, since there are many possible trees of OR-gates for each size of input vector. A
different technique is needed to define such a model.

5.5.2   A type of binary trees

The technique proposed here is to use a concrete recursive type of binary trees to
represent the structure of tree shaped circuits. Using the notation introduced in
section 5.1.2, this type can be described informally by the following equation.

$$btree \quad :: = \quad \textbf{Leaf} \quad | \quad \textbf{Node} \; btree \; btree$$

The data type *btree* defined by this equation has two constructors, **Leaf**:*btree* and
Node:*btree*→*btree*→*btree*. The constant **Leaf** denotes the trivial tree consisting of a
single leaf node. The function **Node** is used to build binary trees from smaller binary
trees; if t_1 and t_2 are trees, then the term '**Node** t_1 t_2' denotes the binary tree with
left subtree t_1 and right subtree t_2. Using **Leaf** and **Node**, it is possible to construct
a binary tree of any shape. For example, the tree

is denoted by the term '**Node Leaf** (**Node Leaf Leaf**) : *btree*'.
    The abstract characterization of the type informally defined by the equation
shown above is the following theorem of higher order logic.

$$\vdash \forall e \, f. \, \exists! fn. \, (fn \; \textbf{Leaf} = e) \wedge (\forall t_1 \, t_2. \, fn \; (\textbf{Node} \; t_1 \; t_2) = f \; (fn \; t_1) \; (fn \; t_2) \; t_1 \; t_2)$$

This theorem states the validity of primitive recursive definitions on binary trees.
It can be proved from a definition of the type constant *btree* using the systematic
method mentioned in section 5.1. All the standard properties of a concrete type
follow from this abstract characterization of binary trees. For example, a structural
induction theorem holds for the type *btree*. As was discussed in section 5.1.2, a
characterization stated in this form can also be used to justify the introduction of
function constants defined by primitive recursion—in this case, primitive recursion
on trees. These facts are used in the sections that follow.

5.5.3   Defining the model

Using the recursive type *btree* defined above, one can define a parameterized model

$$\textbf{Tfztree} \; (t:btree) \; (in:(bool)list, \; out:bool)$$

of the class of all tree-shaped implementations of an n-bit test-for-zero device. The
variables *in* and *out* represent the n-bit input and boolean output of the device.

The variable t ranges over values of type *btree* and represents the shape of the tree of OR-gates in the device. For each tree t, the model describes the tree-shaped test-for-zero device whose internal structure is the same as t. Since the variable t ranges over all binary trees, this model describes the class of all such circuits.

The first step in defining the model is to define an infix function constant '+' for concatenating lists. The definition is done formally by primitive recursion on lists:

$$\vdash [\,] + l = l$$
$$\vdash [h \mid t] + l = [h \mid t + l]$$

These two equations are just the usual recursive definition of concatenation. They can be derived from the characterization of lists given by theorem 5.2.

Using the concatenation function just introduced, a model 'Ortree t (in, o)' can be defined to represent the set of all trees of two-input OR-gates. The variable t in this model has type *btree*, and its value determines the shape of the tree of gates it represents. Each internal node in the tree t corresponds to a two-input OR-gate in the circuit being modelled. Each leaf node corresponds to one of the input wires which make up the bit-vector input. The model is defined by primitive recursion on binary trees as follows:

$$\vdash \mathsf{Ortree}\ \mathsf{Leaf}\ (in, o) = (in = [o])$$
$$\vdash \mathsf{Ortree}\ (\mathsf{Node}\ t_1\ t_2)\ (in, o)\ =$$
$$\exists i_1\ i_2\ o_1\ o_2.$$
$$(in = i_1 + i_2) \wedge \mathsf{Ortree}\ t_1\ (i_1, o_1) \wedge \mathsf{Ortree}\ t_2\ (i_2, o_2) \wedge \mathsf{Or}(o_1, o_2, o)$$

When t is a leaf node, model Ortree t (in, o) simply represents a wire which connects the input in (which must be a bit-vector of length one) directly to the output o. When t is an internal node with two subtrees t_1 and t_2, the bit-vector modelled by the list in is split into two sublists i_1 and i_2 by the expression '$in = i_1 + i_2$'. These sublists become the inputs to the two OR-gate trees constructed recursively from the subtrees t_1 and t_2. The outputs o_1 and o_2 of these two recursively constructed trees are the inputs of a single OR-gate at the root of the entire tree. The specification of the OR-gate is the obvious combinational one:

$$\vdash \mathsf{Or}(i_1, i_2, o) = (o = i_1 \vee i_2)$$

The model Tfztree t (in, out) is defined simply by composing the model defined above with an inverter:

$$\vdash \mathsf{Tfztree}\ t\ (in, out) = \exists o.\ \mathsf{Ortree}\ t\ (in, o) \wedge \mathsf{Not}(o, out)$$

The internal wire represented by o connects the tree of OR-gates modelled by

Ortree t (in, o) to the inverter modelled by Not(o, out). The definition of Not is given on page 78.

The term Tfztree t (in, out) models the class of all tree-shaped test-for-zero devices—both for all possible shapes of the internal tree of OR-gates, and for all possible non-zero sizes of the input bit-vector in. Before basing a correctness proof on this model it is worth checking that it is not inconsistent. The model must in fact be satisfiable for reasonable combinations of values for the variables t and in.

To formulate what is meant by 'reasonable' in this context, a recursive function that computes the number of leaf nodes in a binary tree is needed. The function Leaves:$tree{\rightarrow}num$ is straightforward to define by primitive recursion on trees:

$$\vdash \text{Leaves Leaf} = 1$$

$$\vdash \text{Leaves (Node } t_1 \ t_2) = (\text{Leaves } t_1) + (\text{Leaves } t_2)$$

The validity of this definition follows directly from the abstract characterization of the concrete recursive type $btree$ shown on page 90.

Using Leaves and the Length function defined in section 5.1.1, a theorem can be proved which asserts that the model defined above is consistent for all appropriate combinations of in and t:

$$\vdash \forall t \, in. \, \neg(in = [\,]) \supset ((\exists out. \, \text{Tfztree } t \, (in, out)) = (\text{Leaves } t = \text{Length } in))$$

This says that the model Tfztree t (in, out) can be satisfied by some output value out exactly when the number of leaves in the tree t matches the length of the input word in. This means that the model at least represents *some* consistent design for every value of the parameter t. The proof of this theorem is done by structural induction on the variable t ranging over trees. As was mentioned above, the principle of structural induction on trees follows formally from the abstract characterization of the recursive type $btree$.

5.5.4   The correctness proof

An abstract specification of required behaviour for a device that tests for zero is given by the definition shown below.

$$\vdash \text{Tfz}(in{:}num, \, out{:}bool) = (out = (in = 0))$$

This specification simply states that the boolean output out is true if and only if the numerical value present on the input in is equal to zero.

The behaviour stated by this specification is a data abstraction of the behaviour given by the design model defined above. In the model, the input is an n-bit binary word represented by a variable ranging over $(bool)list$. In the abstract specification, however, the input is simply a number; the free variable *in* in the specification defined above has type *num*. A data abstraction function is therefore needed to formule correctness with respect to this abstract specification.

An appropriate function Val:$(bool)list{\rightarrow}num$, which maps bit-vectors to natural numbers, can be defined by primitive recursion on lists as follows:

$$\vdash \mathsf{Val}\,[\,] = 0$$
$$\vdash \mathsf{Val}\,[b\,|\,l] = (2 \times (\mathsf{Val}\,l)) + (b \Rightarrow 1 \mid 0)$$

It is assumed that an n-bit binary word is represented by a list of booleans ordered from least significant bit (at the start of the list) to most significant bit (at the end of the list).[7] The list $[\mathsf{T};\mathsf{T};\mathsf{F};\mathsf{T}]$, for example, represents the binary number 1011. The equations for Val compute the natural number corresponding to the unsigned binary representation given by any list of boolean values. For example, it follows from these equations that $\vdash \mathsf{Val}\,[\mathsf{T};\mathsf{T};\mathsf{F};\mathsf{T}] = 11$.

As usual, the primitive recursive defining equations for Val can be proved using the characterization of lists given by theorem 5.2. As was mentioned above, this is one of the major pragmatic advantages of the approach taken here to the characterization of concrete recursive data types; recursively-defined data abstraction functions on concrete types are immediately derivable from the theorems that characterize these types in higher order logic.

It remains to show that every device in the class of circuit designs modelled by Tfztree t (in, out) is correct with respect to the abstract specification of required behaviour. The required correctness statement is the theorem shown below:

$$\vdash \forall t\ in\ out.\ \mathsf{Tfztree}\ t\ (in, out) \supset \mathsf{Tfz}(\mathsf{Val}\ in, out)$$

This theorem follows easily by structural induction on the binary tree t. It states that every implementation constructed from an appropriate tree of OR-gates exhibits the functional behaviour stipulated by the relation Tfz. The model is parameterized by the variable t of type *btree*, and this effectively quantifies over all possible shapes that the circuit can have. The theorem also asserts correctness for every possible size of the n-bit input. Finally, the recursively-defined data abstraction function Val relates values of type $(bool)list$ in the model to values of type *num* in the more abstract specification.

---

[7]In the test-for-zero example, of course, it does not matter which is the least significant bit.

5.6   Other approaches

A fundamental requirement for the effective use of data abstraction in reasoning about hardware is, of course, a formal representation of data. This chapter has shown how a wide class of concrete data types can be characterized formally in higher order logic. Two examples were also given to illustrate the approach to data abstraction introduced in chapter 4. A common theme of these examples is the importance of an appropriate choice of types when defining models. Some approaches to data types and data abstraction in other formalisms are briefly discussed below.

Data types in the Boyer-Moore logic

The Boyer-Moore logic includes an axiom-scheme called the *shell principle* which allows one to introduce axioms that describe sets of recursive structures [14]. This was used by Hunt to define several recursive data types[8] for his correctness proof of the FM8501 microprocessor, including a type of lists to represent bit-vectors [73]. Other types axiomatized for the FM8501 proof include the natural numbers and a concrete representation of the integers. The class of types axiomatizable using the shell principle is very similar to the class of concrete data types discussed in this chapter. The main difference between the two approaches is that the shell principle introduces a type by postulating an axiomatization for it, whereas in higher order logic this must derived from a formal definition.

Data types in VERITAS and Nuprl

Types play an important role in the VERITAS+ design logic mentioned in Chapter 3. The type system of this logic includes concrete recursive types, as well as *subtypes* and *dependent* types. Hanna, Daeche and Longley [59] have made a strong case for the utility of subtypes and dependent types for hardware verification. The main advantage is that typing judgements have high information content; subtypes and dependent types may depend on the values of terms rather than only on other types. This is especially convenient where there are many kinds of values that are parameterized by size—for example bit-vectors, or integers mod n. For example, in VERITAS+ one can define a data abstraction function

$$\mathsf{Val} : [n{:}nat] \to word(n) \to nat(2^n)$$

where nat denotes the natural numbers, $word(n)$ denotes the set of n-bit words, and $nat(2^n)$ denotes the set $\{m \in nat \mid m < 2^n\}$. This says that the function Val takes a number n and produces a mapping from n-bit words to natural numbers less than 2^n. This is a much more precise statement than the typing for the Val function

---

[8]Strictly speaking, the Boyer-Moore logic is untyped. In such a setting, however, much of the role of types can easily be played by appropriately-employed predicates.

defined in section 5.5.4. Leeser [81] has also shown how the dependent types of the Nuprl theorem-prover can be used to structure information content in reasoning about hardware.

In a mechanized setting, a disadvantage of using a logic that has dependent types is that type checking is undecidable; it is impossible to devise an algorithm that determines if an arbitrary term is well-typed. Jacobs and Melham [76] describe a translation of dependent type theory into the relatively simpler higher order logic used in this book. In particular, they show how type dependency as found in Martin-Löf's Intuitionistic Type Theory (and VERITAS+) can be mimicked by the use of suitable predicates in higher order logic. The aim is to get the expressive advantages of type dependency while still remaining within the context of a decidable underlying type system. See [76] for the details.

Mechanized reasoning about data types

The logical basis for all the examples in this chapter is the systematic method for defining concrete types explained in [88]. This method has been mechanized in the HOL system by theorem proving tools that can automatically construct a completely rigorous definition for any concrete recursive type. Related HOL tools include programs for proving the structural induction theorem for any concrete type and for defining primitive recursive functions on these types.

Reasoning about recursive types has also been mechanized in other theorem-proving systems. Milner developed a package in LCF for automating the construction of lazy recursive types and the derivation of structural induction [95]. This package was later extended by Monahan [98]. Another development of Milner's package is the structural induction tools in Cambridge LCF [102].

Chapter 6

Temporal Abstraction

Temporal abstraction involves relating formal specifications that describe hardware behaviour using different notions of time. This type of abstraction is used when the design model for a device gives more detail about how it behaves over time than the specification of its required behaviour. With the mechanism of temporal abstraction, information about a device's behaviour at moments of time that are not of interest can be hidden from the specification, allowing it to concentrate on how the device behaves at only significant or interesting points of time.

6.1 Temporal abstraction by sampling

The most common form of temporal abstraction is the signal sampling mechanism introduced in chapter 4. With this kind of abstraction, the specification for a device simply describes its externally observable behaviour at fewer points of time than the design model. The grain of discrete time in the specification is coarser than in the model, and each unit of time at the abstract level of description corresponds to an interval of time at the more detailed level.

The idea of a mapping between time-scales was introduced in section 4.1.3 to express this kind of abstraction relationship in logic. A time mapping describes a correspondence between successive points of time on an abstract time-scale and selected points of time on a concrete time-scale. Given such a mapping $f : num \rightarrow num$, a correctness statement based on temporal abstraction by sampling is formulated in logic as shown below.

$$\vdash M[c_1, \ldots, c_n] \supset S[c_1 \circ f, \ldots, c_n \circ f]$$

The model $M[c_1, \ldots, c_n]$ in this theorem describes the values that appear on each external wire c_i at points of fine-grained or concrete time. The abstract specification is a constraint of the form $S[a_1, \ldots, a_n]$ and specifies the desired behaviour in terms of the values allowed on its external wires at points of coarse-grained or abstract time. The function f defines the intervals of concrete time that correspond to each unit of abstract time. The theorem states that whenever a sequence of values c_i satisfies the temporally detailed model, the sequence $c_i \circ f$ obtained by sampling c_i at the points of concrete time specified by f will satisfy the abstract specification.

To prove a theorem of this form one must show that if the sequences $c_1, \ldots, c_n$ take on the intermediate values defined by the model, then the values of these sequences when sampled at the points of time specified by f will satisfy the specification.

Correctness is formulated by an implication in this theorem because there may be several different ways of implementing the behaviour specified by the constraint $S[a_1, \ldots, a_n]$; the implementation in which the sequences $c_1, \ldots, c_n$ take on the intermediate values defined by the model $M[c_1, \ldots, c_n]$ is only one possibility. In the example given above, each signal in the model is sampled using the same time mapping. In general, however, this need not be the case. Some signals, for example, may be sampled whenever a clock rises while others are sampled when it falls. Examples of this kind occur in the case study presented in section 6.4.

Any correspondence between successive units of abstract time and contiguous intervals of concrete time can be described in logic by a mapping of type $num{\rightarrow}num$. Such a mapping is just a function that assigns a particular point of concrete time to each point of abstract time. Not every function of logical type $num{\rightarrow}num$, however, specifies a valid correspondence between time-scales. A mapping from abstract to concrete time must be a strictly increasing function on the natural numbers. This requirement can be expressed formally by the predicate Incr defined as follows.

$$\vdash \mathsf{Incr}\ f = \forall t_1\ t_2.\ (t_1 < t_2) \supset (f\ t_1 < f\ t_2)$$

The constraint 'Incr f' ensures that if t_1 comes before t_2 on the abstract time-scale, then this relationship also holds between the corresponding points of time $f\ t_1$ and $f\ t_2$ on the concrete time-scale. That is, the order of discrete time is preserved by the function f.

6.1.1   Constructing mappings between time scales

To use temporal abstraction by sampling one must define an appropriate mapping from the abstract time-scale used in the specification to the concrete time-scale used in the model. In general, the points of concrete time that correspond to points of abstract time may depend on the behaviour of the device itself. In this case, a fixed mapping from abstract to concrete time—for example one that maps successive points of abstract time to every tenth point of concrete time—is not possible.

For example, consider the correspondence between time-scales shown in figure 6.1. Here, successive points of abstract time correspond to the points of concrete time at which there is a rising edge of the clock signal ck. The precise correspondence between time-scales depends on the behaviour of this clock signal, and the mapping f must be defined so as to reflect this dependence. This can be done by constructing the time mapping f from a predicate 'Rise ck', which identifies those points of concrete time at which the rising edges of the clock occur.

Any time mapping can be defined using a predicate that specifies which points of concrete time are to correspond to points of abstract time. The idea is to define

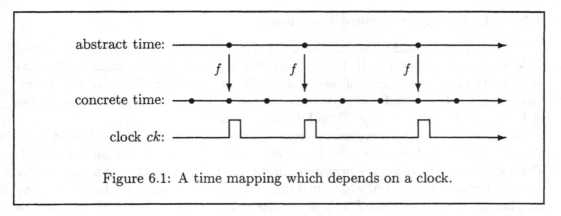

Figure 6.1: A time mapping which depends on a clock.

this predicate such that it is true of precisely those selected points of concrete time which are to be in the image of the time mapping. The free variables in the model can, of course, be used as parameters to this predicate. In synchronous systems the predicate identifying appropriate points of concrete time might involve the value of the clock signal. In asynchronous systems, handshaking signals might be used. This allows the mapping from abstract time to concrete time used in a correctness statement to reflect the time-dependent behaviour of the device itself.

Suppose that P:$num{\rightarrow}bool$ is a predicate which specifies the points of concrete time that are to correspond to points of abstract time. It is possible to construct from P a time mapping f_P which maps each point of abstract time n to the point of concrete time at which P is true for the nth time, as shown in figure 6.2. Formally, we wish to define a function

$$\text{Timeof} : (num{\rightarrow}bool) \rightarrow num \rightarrow num$$

so that for any predicate P and abstract time n, the term 'Timeof P n' denotes the point of concrete time at which P is true for the nth time. The mapping between time-scales f_P shown in figure 6.2 is then just Timeof P. It remains to define the function Timeof formally in higher order logic.

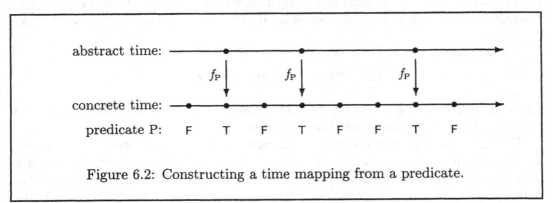

Figure 6.2: Constructing a time mapping from a predicate.

6.1.2   Defining the Timeof function

As informally described above, the value of 'Timeof P n' may in fact be undefined for some values of P and n. If the predicate P true at only a finite number of points of concrete time, then there will be a number N such that for all $n > N$ there is no time at which P is true for the nth time. It seems, therefore, that for some values of P the function denoted by 'Timeof P' must be a partial function.

In higher order logic, however, all functions are total. The function Timeof must therefore be defined to be a total function whose value is only partially specified. This can be done by using the primitive constant ε in the definition, in a way similar to that in which the partially specified function abs was defined in chapter 5. The idea is that if the predicate P is true infinitely often, then 'Timeof P' will denote the required mapping between time-scales. But if P is true only finitely often, then 'Timeof P' will denote a mapping about which nothing significant can be proved.

The formal definition of Timeof is based on a relation Istimeof, defined so that the term 'Istimeof P n t' has the meaning 'P is true for the nth time at time t'. The definition is done by primitive recursion on the natural number n. When n is zero, the defining equation is

$$\vdash \text{Istimeof } P\ 0\ t\ =\ P\ t\ \wedge\ \forall t'.\, t' < t \supset \neg(P\ t')$$

That is, P is true for the first time at concrete time t if it is true at time t and false at every point of time before t. For n greater than zero, the defining equation is

$$\vdash \text{Istimeof } P\ (\text{Suc } n)\ t\ =\ \exists t'.\, \text{Istimeof } P\ n\ t'\ \wedge\ \text{Next } t'\ t\ P$$

where the auxiliary predicate Next is defined by

$$\vdash \text{Next } t'\ t\ P\ =\ t' < t\ \wedge\ P\ t\ \wedge\ \forall t''.\, (t' < t'' \wedge t'' < t) \supset \neg(P\ t'')$$

This says that t is the n+1th time at which P is true if P was true for the nth time at time t' and t is the next time after t' at which P is true. To summarize, the primitive recursive definition of Istimeof is given by the two equations shown below.

$$\vdash \text{Istimeof } P\ 0\ t\ =\ P\ t\ \wedge\ \forall t'.\, t' < t \supset \neg(P\ t')$$

$$\vdash \text{Istimeof } P\ (\text{Suc } n)\ t\ =\ \exists t'.\, \text{Istimeof } P\ n\ t'\ \wedge\ \text{Next } t'\ t\ P$$

Formally, this recursive definition is justified using the method for proving primitive recursive defining equations discussed in chapter 2.

The term 'Istimeof P n t' expresses the proposition that the predicate P is true for the nth time at concrete time t. There is no guarantee, however, that such a time exists for all values of P and n. But if the predicate P is true infinitely often, then there is a unique value t for each value of n such that Istimeof P n t holds. In this case, the relation Istimeof P in fact represents a well-defined total function that maps n to t.

The condition that P is true at an infinite number of points of concrete time is stated formally by the predicate Inf defined below.

$$\vdash \text{Inf } P = \forall t. \exists t'. t' > t \wedge P\, t'$$

It is straightforward to show that if P satisfies this predicate, then for all n there exists a unique time t at which P is true for the nth time:

$$\vdash \forall P. \text{Inf } P \supset \forall n. \exists!\, t. \text{Istimeof } P\, n\, t \tag{6.1}$$

The proof of this theorem proceeds by proving the existence and uniqueness parts separately. The existence of t follows by induction on n, using the well ordering property of the natural numbers

$$\vdash \forall P. (\exists n. P\, n) \supset \exists n. P\, n \wedge \forall m. m < n \supset \neg(P\, m)$$

to infer from the assumption Inf P that whenever P is true, there is always a *smallest* next time at which P is true. The uniqueness of t also follows by induction on n.

Having defined the relation Istimeof and proved theorem 6.1, the function Timeof can be defined formally using ε as shown below.

$$\vdash \text{Timeof } P\, n = \varepsilon t. \text{Istimeof } P\, n\, t$$

This defines Timeof $P\, n$ to be the time t such that Istimeof $P\, n\, t$ is true—i.e. such that P is true for the nth time at time t. If no such time exists, then 'Timeof $P\, n$' denotes an arbitrary time. Using the primitive constant ε makes the term 'Timeof P' denote a total function, but one which may be only partially specified for some values of P. The term 'Timeof $P\, n$' therefore always denotes *some* time, even when P is true at only a finite number of points of time.

As theorem 6.1 shows, if the predicate P is true infinitely often then for all n there is a unique time t such that 'Istimeof $P\, n\, t$' is true. Thus if Inf P holds, then Timeof $P\, n$ will in fact be the time at which P is true for the nth time, as desired. More formally, an immediate consequence of the existence part of theorem 6.1 is

$$\vdash \forall P. \text{Inf } P \supset \forall n. \text{Istimeof } P\, n\, (\text{Timeof } P\, n) \tag{6.2}$$

from which it follows by an easy case analysis that

$$\vdash \forall P. \text{Inf } P \supset \forall n. P(\text{Timeof } P\, n)$$

That is, if the predicate P is true infinitely often, then Timeof $P\, n$ always denotes a point of time at which P is in fact true. Furthermore, it follows immediately from theorem 6.2 that Timeof P maps 0 to the first time at which P is true:

$$\vdash \forall P.\, \text{Inf } P \supset \forall t.\, t < (\text{Timeof } P\ 0) \supset \neg(P\ t)$$

From the uniqueness part of theorem 6.1 it also follows that Timeof P denotes an increasing function from abstract to concrete time, and that this function does not skip any points of concrete time identified by the predicate P:

$$\vdash \forall P.\, \text{Inf } P \supset \forall n.\, (\text{Timeof } P\ n) < (\text{Timeof } P\ (n{+}1))$$

$$\vdash \forall P.\, \text{Inf } P \supset \forall n\ t.\, ((\text{Timeof } P\ n) < t \wedge t < (\text{Timeof } P\ (n{+}1))) \supset \neg(P\ t)$$

These theorems about Timeof show that if the predicate P is true infinitely often, then the term 'Timeof P' is a well defined total function that maps each point of abstract time n to the point of concrete time at which P is true for the nth time, as required.

6.1.3   Using Timeof to formulate correctness

The Timeof function just defined is the fundamental logical tool for formulating correctness theorems using temporal abstraction by sampling. The time mapping required for such a theorem is always an increasing function of type $num{\rightarrow}num$. Any such function can be defined by applying Timeof to an appropriate predicate which indicates the points of concrete time of interest. Formally, we have that any strictly increasing function f can be constructed using Timeof from a predicate P for which Inf P holds:

$$\vdash \forall f.\, \text{Incr } f = \exists P.\, \text{Inf } P \wedge (f = \text{Timeof } P)$$

This follows from the definition of Incr and the properties of Timeof discussed in the preceding section.

Suppose that $M[c_1, \ldots, c_n]$ is a design model and that P denotes a predicate which specifies the points of concrete time in this model that are to correspond to points of abstract time. Then a correctness theorem which relates the model to an abstract specification $S[a_1, \ldots, a_n]$ can be formulated in logic as shown below.

$$\vdash \forall c_1 \ldots c_n.\, \text{Inf } P \supset M[c_1, \ldots, c_n] \supset S[c_1 \circ (\text{Timeof P}), \ldots, c_n \circ (\text{Timeof P})]$$

This theorem states that whenever the signals c_1, ..., c_n satisfy the model, the abstractions constructed by sampling these signals when the predicate P is true will satisfy the specification. The predicate P can, of course, be defined in terms of the variables c_1, ..., c_n. And this will make the times at which the values in the model are sampled depend on the time-varying behaviour of the device itself.

The term 'Inf P' in the above correctness theorem is a validity condition on the abstraction it expresses. This condition is necessary to ensure that the time-mapping Timeof P is correctly constructed. In some cases, however, the validity condition may just be satisfied by the model itself:

$$\vdash M[c_1, \ldots, c_n] \supset \mathsf{Inf}\ P$$

In this case, the correctness theorem can be simplified to

$$\vdash \forall c_1 \ldots c_n.\ M[c_1, \ldots, c_n] \supset S[c_1 \circ (\mathsf{Timeof}\ P), \ldots, c_n \circ (\mathsf{Timeof}\ P)]$$

The formal justification for this simplification is essentially the VCOND rule discussed in chapter 4.

Suppose that when is an infix function constant defined as follows.

$$\vdash \forall s:num \to \alpha.\ \forall P.\ s\ \mathsf{when}\ P = s \circ (\mathsf{Timeof}\ P)$$

Then the correctness statement shown above can be written in the more intuitively clear form below.

$$\vdash \forall c_1 \ldots c_n.\ \mathsf{Inf}\ P \supset M[c_1, \ldots, c_n] \supset S[c_1\ \mathsf{when}\ P, \ldots, c_n\ \mathsf{when}\ P]$$

Any correctness relationship based on temporal abstraction by sampling can also be expressed in this form. Note that the type of the constant when is polymorphic:

$$\mathsf{when} : (num \to \alpha) \to (num \to bool) \to (num \to \alpha)$$

The when operator can therefore be used for temporal abstraction of sequences of values of any type, and not just for boolean signals.

The example in the next section shows how the when operator just defined can be used to formulate the correctness of a D-type flip-flop with respect to the abstract specification of a one-bit unit delay register.

6.2   An example: abstracting to unit delay

A commonly used register-transfer level device is the unit delay, described formally by the specification shown below.

$$\vdash \mathsf{Del}(i, o) = \forall t.\ o(t+1) = i\ t$$

This specification simply states that the value on the output o is equal to the value on the input i delayed by one unit of discrete time.

The delay device described by this specification is an abstraction—there are many circuits that can implement the behaviour given by 'Del(i, o)'. One possiblity is the rising edge triggered D-type flip-flop specified in chapter 3. The sequential behaviour of this device is modelled in logic by the term Dtype(ck, d, q) defined below.

d —|Dtype|— q

ck —▷

$\vdash$ Rise $ck\ t = \neg ck(t) \wedge ck(t{+}1)$

$\vdash$ Dtype$(ck, d, q) = \forall t.\ q(t{+}1) = ($Rise $ck\ t \Rightarrow d\ t \mid q\ t)$

The D-type device implements a unit delay by sampling the input value d when the clock rises and holding this value on the output q until the next rise of the clock. In this way the D-type delays by one clock period the sequence of values present on the input d at successive rising edges of the clock ck. This suggests that a time mapping which maps successive points of abstract time to the points of concrete time where the clock rises can be used to relate the model Dtype(ck, d, q) to the abstract specification Del(i, o). In fact, the required time mapping is just the function

      Timeof (Rise ck) : $num \to num$

constructed from the predicate Rise ck by the function Timeof.

    Using this mapping between time-scales, a correctness statement that relates the D-type model to the unit delay specification can be formulated as shown below.

$\vdash \forall ck.$ Inf(Rise ck) $\supset$
    $\forall d\ q.$ Dtype$(ck, d, q) \supset$ Del$(d$ when (Rise ck), q when (Rise ck))   (6.3)

This says that if the signals ck, d, and q satisfy the model, then the abstract signals obtained by sampling d and q at successive rising edges of the clock ck will satisfy the specification. Note that there is actually an infinite family of sampling functions used to relate the model to the specification in this correctness theorem. For each possible value of the clock ck, the term 'Rise ck' denotes a predicate that identifies when the clock rises. The **when** operator then samples the signals d and q whenever this predicate is true.

    The assumption that the clock rises infinitely often is a validity condition on the abstraction relationship expressed by this theorem. The theorem asserts that the specification represents a valid abstract view of the behaviour of a D-type flip-flop only if this condition is satisfied by the environment in which it is placed. The condition is as unrestrictive as possible; the clock is not requiredto be regular or have a minimum period, but merely to be 'live'.

    The proof of this correctness theorem is straightforward. The main step is an induction on the time between adjacent rises of the clock, with the aim of proving that the value on d sampled at each rising edge is held on the output q until the next rising edge. More precisely, one first proves the following lemma.

$$\vdash (\forall t.\, q(t+1) = (P\, t \Rightarrow d\, t \mid q\, t)) \supset$$
$$\forall t.\, P\, t \supset \forall n.\, (\forall t'.\, t < t' \wedge t' < t{+}n{+}1 \supset \neg(P\, t')) \supset (q\, (t{+}n{+}1) = d\, t)$$

The proof is an easy mathematical induction on the natural number n. This lemma can then be re-expressed in the following form

$$\vdash (\forall t.\, q(t+1) = (P\, t \Rightarrow d\, t \mid q\, t)) \supset$$
$$\forall t_1\, t_2.\, P\, t_1 \supset t_1 < t_2 \supset (\forall t.\, t_1 < t \wedge t < t_2 \supset \neg(P\, t)) \supset (q\, t_2 = d\, t_1)$$

since the condition '$t_1 < t_2$' is equivalent to the existence of a number n such that $t_2 = t_1 + n + 1$. The correctness result stated by theorem 6.3 then follows easily from this lemma. Instantiating the predicate variable P to 'Rise ck' and specializing the variables t_1 and t_2 to the times of successive rising edges of the clock gives

$$\vdash (\forall t.\, q(t+1) = (\text{Rise } ck\ t \Rightarrow d\, t \mid q\, t)) \supset$$
$$\text{Rise } ck\ (\text{Timeof } (\text{Rise } ck)\ t) \supset$$
$$(\text{Timeof } (\text{Rise } ck)\ t) < (\text{Timeof } (\text{Rise } ck)\ (t{+}1)) \supset$$
$$(\forall t'.\, (\text{Timeof } (\text{Rise } ck)\ t) < t' \wedge t' < (\text{Timeof } (\text{Rise } ck)\ (t{+}1)) \supset \neg(\text{Rise } ck\ t'))$$
$$\supset$$
$$(q\, (\text{Timeof } (\text{Rise } ck)\ (t{+}1)) = d\, (\text{Timeof } (\text{Rise } ck)\ t))$$

The first line of this theorem is just the definition of the model $\text{Dtype}(ck, d, q)$ and the last line is essentially the required instance of the specification. The remaining lines are among the properties of Timeof listed in the preceding section, and these are all implied by the validity condition 'Inf (Rise ck)' of theorem 6.3.

The D-type proof just described is typical of a very common type of temporal abstraction—namely one in which contiguous intervals of concrete time correspond to successive units of abstract time. Proofs involving detailed timing information or several different time mappings may be much more complex than this very simple example; but, as far as the abstraction relationship itself is concerned, more complex uses of temporal abstraction by sampling employ the same general approach.

6.3   A synchronizing temporal abstraction

The Timeof function can be used to define other abstraction operators in addition to the sampling operator when. One example, used in the case study presented later, is a temporal abstraction operator that synchronizes one signal with another (e.g. with a clock). This is the 'between' operator, defined formally as follows:

$$\vdash (s \text{ between } P)\, n = \exists t.\, (\text{Timeof } P\, n) \leq t \wedge t < (\text{Timeof } P\, (n{+}1)) \wedge s\, t$$

The predicate P in this definition identifies points of concrete time which are of interest at the abstract level—in the same way that the predicate P is used in the sampling construct s when P. As in temporal abstraction by sampling, this predicate defines the intervals of concrete time that correspond to successive units of abstract time. The variable $s{:}num{\rightarrow}bool$ stands for a sequence of boolean values at the concrete level of abstraction. The abstract signal s between P is constructed from s and is true at abstract time n if the signal s is true at some intermediate point of concrete time between the nth and the $n{+}1$th time P is true. This 'synchronizes' the asynchronous signal s with the abstract time-scale defined by P—the abstract signal s between P is true at time n if there was an event on s at some time within the nth cycle. A similar function is performed by the 'some' abstraction operator defined by Fourman and Hexsel in [39].

6.4 A case study: the T-ring

The T-ring is a very simple ring communication network, designed and built in TTL by D. Gaubatz and M. Burrows at the University of Cambridge. It was originally designed to provide a simplified network which could be specified and proved correct as a prelude to attempting the much more difficult verification of the Cambridge Fast Ring network [72]. A correctness proof for the Fast Ring was never actually attempted, but an ECL chip used as a part of the network has been verified by John Herbert [65]. The TTL implementation of the T-ring was deliberately designed to present certain typical difficulties to verification; as the reader will see, it was never intended as an example of good TTL design.

This section outlines the main steps in a proof of correctness for the design of the T-ring. The aim is to give an overview of a relatively complex example of temporal abstraction, without burdening the reader with the details of the intricate (but generally shallow) formal proofs that are involved. This section is therefore mainly concerned with the overall structure of the proof and how it fits together.

6.4.1 Informal description of the T-ring

The T-ring has three major components, called the *transmitter*, the *receiver*, and the *monitor*. These are connected together to form a data transmission network in the shape of ring, as shown in figure 6.3. The transmitter sends messages (clockwise) around the ring to the receiver. Each message contains only one bit of information; no source or destination address is included in a message, since in the T-ring network there is only one transmitter and one receiver.

Storage for messages in a ring network is normally provided by delay in the transmission wires which run between the devices connected to it. In the TTL implementation of T-ring, however, these transmission wires are very short, and they impose virtually no delay between the components connected to the ring. Storage is therefore artificially supplied in the T-ring by special delay devices inserted between the other components in the ring. These are the devices labelled Del in figure 6.3,

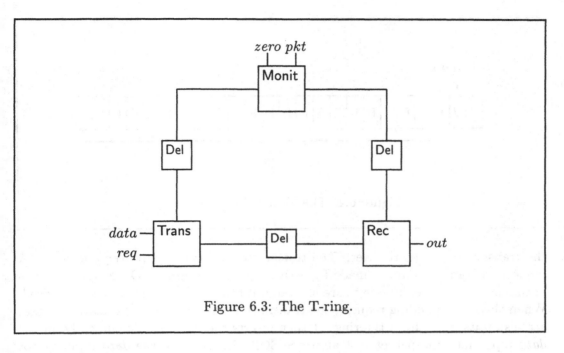

Figure 6.3: The T-ring.

each of which is simply a shift register that imposes eight bits of delay between its input and output. These registers supply the T-ring network with the storage for circulating messages which in a more realistic ring network is provided by delay in the transmission wires. The transmitter, receiver, and monitor contribute no delay to the ring, so the T-ring network has a total of 24 bits of storage.

Messages are transmitted serially around the ring encoded in a simple format called a *packet*. A packet consists of only two bits, a start-of-packet (SOP) bit followed by a data bit. The start-of-packet bit is always a boolean T. There is only one such packet circulating in the ring at any time. The other 22 bits of storage in the ring constitute a gap, each bit of which has the value F. This pattern of bits—a single packet followed by the gap—is called the *slot structure* of the ring; it is shown in figure 6.4 (overleaf). The circulating packet is a slot in the circular bit pattern, where data can be inserted into the ring and read from the ring. The devices connected to the ring detect the presence of the packet by sensing a transition from F (the end of the gap) to T (the SOP bit).

The monitor is used to create the slot structure of the T-ring. The monitor has two inputs, *zero* and *pkt*. When the *zero* input is activated, a boolean F is inserted into the bit pattern on the ring at the monitor's output. The first step in creating the slot structure is to activate *zero* long enough to set each bit in the ring to F. The *pkt* input is then activated once, and a single start-of-packet bit is inserted into the bit pattern on the ring. This creates one packet on the ring, and completes the creation of the T-ring slot structure.

Once the slot structure exists, the ring is ready to carry one-bit messages from

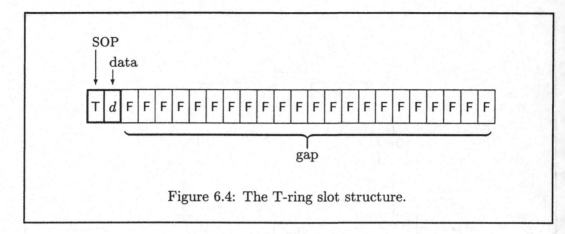

Figure 6.4: The T-ring slot structure.

the transmitter to the receiver. The transmitter has two inputs, *req* and *data*. A request to transmit data is made by activating the *req* input. Once a request has been made, subsequent requests are ignored until the pending one has been serviced. When there is a pending request, the transmitter waits until the circulating packet arrives on its input from the ring. It then inserts the bit which is currently on the *data* input into the packet just after the SOP bit. Because the *data* input is not read until the packet arrives at the transmitter, the data bit which is sent to the receiver will not necessarily be the value on the *data* line at the time of the request. The receiver simply reads the data bit in the circulating packet each time it comes around and makes this value available on the output wire *out*.

The proof of correctness for the T-ring is structured into a two-level hierarchy. At the lower level, called the *timing level*, there is a correctness theorem for each of the four kinds of component in the design—namely, the delay devices, the receiver, the transmitter, and the monitor. The correctness results at this level are discussed in sections 6.4.3–6.4.6. The next level of the proof is the *register-transfer* level, where a model for the entire network is defined and proved correct with respect to a top-level specification that captures the data transmission behaviour just described. The proof at this level is discussed in sections 6.4.7 and 6.4.8. Finally, section 6.4.9 shows how the results for the two levels are combined to obtain a theorem that relates the timing level design to the top-level specification. The discussion begins with an overview of the timing scheme for the TTL implementation of the T-ring and a description of the hardware primitives that are used.

6.4.2   The T-ring timing scheme and TTL primitives

The T-ring is a synchronous TTL system driven by a single master clock. Values on the ring change on the falling edges of the clock and are sampled by the transmitter, receiver, and monitor on the rising edges of the clock. (See figure 6.5.) The idea of this timing scheme is to ensure that the value on the ring is sampled when it is

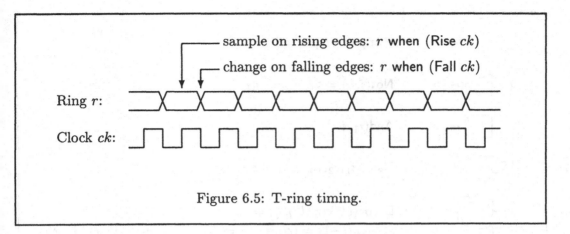

sample on rising edges: r when (Rise ck)

change on falling edges: r when (Fall ck)

Ring r:

Clock ck:

Figure 6.5: T-ring timing.

most likely to be stable—namely, half-way between two falling edges of the clock. This is done by having the primitive components that read from the ring triggered on the rising edges of the clock and the primitive components that write to the ring triggered on the falling edges. A consequence is that the proof involves temporal abstraction by sampling on both rising and falling edges of the clock.

In the T-ring TTL approximation to a real network, the delay devices represent 'the ring' itself. The principle of sampling on rising edges therefore does not apply to the delay devices; they are instead just triggered on falling edges.

There are four combinational primitives used in the T-ring design—the power source, the inverter, the AND-gate, and the NAND-gate. The specifications of these devices are simple, as shown in figure 6.6 (overleaf). The only primitive device with state is the rising edge triggered D-type flip-flop) with asynchronous clear. The specification of this device, also shown in figure 6.6, is similar to that of the D-type discussed earlier in this chapter. The only differences are the addition of an active-low 'clear' input and an additional inverted output.

The D-type flip-flop is often used with the asynchronous clear disabled. In this case, the (active low) clear input is just driven by the power source, and the resulting model simplifies as follows:

$$\vdash (\exists clr.\, \mathsf{Pwr}\; clr \wedge \mathsf{Dtype}(ck, clr, d, q, \bar{q})) =$$
$$\forall t.\, q(t+1) = (\mathsf{Rise}\; ck\; t \Rightarrow d\; t \mid q\; t) \wedge \forall t.\, \bar{q}\; t = \neg(q\; t)$$

Note that the simplified equation for q is just the D-type model of section 6.2. The correctness theorem proved in that section therefore also applies here.

For clarity, the clear inputs to D-type flip-flops are not shown in circuit diagrams when they are disabled. Similarly, the inverted output of a flip-flop is also omitted if it is not used. The power source is sometimes used to drive other internal wires in the design. This is indicated in the circuit diagrams shown in the following sections by writing the constant 'T' beside these wires.

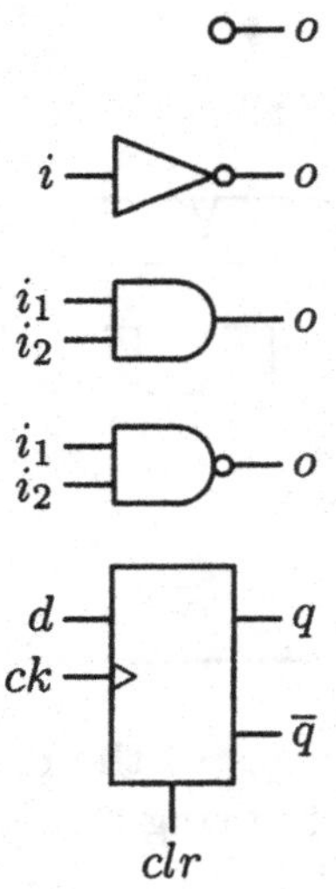

o—o $\vdash$ Pwr $p = \forall t.\, p\, t = \mathsf{T}$

i —▷o—o $\vdash$ Not$(i, o) = \forall t.\, o\, t = \neg(i\, t)$

$\begin{array}{c} i_1 \\ i_2 \end{array}$ D—o $\vdash$ And$(i_1, i_2, o) = \forall t.\, o\, t = (i_1\, t \wedge i_2\, t)$

$\begin{array}{c} i_1 \\ i_2 \end{array}$ Do—o $\vdash$ Nand$(i_1, i_2, o) = \forall t.\, o\, t = \neg(i_1\, t \wedge i_2\, t)$

d —| |— q $\vdash$ Dtype$(ck, clr, d, q, \bar{q}) =$
ck —▷| | $\qquad \forall t.\, q(t{+}1) = (clr(t{+}1) \Rightarrow (\text{Rise } ck\, t \Rightarrow d\, t \mid q\, t) \mid \mathsf{F}) \wedge$
   | |— $\bar{q}$ $\qquad \forall t.\, \bar{q}\, t = \neg(q\, t)$

clr

Figure 6.6: Primitive devices used in the T-ring.

6.4.3   Correctness of the delay devices

The simplest devices in the T-ring are the delay devices inserted between the other three components connected to the ring. These provide data storage for the ring by imposing a delay of 8 bits between their inputs and outputs. The register-transfer level specification for these devices is shown below.

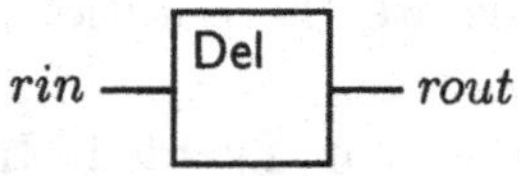

rin —| Del |— $rout$ $\vdash$ Del $rin\ rout = \forall t.\, rout(t{+}8) = rin\, t$

Each of the three delay devices used in the T-ring is implemented by a shift register of eight flip-flops driven by an inverted clock signal, as shown in figure 6.7. In order take advantage of induction in the proof, the model 'Delay $ck\ rin\ rout$' that describes this device is defined in the following slightly indirect way. The first step is to define a parameterized model of a string of $n{+}1$ flip-flops by primitive recursion on n, as shown below.

$\qquad \vdash$ Shift 0 $ck\ clr\ rin\ rout = \exists \bar{q}.\ \text{Dtype}(ck, clr, rin, rout, \bar{q})$

$\qquad \vdash$ Shift $(n{+}1)\ ck\ clr\ rin\ rout =$
$\qquad\qquad \exists \bar{q}\ c.\ \text{Dtype}(ck, clr, rin, c, \bar{q}) \wedge \text{Shift } n\ ck\ clr\ c\ rout$

This use of primitive recursion to define Shift is similar to the way in which the n-bit multiplexer model was defined by recursion in chapter 5. The model for the

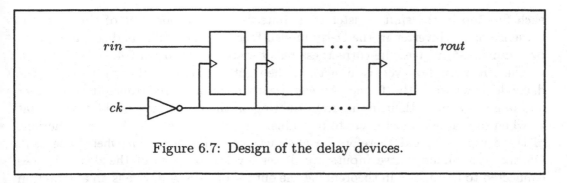

Figure 6.7: Design of the delay devices.

delay devices is defined by composing an instance of this parameterized shift register model with an inverter and a power source:

$\vdash$ Delay $ck\ rin\ rout = \exists clr\ c.$ Not$(ck, c) \land$ Pwr $clr \land$ Shift 8 $ck\ clr\ rin\ rout$

The power source simply disables the asynchronous clear inputs to the flip-flops, and the inverter effectively makes them triggered on falling edges of the clock.

Once the Delay model has been defined, one can prove that the design shown in figure 6.7 correctly implements the specification for an 8-bit delay. Following the pattern set by the D-type proof already described, the naïve correctness statement is the following theorem:

$\vdash \forall ck\ rin\ rout.$
    Inf(Rise ck) $\supset$
    Delay $ck\ rin\ rout \supset$
    Del $(rin$ when (Fall ck)) $(rout$ when (Fall ck))   (6.4)

The input *rin* and output *rout* are sampled on falling edges of the clock, where the function Fall is defined formally by

$\vdash$ Fall $ck\ t = ck(t) \land \neg ck(t+1)$

The theorem says that the sampled values of the input *rin* and output *rout* satisfy the temporally abstract specification for an 8-bit delay device.

The proof of theorem 6.4 is done by first proving the following property of the shift register model given by Shift:

$\vdash \forall ck\ rin\ rout.$
    Inf(Rise ck) $\land$ Pwr $clr \supset$
    $\forall n.$ Shift $n\ ck\ clr\ rin\ rout \supset$
        $\forall t.\ (rout$ when (Rise ck)) $(t+n+1) = (rin$ when (Rise ck)) t

The proof is an easy induction on the length n of the shift register. The D-type correctness result already proved (theorem 6.3 of section 6.2) is used to show that each flip-flop in the shift register contributes a delay of one unit of time. In the presence of the inverter in the Delay model, Rise becomes Fall,[1] and so taking n to be 8 immediately gives the correctness result stated by theorem 6.4.

This theorem, however, is in fact *not* the right formulation of correctness for the delay devices used in the T-ring. As was already mentioned, the transmitter, receiver and monitor sample their inputs from the ring on the *rising* edge of the clock—that is, when the value is most likely to be stable. The register-transfer level abstractions of these inputs should therefore be abstractions of the form '*in* when (Rise ck)'. On the other hand, these inputs are driven by the outputs of the delay devices connected to them, and in theorem 6.4 the output of a delay device is an abstraction of the form '*out* when (Fall ck)'. But when the delay devices are connected to the other components of the T-ring, these abstractions must correspond. It is therefore necessary to sample the output of the delay device on rising edges of the clock, rather than falling edges.

This suggests that the correctness theorem for the 8-bit delay devices in the T-ring should have the form shown below.

$\forall ck\ rin\ rout.$
  Inf(Rise ck) $\supset$
  Delay $ck\ rin\ rout$ $\supset$
  Del $(rin$ when (Fall ck)) $(rout$ when (Rise ck))

The input *rin* is sampled on the falling edges of the clock and the output *rout* on the rising edges. The output of a delay device is therefore an abstraction that will match the inputs it drives—namely, the ring inputs of the receiver, the transmitter, and the monitor.

This revised correctness statement, however, does not hold. Because *rout* is driven by a D-type device, it is possible to show (by induction) that it remains stable until just after each fall of the clock. The value of this output at the time of the nth rise of the clock is therefore the same as its value at the time of the fall after the nth rise. But because the clock may start out (i.e. at time zero) either high or low, this fall of the clock may be either the nth falling edge or the $n+1$th falling edge. If the fall is the nth, then the output of a delay device is the same when sampled on the either the rising or the falling edges of the clock. That is, we have

$$rout(\mathsf{Timeof}\ (\mathsf{Rise}\ ck)\ n) = rout(\mathsf{Timeof}\ (\mathsf{Fall}\ ck)\ n).$$

In this case, the implication shown above holds. But if the falling edge after the nth rise is the falling edge numbered $n+1$, then it follows that

$$rout(\mathsf{Timeof}\ (\mathsf{Rise}\ ck)\ n) = rout(\mathsf{Timeof}\ (\mathsf{Fall}\ ck)\ (n+1))$$

in which case the implication will not be true.

---

[1]Note that $\vdash \forall ck.\ \mathsf{Inf}(\mathsf{Rise}\ ck) = \mathsf{Inf}(\mathsf{Fall}\ ck)$.

The solution to this problem is to operate under a standard notion of the relative positions of the nth rising and falling edges. One way of doing this is to consider only falling edges which are preceded by rising edges—i.e. to ignore the initial falling edge if the clock happens to be high at time zero. Suppose that Fall is given the definition shown below.

$$\vdash \text{Fall } ck\ t = ck(t) \wedge \neg ck(t{+}1) \wedge \exists t'.\, t' < t \wedge \text{Rise } ck\ t'$$

According to this 'standardized' notion of falling edges, the nth falling edge always lies between the rising edges numbered n and $n{+}1$. Formally, we have the following theorems about rising and falling edges.[2]

$$\vdash \text{Inf}(\text{Rise } ck) \supset \forall n.\ \text{Timeof }(\text{Rise } ck)\ n < \text{Timeof }(\text{Fall } ck)\ n$$

$$\vdash \text{Inf}(\text{Rise } ck) \supset \forall n.\ \text{Timeof }(\text{Fall } ck)\ n < \text{Timeof }(\text{Rise } ck)\ (n{+}1)$$

Because the last D-type flip-flop in the delay device keeps the output *rout* stable between falling edges of the clock, it follows from these two theorems that

$$\vdash \forall ck\ rin\ rout.$$
$$\text{Inf}(\text{Rise } ck) \wedge \text{Delay } ck\ rin\ rout \supset \tag{6.5}$$
$$\forall n.\ (rout \text{ when } (\text{Fall } ck))\ (n{+}1) = (rout \text{ when } (\text{Rise } ck))\ (n{+}1)$$

By a proof similar to the one was sketched above for theorem 6.4, one can derive a version of this theorem in which 'Fall' is the standardized notion of falling edge just introduced. This, together with theorem 6.5, implies the result shown below.

$$\vdash \forall ck\ rin\ rout.$$
$$\text{Inf}(\text{Rise } ck) \supset$$
$$\text{Delay } ck\ rin\ rout \supset \tag{6.6}$$
$$\text{Del }(rin \text{ when } (\text{Fall } ck))\ (rout \text{ when } (\text{Rise } ck))$$

This is the final form of correctness for the 8-bit delay devices in the T-ring.

6.4.4   Correctness of the receiver

At the register-transfer level, the receiver is a device with one boolean input *rin*, two boolean outputs *rout* and *out*, and a boolean state (or output) *sop*:

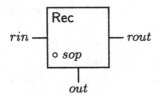

The abstract specification for the receiver at the register-transfer level is given by

---

[2]Cf. the 'well imbrication' conditions in Amblard, Caspi, and Halbwachs [1].

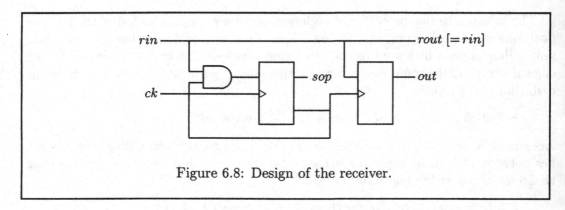

Figure 6.8: Design of the receiver.

the predicate Rec defined below.

⊢ Rec *sop rin rout out* =
  $\forall t.\,sop(t{+}1) = rin(t{+}1) \wedge \neg sop\ t\ \wedge$
  $\forall t.\,rout(t{+}1) = rin(t{+}1)\ \wedge$
  $\forall t.\,out(t{+}1) = (sop\ t \Rightarrow rin(t{+}1)\ |\ out\ t)$

The device is modelled as a state-machine; the outputs at time $t{+}1$ are defined in terms of the input at time $t{+}1$ and the outputs at time t.

 The variables *rin* and *rout* model the input from the ring and the output to the ring respectively. The receiver does not change the value on the ring, and there is no delay between *rin* and *rout*.[3] The variable *sop* represents an output that indicates whether the bit currently on the ring input *rin* is the start-of-packet bit. The equation for *sop* states that the bit currently on the ring is the SOP bit exactly when it has the value T and the previous bit was not the SOP bit. The variable *out* represents the data output of the receiver. This gets the value in the data part of a packet whenever it appears on the ring input *rin*.

 The circuit diagram for the receiver is shown in figure 6.8. The device contains two D-type flip-flops used as registers to store the *sop* and *out* values between clock cycles. The clocking of these flip-flops is consistent with the timing scheme explained above—i.e. the ring is sampled on rising clock edges. The *sop* flip-flop is triggered by the rising edges of the clock. The output flip-flop, however, is driven by the inverted *sop* signal. This signal changes at rising edges, and so this flip-flop also samples the data on the ring input at rising edges.

 A design model 'Receiver *ck sop rin out*' which represents the circuit shown in figure 6.8 is straightforward to define in the usual way—i.e. by applying composition ('∧') and hiding ('∃') to specifications of the components in the design. The actual definition will therefore not be given here.

---

[3]The relationship between *rin* and *rout* at time zero is unimportant to the correct operation of the T-ring. It is left unspecified in order to simplify the correctness proof.

The correctness statement for the receiver involves the concept of the value of a signal being stable between two falling edges of the clock. The predicate Stable defined below expresses this property in logic.

> ⊢ Stable s ck =
> $\forall n\, t.\,((\text{Timeof (Fall } ck)\ n) < t \wedge t \leq (\text{Timeof (Fall } ck)\ (n+1))) \supset$
> $(s\, t = s(\text{Timeof (Fall } ck)\ (n+1))))$

Note that the outputs of the D-type flip-flops in the delay devices are stable in exactly the way stipulated by this predicate; these outputs change just after a falling edge of the clock and remain stable until the next falling edge. In fact, one can prove

> ⊢ $\forall ck\ rin\ rout.\ \text{Inf}(\text{Rise } ck) \supset \text{Delay } ck\ rin\ rout \supset \text{Stable } rout\ ck$ $\qquad$ (6.7)

It is therefore always legitimate to assume that data being read from the ring is stable in this sense.

The formal correctness statement for the receiver is the following theorem:

> ⊢ $\forall ck\ sop\ rin\ out.$
> $\text{Inf}(\text{Rise } ck) \wedge \text{Stable } rin\ ck \supset$
> $\text{Receiver } ck\ sop\ rin\ out \supset$
> $\text{Rec } (sop \text{ when } (\text{Fall } ck))$
> $\qquad (rin \text{ when } (\text{Rise } ck))$
> $\qquad (rin \text{ when } (\text{Fall } ck))$
> $\qquad (out \text{ when } (\text{Fall } ck))$

This expresses correctness as a relationship of temporal abstraction between the design model and the specification. Note that the ring input rin is sampled on rising edges of the clock—in agreement with the T-ring timing scheme explained in section 6.4.2. All other signals are sampled on falling edges. The usual validity condition Inf(Rise ck) states that the clock must be live. An additional validity condition requires rin to be stable between falling edges of the clock. This ensures that the output driving the ring, which is in fact just the same wire as the input rin, can be sampled on falling edges of the clock.

The details of the proof of this correctness statement will not be given here. Very briefly, the main steps are as follows. The D-type correctness theorem already discussed (theorem 6.3) is used as a lemma to derive the specified state equation for sop, and a proof very similar to the one for sketched in section 6.2 for theorem 6.3 is used to derive the state equation for out. In proving these state equations, the fact that the D-types keep their outputs stable between rising edges is used to equate sampling sop and out on rising edges with sampling them on falling edges. Finally, the specified equation for $rout$ follows directly from the stability validity condition.

6.4.5   Correctness of the transmitter

At the register-transfer level, the transmitter looks like

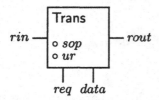

and is specified by the predicate Trans defined below.

$\vdash$ Trans *sop ur data req rin rout* =
$\qquad \forall t.\, sop(t{+}1) = rin(t{+}1) \wedge \neg sop\ t\ \wedge$
$\qquad \forall t.\, ur(t{+}1) = ((sop\ t \wedge ur\ t) \Rightarrow \mathsf{F} \mid (req\ t \Rightarrow \mathsf{T} \mid ur\ t))\ \wedge$
$\qquad \forall t.\, rout(t{+}1) = ((sop\ t \wedge ur\ t) \Rightarrow data(t{+}1) \mid rin(t{+}1))$

Like the receiver, the transmitter has a state *sop* which indicate the presence of the start-of-packet bit. The additional state *ur* is true whenever there is a pending request to transmit data. The state equation specifies that *ur* becomes false when there is a pending request and the packet arrives (at which point the request is serviced). If there is no request already pending, *ur* becomes true whenever a new request is made and otherwise remains the same. The equation for the output *rout* specifies how the bit on the *data* input is inserted into data part of the packet. If there is a pending request when the packet arrives, then the value on the *data* input is inserted into the data bit of the packet on ring output *rout*. Otherwise, the value on the ring is transmitted unchanged from *rin* to *rout*.

The design of the transmitter is shown in figure 6.9. The circuitry used to detect the start-of-packet bit is the same as in the receiver. The output flip-flop, however, in this case drives a multiplexer which selects between the *data* and *rin* inputs. This D-type is clocked by an inverted clock signal, in keeping with the timing scheme in which values on the ring change on falling edges of the clock. The request line drives the clock input of the lower D-type, which is used to generate and store the pending request signal *ur*. This is cleared (on falling edges of the clock) by a signal coming from the $\bar{q}$ output of the D-type on the right. This rather tricky style of TTL design, in which flip-flops are triggered by signals other than the clock, somewhat complicates the proof of correctness.

The most interesting aspect of the transmitter correctness proof is that it uses not only temporal abstraction by sampling, but also the synchronizing temporal abstraction introduced in section 6.3. The request wire drives the clock input of a D-type flip-flop. This means that a request to transmit data in fact consists of a rising edge on the *req* input. This rising edge may occur asynchronously—at any time during a clock cycle—so the sampling operator when cannot be used to

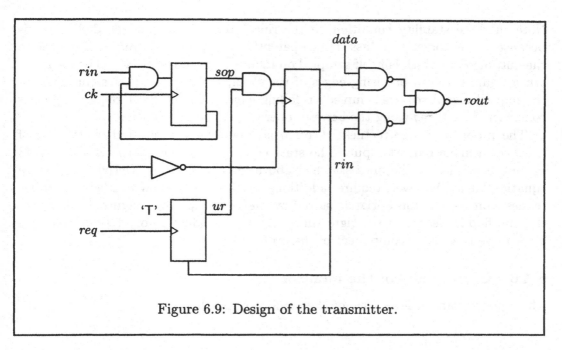

Figure 6.9: Design of the transmitter.

construct a register-transfer level abstraction of *req*. An appropriate abstraction can, however, be defined using the **between** operator as follows:

(Rise *req*) **between** (Fall *ck*)

This abstract signal is true at some abstract time n if there is a rising edge on the request signal *req* at any time during the nth clock cycle—that is, at any time between the nth falling clock edge and the next falling edge. Thus, a 'request' at the register-transfer level corresponds to the occurrence of a rising edge on the physical *req* input at any time between falling edges of the clock.

Suppose that 'Transmitter *ck sop ur req data rin rout*' is a design model for the transmitter circuit shown in figure 6.9. The correctness of the transmitter design is then stated formally by the theorem shown below.

⊢ ∀*ck sop ur req data rin rout*.
    Inf(Rise *ck*) ∧ Stable *rin ck* ⊃
    Transmitter *ck sop ur req data rin rout* ⊃
    Trans (*sop* when (Fall *ck*))
          (*ur* when (Fall *ck*))
          (*data* when (Fall *ck*))
          ((Rise *req*) between (Fall *ck*))
          (*rin* when (Rise *ck*))
          (*rout* when (Fall *ck*))

The validity conditions on this correctness statement are the same as for the receiver.

Note that the stability condition on the ring input rin is again needed. This is because rin is sometimes passed transparently through the output multiplexer to the output $rout$, which is itself sampled on falling edges of the clock. The ring input rin is again sampled on rising edges of the clock, and all the other signals except the request signal req are sampled on falling edges. The abstract request signal is constructed from req using the **between** operator introduced above.

The proof of this correctness theorem is somewhat complicated by the use of an asynchronous request input. The state equations for sop and $rout$ are derived by proofs similar to the ones sketched above for the receiver. Deriving the state equation for ur, however, requires additional arguments to show that asynchronous requests on req are appropriately stored by the lower flip-flop in figure 6.9 and that this flip-flop is cleared at the right times. As usual, induction on the duration of a clock cycle is a major component of the proofs.

6.4.6   Correctness of the monitor

The register-transfer level view of the monitor is as follows:

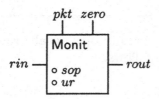

The specification of the monitor is similar to that of the transmitter, but slightly more complex. It is given by the predicate Monit defined below.

$\vdash$ Monit $sop\ ur\ pkt\ zero\ rin\ rout =$
$\quad \forall t.\, sop(t{+}1) = rin(t{+}1) \land \neg sop\ t\ \land$
$\quad \forall t.\, ur(t{+}1) = ((\neg sop\ t \land ur\ t) \Rightarrow \mathsf{F} \mid (pkt\ t \Rightarrow \mathsf{T} \mid ur\ t))\ \land$
$\quad \forall t.\, rout(t{+}1) = ((\neg sop\ t \land ur\ t) \Rightarrow \mathsf{T} \mid (\neg zero(t{+}1) \Rightarrow \mathsf{F} \mid rin(t{+}1)))$

The sop output for the monitor is defined in the same way as it is in the receiver and transmitter. The additional state variable ur records pending requests by the user to create a packet by inserting a start-of-packet bit into the bit pattern in the ring. The equation for the ring output $rout$ shows that an SOP bit will be inserted when the previous bit was not an SOP bit and there is a pending request to do so. In this case, the ur state is also cleared. The $zero$ input can be activated to clear the ring provided there is not also a pending request to create a packet.

The monitor is rather more complex than it needs to be simply in order to create the one-packet slot structure shown above in figure 6.4. In fact, the monitor was originally designed to allow the creation of a T-ring slot structure with several packets. But this does not work. As can be seen from the equation for $rout$ given

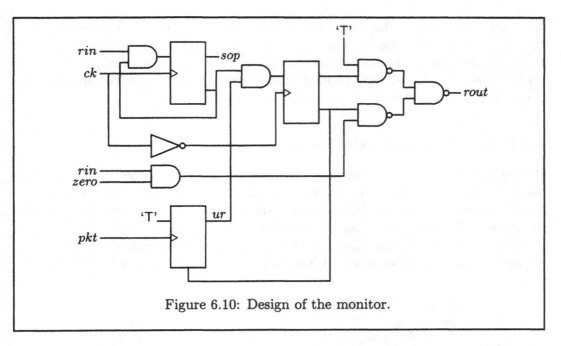

Figure 6.10: Design of the monitor.

above, the monitor cannot reliably create a new packet on the ring without the danger of overwriting the *data* bit of an already existing packet. Formal verification of the monitor with respect to the Monit specification makes this defect clear.

The monitor circuit design is shown in figure 6.10. This is a minor variation on the design of the transmitter—as in the transmitter, a request input (in this case *pkt*) is used to trigger a D-type flip-flop, and the pending request flag *ur* generated by this flip-flop is cleared using its asynchronous clear input. The main differences are the addition of an AND-gate to implement the active-low clear input *zero* and the presence of 'T' on the upper input of the multiplexer that drives the ring to implement the insertion of an SOP bit.

The correctness theorem for the monitor also similar to the correctness statement for the transmitter. Let 'Monitor *ck sop ur pkt zero rin rout*' be a model of the monitor design shown in figure 6.10. Then the correctness of this design is stated by the theorem shown below.

⊢ ∀*ck sop ur pkt zero rin rout*.
    Inf (Rise *ck*) ∧ Stable *rin ck* ⊃
    Monitor *ck sop ur pkt zero rin rout* ⊃
    Monit (*sop* when (Fall *ck*))
        (*ur* when (Fall *ck*))
        ((Rise *pkt*) between (Fall *ck*))
        (*zero* when (Fall *ck*))
        (*rin* when (Rise *ck*))
        (*rout* when (Fall *ck*))

As usual, the temporal abstractions employed in this theorem are the ones dictated by the T-ring timing scheme. The ring input is sampled on the rising edges of the clock and the abstract request signal is constructed using the **between** operator. All other values are sampled on the falling edges of the clock. The proof of this theorem is very similar to the proof of correctness for the transmitter.

6.4.7   Specification of the T-ring

Having completed the verification of the main components of the T-ring—i.e. the delay devices, the receiver, the transmitter, and the monitor—the next step in the correctness proof is to use the abstract specifications for these components to verify the system with respect to a top-level specification of the entire network.

A top-level specification of the T-ring network which describes the behaviour informally explained in section 6.4.1 is given by the predicate **Network** defined below.

$$
\begin{aligned}
&\vdash \textbf{Network}\ zero\ pkt\ data\ req\ out = \\
&\quad \forall t_i.\ \textsf{Init}\ pkt\ zero\ t_i \supset \\
&\qquad \forall t'.\ t' \geq t_i \land req\ t' \supset \\
&\qquad\quad \exists n.\ (0 \leq n \land n \leq 24) \land (out(t'{+}17{+}n) = data(t'{+}n{+}1))
\end{aligned}
$$

The specification is stated in the form of an implication. The antecedent describes the values that must appear on the monitor inputs *pkt* and *zero* in order to initialize the T-ring slot structure. The variable t_i refers to the time at which the T-ting is initialized and ready to transmit data. (The definition of Init is given later.) The consequent of the implication describes the transmission of data through the T-ring network once the slot structure exists. The specification says that whenever there is a request on the *req* input on or after time t_i, the value on the *data* input will be read within 24 time units and will appear on the output *out* 16 time units after it is read. That is, the data bit present on the transmitter *data* input will be sent to the receiver output *out*, with a transmission delay of 16 bits.

Two auxiliary predicates During and After are used to describe the values that the T-ring inputs *pkt* and *zero* must have in order to initialize the slot structure of the ring. These predicates have the definitions shown below.

$$
\vdash \textsf{During}\ t_1\ t_2\ s\ v = \forall t.\ (t_1 \leq t \land t \leq t_2) \supset s\ t = v
$$

$$
\vdash \textsf{After}\ t\ s\ v = \forall t'.\ (t' > t) \supset (s\ t' = v)
$$

The term During t_1 t_2 s v says that the signal s has a constant value v during an interval of time from time t_1 to time t_2 (inclusive). The term After t s says that the signal s has a constant value v after time t.

Using these two auxiliary predicates, the initialization sequence for the T-ring can be described by the predicate Init defined as follows:

⊢ Init *pkt zero* t_i =
  ∃ *t n m*. During *t* $(t+26+n)$ *zero* F ∧
      During *t* $(t+27+n+m)$ *pkt* F ∧
      $pkt(t+27+n+m)$ ∧
      After$(t+28+n+m)$ F *pkt* ∧
      After$(t+29+n+m)$ T *zero* ∧
      $t' \geq t+22+n+m$

This says that the T-ring initialization sequence consists of the following steps:

1. Starting at some time t, activate the *zero* input for at least 26 units of time in order to clear the entire bit pattern in the ring. While doing this, do not activate the *pkt* input. After the ring has been cleared, the *pkt* input can remain inactive as long as desired. The *zero* input is active low and the *pkt* input is active high, so the required input sequence is given by

   During *t* $(t+26+n)$ *zero* F ∧ During *t* $(t+27+n+m)$ *pkt* F

2. Activate the *pkt* input once to create a single a packet in the circulating bit pattern in the ring. This completes the T-ring slot structure. The *pkt* input can be activated any time after the ring has been cleared:

   $pkt(t+27+n+m)$

3. Do not activate the *pkt* and *zero* inputs again after the T-ring slot structure has been created:

   After$(t+28+n+m)$ F *pkt* ∧ After$(t+29+n+m)$ T *zero*

The particular numerical constants which appear in this initialization sequence (e.g. '26' and '27' in step 1) were derived in the course of the correctness proof for the design of the T-ring. These numbers represent the shortest periods of time for which the *pkt* and *zero* inputs must have the required values to initialize the ring. The variable n stands for an arbitrarily long additional period of time during which the *zero* input can remain active once the ring is cleared. Likewise, the variable m stands for an arbitrarily long period of time between the time at which the ring is cleared and the time at which the *pkt* input is activated. The ring is able to receive requests on the *req* input as early as 5 time units before the packet is inserted during the initialization sequence. Hence t' is defined to be at least $(t+22+n+m)$.

Note that the top-level specification Network is only a partial specification of the behaviour of the T-ring. It leaves unspecified, for example, the behaviour of the ring when uninitialized. Furthermore, it covers only the most basic requirement for the correct operation of the device—namely, the ability to transmit one bit of data from the receiver to the transmitter whenever requested to do so. This specification therefore represents a behavioural abstraction of the more detailed behaviour given by the T-ring design model.

6.4.8   Correctness of the register-transfer design

The correctness proof at the register-transfer level begins with the definition of a design model for the T-ring network at that level. This model, which describes the network shown in figure 6.3, is defined as follows:

$\vdash$ TringRt *pkt zero data req out* =
$\qquad \exists sop_1 \ sop_2 \ sop_3 \ ur_1 \ ur_2 \ l_1 \ l_2 \ l_3 \ l_4 \ l_5 \ l_6.$
$\qquad\qquad$ Trans $sop_1 \ ur_1 \ data \ req \ l_6 \ l_1 \ \wedge$
$\qquad\qquad$ Del $l_1 \ l_2 \ \wedge$
$\qquad\qquad$ Monit $sop_2 \ ur_2 \ pkt \ zero \ l_2 \ l_3 \ \wedge$
$\qquad\qquad$ Del $l_3 \ l_4 \ \wedge$
$\qquad\qquad$ Rec $sop_3 \ l_4 \ l_5 \ out \ \wedge$
$\qquad\qquad$ Del $l_5 \ l_6$

The model is constructed from the abstract specifications of the six components in the T-ring network, rather than the timing level models of these components. It is this concise model of the ring that is to be proved correct with respect to the top-level specification. The resulting correctness theorem will later be combined with the correctness results for the each of the six components in the ring to obtain a correctness theorem for the concrete T-ring design.

The register-transfer level correctness theorem is simple:

$$\vdash \text{TringRt } pkt \ zero \ data \ req \ out \supset \text{Network } pkt \ zero \ data \ req \ out \qquad\qquad (6.8)$$

This theorem states that the T-ring specification defined in the previous section is a behavioural abstraction of the design model just defined.

The full proof of this correctness statement will not be given here. Very briefly, however, the proof proceeds as follows. One first proves that a circulating bit pattern is created by setting up the slot structure using the initialization sequence explained in the previous section. One then proves that this can be used to store a packet in the ring for an indefinite period of time between data transmission requests. This is done essentially by symbolically 'simulating' the transmission of a packet through one complete cycle around the ring. This gives an assertion about the values on the transmission wires which is invariant every 24 units of time. The data transmission part of the correctness statement then follows from this assertion together with some simple facts about modulo arithmetic.

6.4.9 Putting the proof together

In the preceding sections, the verification of the T-ring was structured into a two-level hierarchy of correctness results. To complete the proof, it is necessary to combine these results to show that the circuit design at the timing level—i.e. a model of the entire T-ring constructed from the primitive specifications for gates and flip-flops—is correct with respect to the top-level specification.

The complete T-ring design is modelled by the predicate TringTTL:

$\vdash$ TringTTL *ck zero pkt data req out* =
  $\exists sop_1 \ sop_2 \ sop_3 \ ur_1 \ ur_2 \ l_1 \ l_2 \ l_3 \ l_4 \ l_5 \ l_6.$
    Transmitter *ck sop$_1$ ur$_1$ req data l$_6$ l$_1$* $\wedge$
    Delay *ck l$_1$ l$_2$* $\wedge$
    Monitor *ck sop$_2$ ur$_2$ pkt zero l$_2$ l$_3$* $\wedge$
    Delay *ck l$_3$ l$_4$* $\wedge$
    Receiver *ck sop$_3$ out l$_4$ l$_5$* $\wedge$
    Delay *ck l$_5$ l$_6$*

The timing level models for the transmitter, the monitor, the receiver, and the three delay devices are just combined using composition to obtain a model of the entire design. The data transmission wires $l_1, \ldots, l_6$ are hidden, as are the start-of-packet and user request state variables.

Using the correctness theorems already presented and the rules[4] given in chapter 4 for putting together hierarchical proofs, it is straightforward to derive a correctness statement for this concrete design model of the entire T-ring network. The first step is to use the (extended) $\wedge$-MONO rule to combine the correctness theorems for the components of the T-ring into a single correctness theorem for their composition. This yields the theorem shown overleaf.

The stability conditions on the wires l_6, l_2 and l_4 in this theorem are just satisfied by the Delay devices which drive them. As was mentioned in section 6.4.4, one can prove that

$\vdash \forall ck \ rin \ rout.$
  Inf(Rise *ck*) $\supset$ Delay *ck rin rout* $\supset$ Stable *rout ck*

This allows the stability conditions to be dropped. Formally, we use this theorem and the VCOND rule explained in chapter 4 to simplify the validity condition in the composite correctness theorem derived using $\wedge$-MONO.

---

[4]See page 65 for a list of these rules.

⊢ (Inf (Rise ck) ∧ Stable l_6 ck ∧ Stable l_2 ck ∧ Stable l_4 ck) ⊃
    (Transmitter ck sop_1 ur_1 req $data$ l_6 l_1 ∧
    Delay ck l_1 l_2 ∧
    Monitor ck sop_2 ur_2 pkt; $zero$ l_2 l_3 ∧
    Delay ck l_3 l_4 ∧
    Receiver ck sop_3 out l_4 l_5 ∧
    Delay ck l_5 l_6) ⊃
    Trans (sop when (Fall ck))
         (ur when (Fall ck))
         ($data$ when (Fall ck))
         ((Rise req) between (Fall ck))
         (l_6 when (Rise ck))
         (l_1 when (Fall ck)) ∧
    Del (l_1 when (Fall ck)) (l_2 when (Rise ck)) ∧
    Monit (sop when (Fall ck))
         (ur when (Fall ck))
         ($zero$ when (Fall ck))
         ((Rise pkt) between (Fall ck))
         (l_2 when (Rise ck))
         (l_3 when (Fall ck)) ∧
    Del (l_3 when (Fall ck)) (l_4 when (Rise ck)) ∧
    Rec (sop when (Fall ck))
         (out when (Fall ck))
         (l_4 when (Rise ck))
         (l_5 when (Fall ck)) ∧
    Del (l_5 when (Fall ck)) (l_6 when (Rise ck))

The next step is to existentially quantify the hidden wires in both the antecedent and the consequent of the correctness theorem using the rule ∃-EXT. Abbreviating the resulting theorem with TringRt and TringTTL yields

   ⊢ Inf (Rise ck) ⊃
    TringTTL ck $zero$ pkt $data$ req out ⊃
    TringRt ($zero$ when (Fall ck))
            ((Rise pkt) between (Fall ck))
            ($data$ when (Fall ck))
            ((Rise req) between (Fall ck))
            (out when (Fall ck))

Using the transitivity of implication (i.e. the rule sat-TRANS) this theorem, together with the top-level result stated by theorem 6.8, give a correctness statement for the entire T-ring design:

$\vdash$ Inf (Rise ck) $\supset$
    TringTTL ck $zero$ pkt $data$ req out $\supset$
    Network ($zero$ when (Fall ck))
            ((Rise pkt) between (Fall ck))
            ($data$ when (Fall ck))
            ((Rise req) between (Fall ck))
            (out when (Fall ck))

This theorem states the correctness of the actual TTL design of the T-ring and completes the T-ring verification.

6.5   Other approaches

This chapter has described an approach to temporal abstraction in higher order logic based on two fundamental operators—namely, the sampling and synchronizing operators **when** and **between**. Some other approaches to temporal abstraction for hardware verification are sketched below.

Temporal abstraction in LCF_LSM

LCF_LSM is a special-purpose formalism for hardware specification and verification based on denotational semantics and due to Mike Gordon [43]. LCF_LSM includes an inference rule for temporal abstraction by sampling. This is based on an operator on state machines which merges state transitions, yielding a machine which runs at a 'coarser grain' of discrete time. The operator uses a predicate on the outputs of the state machine to mark which sequences of transitions are to be coalesced into a single one. There is an implicit assumption that all inputs remain stable during the merged state transitions. The mechanism for temporal abstraction provided by this operator was implemented in the LCF_LSM theorem prover and used by Gordon in the verification of a simple microcoded computer [44].

Projection in interval temporal logic

Moszkowski [100], writing on future research directions for interval temporal logic, defines a *projection* operator for describing the behaviour of digital hardware over intervals consisting of only selected points of time. Predicates containing 'marker' variables are used to identify the states which are of interest. The role of these predicates is analogous to the role of the predicate P in the sampling construct s when P defined in this chapter. In Tempura [99], the projection operator is given a slightly different definition, in which the predicates mentioned above describe a series of consecutive subintervals of time. This version of the ITL projection operator can executed by the Tempura interpreter. The dual of this executable projection operator (which is not itself executable) can be used to describe the behaviour of a device over subintervals of time corresponding to a series of clock cycles.

Temporal projection in ITL and Tempura is also discussed by Hale in [53, 54]. The paper [53] shows how the T-ring network verified in this chapter can be specified in ITL and executed in Tempura to simulate its operation. A formulation of correctness in ITL for the receiver node of the T-ring is also discussed. The Tempura version of the temporal projection operator is used to state the correctness of the receiver with respect to a specification at a higher level of temporal abstraction. The receiver circuit design in this correctness statement differs from the circuit verified in this chapter; in particular, Hale avoids the complexity introduced by the T-ring timing scheme discussed in section 6.4.2 by having values on the ring change on the rising edges of the clock. The correctness of the monitor and transmitter designs are not considered in [53].

Higher order logic

The work on temporal abstraction reported by Herbert in [65, 67] is closely related to the approach developed in this chapter. In his Ph.D. dissertation, Herbert defines a special-purpose higher order predicate 'UP_OF ck n t' which is equivalent to the predicate 'Istimeof (Rise ck) n t' defined using the more general Istimeof function. Herbert also defines a sampling function ABS by the equation

$$\vdash \text{ABS } select\ sig\ n = sig(\varepsilon t.\ select\ n\ t)$$

and uses it to construct an abstract signal 'ABS(UP_OF ck) sig' by sampling the signal sig on the rising edges of the clock ck. This is equivalent to 'sig when (Rise ck)', where the signal sig is sampled using the when operator. The examples presented by Herbert involve a detailed analysis of the timing conditions that must hold for a temporal abstraction to be valid (e.g. conditions on clock periods, set-up and hold times, etc.). A formal approach to timing analysis is one of the main contributions of Herbert's work. By contrast, details about system timing were for the most part ignored in the T-ring example presented here.

In both Herbert's work and the T-ring example, temporal abstraction is based on a single phase clocking scheme. Dhingra [32] shows how the when operator can be used for temporal abstraction where circuits are implemented in a design style based on two-phase clocking.

Retiming functions

Harman and Tucker [62, 63] describe an approach to temporal abstraction based on *retiming* functions. A retiming function is a mapping $f:num{\rightarrow}num$ from concrete time to abstract time with the following properties:

$$\vdash f\,0 = 0$$

$$\vdash \forall t_a.\, \exists t_c.\, f\, t_c = t_a \qquad\qquad \text{(surjective)}$$

$$\vdash \forall t_1\, t_2.\, (t_1 \le t_2) \supset (f\, t_1 \le f\, t_2) \qquad \text{(monotonic)}$$

A typical example is the function shown in figure 6.11.

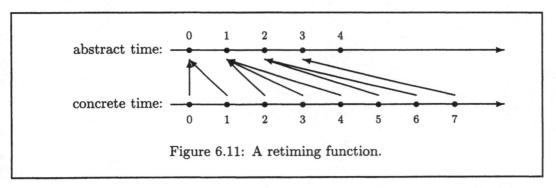

Figure 6.11: A retiming function.

The time mappings in the higher order logic approach explained in this chapter are (increasing) functions from abstract to concrete time; by contrast, retimings map concrete to abstract time. Harman and Tucker also, however, introduce the *immersion* $\bar{f}$ of a retiming f by the definition

$$\vdash \bar{f}(t_a) = \text{the least } t_c \text{ such that } f\, t_c = t_a$$

The immersion of a retiming plays the same role as the time mapping in temporal abstraction by sampling. A signal $s{:}num{\rightarrow}bool$ is sampled by composition on the right with the immersion of a retiming—as, for example, in '$s \circ \bar{f}$'. Harman and Tucker illustrate the utility of retimings in the design, specification, and analysis of a UART [62] and a digital correlator [63].

Chapter 7 ————————————————————

Abstraction between Models

This chapter gives an example to illustrate the idea of an abstraction relationship between two hardware models which was introduced in chapter 4. The two models considered are the threshold switching model of CMOS transistor behaviour defined in chapter 5 and the simpler switch model defined in chapter 2.

Both of these models of the CMOS technology are, of course, abstractions of the physical reality they represent, and both models are therefore bound to be inaccurate in some respects. But the switch model is also an abstraction of the threshold switching model, in the sense that both models describe the same set of primitive components—power, ground, N-type and P-type transistors—but the switch model presents a more abstract view of these components. The threshold switching model reflects the fact that real CMOS transistors do not pass both logic levels equally well. But in the more abstract (and therefore simpler) switch model, this aspect of transistor behaviour is ignored.

The switch model is less accurate than the threshold switching model; a circuit that can be proved correct using the switch model may in fact be incorrect according to the threshold switching model. For certain circuits, however, the two models are effectively equivalent. For these circuits, a proof of correctness in the switch model amounts to a proof of correctness in the threshold switching model. The switch model is an adequate basis for verification of these circuits, and the extra accuracy of the more complex threshold switching model is not needed.

In this chapter, the abstraction relationship between these two models of CMOS is formalized by means of semantic functions defined on a concrete recursive type *circ*. This is an instance of the general class of concrete types discussed in chapter 5, and can be defined formally (and, in the HOL system, automatically) using the method explained in [88]. The type *circ* is used to formulate a theorem that describes the conditions under which correctness results obtained in the two models of transistor behaviour are effectively equivalent.

7.1   Representing the structure of CMOS circuits

This section introduces a specially-defined recursive data type 'circ' to provide an explicit representation in logic for (the *structure* of) the class of all CMOS circuit designs. The motivation for introducing this type is that it allows assertions about the abstraction relationship between the two transistor models considered in this chapter to be stated and proved as *theorems* of higher order logic, rather than meta-theorems about provability in the logic. The advantage of this approach is that it allows the formal proofs of these theorems to be checked mechanically using a theorem prover like the HOL system.

Formally, a transistor model is just a set of logical terms, each of which describes one of the primitive components from which CMOS circuits are built. The model of any particular circuit design is also a logical term, constructed by applying the syntactic operations of composition $\wedge$ and hiding $\exists$ to instances of these primitives. The syntactic structure of such a model mirrors the structure of the circuit that it describes; where the circuit contains two parts wired together, the model contains a subterm of the form '$P_1 \wedge P_2$', and where the circuit contains an internal wire, the model contains a subterm of the form '$\exists w. P$'.

The set of all CMOS design models is a set of logical terms—i.e. a subset of the formal language of terms in higher order logic. For example, the set of all design models constructed from the switch model primitives defined in chapter 2 is the smallest set of terms that contains every instance of the primitive specifications '$Pwr\ p$', '$Gnd\ g$', '$Ntran(g, s, d)$' and '$Ptran(g, s, d)$' and is closed under the syntactic operations of conjunction '$\wedge$' and existential quantification '$\exists$'. Similarly, the set of all design models in the threshold switching model is the smallest set of logical terms that can be built up using $\wedge$ and $\exists$ from instances of the threshold switching primitives defined in chapter 5.

The idea proposed in this chapter is to use a specially-defined concrete recursive type *circ* to embed the (abstract) syntax of these subsets of higher order logic within the logic itself. This allows metalinguistic quantification over all design models to be replaced by explicit quantification *within* the logic over values of type *circ*. The set denoted by *circ* provides a representation of the syntax of a language of *circuit terms*, whose expressions describe how circuits are built up from their constituent parts.[1] A circuit term is either a primitive expression that denotes a basic component (i.e. power, ground, an N-type or P-type transistor), or a composite expression that denotes a circuit built up by the operations of composition and hiding. Thus *circ* models exactly the structural aspect of the class of all CMOS design models.

7.1.1   The type of ascii character strings

With the direct approach to modelling hardware behaviour in logic, where a design model is just a boolean-valued logical term, externally visible values are simply represented by free variables. The first step in the formal definition of the type *circ*, which embeds the syntax of design models within the logic, is to define a type of

---

[1]The type *circ* defined in this section is a formalization in higher order logic of the algebraic approach used by Cardelli [22] and Winskel [118] to model circuit designs.

ascii character strings to represent the names of wires in CMOS designs. This type is an instance of the class of concrete recursive types discussed in chapter 5 and can be defined as follows.

Using the notation introduced in chapter 5, a logical type *ascii* which denotes the set of all 7-bit ascii character codes can be defined (informally) by the equation shown below.

$$ascii \ :: = \ \ \mathsf{Ascii} \ bool \ bool \ bool \ bool \ bool \ bool \ bool$$

Each character is represented by a value of type *ascii* obtained by applying the function Ascii to the seven boolean values in its ascii character code. The letter 'a', for example, has the 7-bit ascii code '1100001' and is represented formally by the term 'Ascii T T F F F F T'. The ascii code for any other character can likewise be represented in logic by a value constructed using the function Ascii.

Using this representation of 7-bit ascii character codes, a type of ascii character *strings* can be defined informally by the equation shown below.

$$str \ :: = \ \ \mathsf{Empty} \ | \ \ \mathsf{String} \ ascii \ str$$

The type described by this equation is similar to the type of lists defined in chapter 5. Every value of type *str* is a finite sequence of ascii character codes constructed using the function String from the empty string represented by the constant Empty. For example, the character string 'ab' is represented by the term

$$\mathsf{String} \ (\mathsf{Ascii} \ \mathsf{T} \ \mathsf{T} \ \mathsf{F} \ \mathsf{F} \ \mathsf{F} \ \mathsf{F} \ \mathsf{T}) \ (\mathsf{String} \ (\mathsf{Ascii} \ \mathsf{T} \ \mathsf{T} \ \mathsf{F} \ \mathsf{F} \ \mathsf{F} \ \mathsf{T} \ \mathsf{F}) \ \mathsf{Empty})$$

Any finite-length string of ascii characters can be represented in logic by a value of type *str* constructed in a similar way.

To provide a concise way of writing terms that denote ascii character strings, the following notation for *string constants* is introduced. A string constant is a constant of type *str* written between single quotes as follows: $'c_1 \ldots c_n'$. This should be regarded as an object language abbreviation for the value of type *str* that represents the ascii character string '$c_1 \ldots c_n$'. String constants written in this notation are just ordinary defined constants introduced to abbreviate terms of type *str* constructed using T and F, and the constructors String, Ascii, and Empty. For example, the string constant 'ab' is defined by the equation

$$\vdash \mathsf{'ab'} = \mathsf{String} \ (\mathsf{Ascii} \ \mathsf{T} \ \mathsf{T} \ \mathsf{F} \ \mathsf{F} \ \mathsf{F} \ \mathsf{F} \ \mathsf{T}) \ (\mathsf{String} \ (\mathsf{Ascii} \ \mathsf{T} \ \mathsf{T} \ \mathsf{F} \ \mathsf{F} \ \mathsf{F} \ \mathsf{T} \ \mathsf{F}) \ \mathsf{Empty})$$

and abbreviates the term of type *str* which represents the string 'ab'.

The theorems of higher order logic which characterize the defined types *ascii* and *str* have the form discussed in section 5.1.2 of chapter 5:

$$\vdash \forall f.\, \exists! fn.\, \forall b_7\, b_6\, b_5\, b_4\, b_3\, b_2\, b_1.\, fn(\mathsf{Ascii}\ b_7\ b_6\ b_5\ b_4\ b_3\ b_2\ b_1) = f\ b_7\ b_6\ b_5\ b_4\ b_3\ b_2\ b_1$$

$$\vdash \forall e\, f.\, \exists! fn.\, (fn\ \mathsf{Empty} = e) \wedge (\forall c\, s.\, fn(\mathsf{String}\ c\ s) = f\ (fn\ s)\ c\ s)$$

The standard properties of concrete types explained in section 5.1.2 follow from these characterizations of *ascii* and *str*. In particular, it follows from these theorems that the functions Ascii and String are one-to-one and that every value of type *str* can be obtained using these functions and the constant Empty. Two values of type *str* are therefore equal exactly when they represent the same sequence of ascii characters.

7.1.2   The type of circuit terms

Using the type *str* just defined, the syntax of circuit terms can be represented in logic by the recursive type *circ* defined by the following equation:

circ	::=	Pwr *str*	(power)
	|	Gnd *str*	(ground)
	|	Ntran *str str str*	(N-type transistor)
	|	Ptran *str str str*	(P-type transistor)
	|	Join *circ circ*	(composition)
	|	Hide *str circ*	(hiding)

This defines a recursive type *circ* with six constructors, corresponding to the six different syntactic constructs in the abstract syntax of the language it represents. The first four constructors represent the primitive CMOS devices power, ground, N-type transistors, and P-type transistors. These four constructors are functions that map wire names (modelled by strings) to values of type *circ* that represent primitive components. For example, the circuit term 'Ntran $g\ s\ d$' represents an N-type transistor with gate g, source s, and drain d.

The other two constructors, Join and Hide, represent the composition and hiding operations. If c_1 and c_2 are two values of type *circ*, then the circuit term 'Join $c_1\ c_2$' represents the composition of the two circuits represented by c_1 and c_2. If c is a circuit term and s is a string, then the circuit term 'Hide $s\ c$' represents the circuit obtained by hiding the wire labelled s in the circuit represented by c.

The recursive type *circ* provides an explicit representation in logic for the class of all CMOS circuit designs.[2] A circuit term that models the structure of any particular circuit can built up using the six constructors of *circ*. For example, a circuit term Inv which models the structure of an inverter can be defined as shown in figure 7.1. The circuit term for any other CMOS design can also be constructed (in the obvious way) using the functions Pwr, Gnd, Ntran, Ptran, Join, and Hide.

---

[2]The type *circ* is an example of what Boulton et al. [13] call a *deep embedding* of an HDL in higher order logic. See also the work of Brock and Hunt [15].

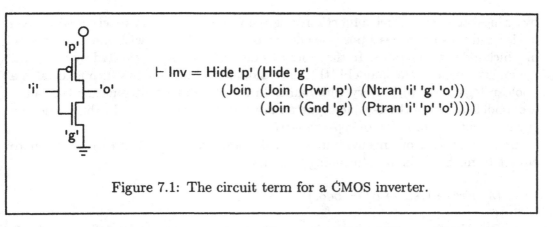

Figure 7.1: The circuit term for a ĊMOS inverter.

As was discussed in chapter 5, the type *circ* described informally by the above equation can be introduced formally in higher order logic by an appropriate type definition. The abstract characterization for the type *circ* is a primitive recursion theorem of the kind discussed in section 5.1.2:

$$\vdash \forall f_1\ f_2\ f_3\ f_4\ f_5\ f_6.\ \exists!\ fn.$$
$$\forall p.\ fn(\mathsf{Pwr}\ p) = f_1\ p\ \wedge$$
$$\forall g.\ fn(\mathsf{Gnd}\ g) = f_2\ g\ \wedge$$
$$\forall g\ s\ d.\ fn(\mathsf{Ntran}\ g\ s\ d) = f_3\ g\ s\ d\ \wedge \qquad\qquad (7.1)$$
$$\forall g\ s\ d.\ fn(\mathsf{Ptran}\ g\ s\ d) = f_4\ g\ s\ d\ \wedge$$
$$\forall c_1\ c_2.\ fn(\mathsf{Join}\ c_1\ c_2) = f_5\ (fn\ c_1)\ (fn\ c_2)\ c_1\ c_2\ \wedge$$
$$\forall s\ c.\ fn(\mathsf{Hide}\ s\ c) = f_6\ (fn\ c)\ s\ c$$

This theorem asserts the unique existence of any primitive recursive function defined by cases on the constructors of the type *circ*. This property can be used to justify the introduction of function constants that denote primitive recursive functions on *circ*. The principle of structural induction for *circ* also follows from this theorem.

7.2 Defining the semantics of CMOS circuits

The type *circ* defined in the previous section denotes a set of values whose structure mirrors the way in which CMOS circuits are built up from their primitive parts. This provides an embedded language of circuit terms in higher order logic for modelling the purely structural aspects of the class of all CMOS designs. The following sections show how the behaviour of these designs can also be modelled by defining a formal semantics for this language. The semantics of circuit terms will be defined in two different ways. One of these corresponds to the switch model of transistor behaviour, and the other corresponds to the threshold switching model.

For both models, the semantics of circuit terms will be based on the idea of an *environment*. An environment is a function $e{:}str{\rightarrow}\sigma$ that maps wire names (modelled

by strings) to values. Such a function assigns a value 'es' to every external wire s of a
device and thus describes a possible pattern of communication with the environment
in which a device operates. In the switch model, values are represented by booleans.
An environment in this model is therefore a function e:$str{\rightarrow}bool$ which associates a
boolean logic level with every wire name. In the threshold switching model, values
are modelled by the three-valued type tri introduced in chapter 5. In this model, an
environment is a function of type $str{\rightarrow}tri$.

Using this idea of an environment, a denotational semantics can be given to
circuit terms by defining a 'meaning' function

$$\mathsf{M} : circ \rightarrow ((str \rightarrow \alpha) \rightarrow bool)$$

that maps circuit terms to predicates on environments. The precise definition of this
function will depend on the model of transistor behaviour which is used, but the idea
is to define M such that for every circuit term c the predicate M c is satisfied only by
environments that represent allowable configurations of values on the external wires
of the circuit represented by c.

7.2.1   The switch model semantics

The meaning function Sm for the switch model is defined by primitive recursion
on circuit terms. This function has logical type $circ{\rightarrow}((str{\rightarrow}bool){\rightarrow}bool)$; when
applied to a circuit term, it yields a predicate on environments of type $str{\rightarrow}bool$.
The primitive recursive definition of Sm is the following:

$$
\begin{aligned}
&\vdash \mathsf{Sm}\ (\mathsf{Pwr}\ p)\ e &&= (e\,p = \mathsf{T})\\
&\vdash \mathsf{Sm}\ (\mathsf{Gnd}\ g)\ e &&= (e\,g = \mathsf{F})\\
&\vdash \mathsf{Sm}\ (\mathsf{Ntran}\ g\ s\ d)\ e &&= e\,g \supset (e\,d = e\,s)\\
&\vdash \mathsf{Sm}\ (\mathsf{Ptran}\ g\ s\ d)\ e &&= \neg(e\,g) \supset (e\,d = e\,s)\\
&\vdash \mathsf{Sm}\ (\mathsf{Join}\ c_1\ c_2)\ e &&= \mathsf{Sm}\ c_1\ e \wedge \mathsf{Sm}\ c_2\ e\\
&\vdash \mathsf{Sm}\ (\mathsf{Hide}\ s\ c)\ e &&= \exists b.\, \mathsf{Sm}\ c\ \lambda st.\, ((st = s) \Rightarrow b\,|\,e\,st)
\end{aligned}
$$

The validity of this definition is justified formally by the characterization of the
defined type $circ$ given by theorem 7.1 on page 133.

The first four equations in the definition of Sm define the semantics of primitive
CMOS devices—power, ground, N-type transistors, and P-type transistors. Each
equation states what must be true of an environment in which the corresponding
component is operating. For example, the equation for 'Ntran g s d' imposes the
constraint that any environment which assigns the value T to g must also assign
equal values to d and s. The semantics of power, ground, and P-type transistors are
defined in a similar way.

The last two equations define the semantics of composition and hiding. The
equation for the constructor Join states that an environment is a possible assignment

of values to the wires in a composition of two circuits exactly when it is a possible assignment of values to the wires of *both* subcircuits. The equation for Hide uses existential quantification to isolate the hidden wire from the environment. It states that e is a possible environment for the circuit represented by 'Hide s c' exactly when there exists *some* environment which is allowed by the semantics of c and which differs from e only in the boolean value it assigns to s.

The theorems shown above define the value of the function Sm for any circuit term c and environment e, and so they give a semantics to the class of all CMOS circuit designs. The semantics of any particular circuit design can derived using these defining equations for Sm. For example, one can prove the following theorem about the semantics of the circuit term Inv defined above in figure 7.1:

$$\vdash \mathsf{Sm}\ \mathsf{Inv}\ e = (e\ \mathsf{'o'} = \neg(e\ \mathsf{'i'}))$$

This is exactly analogous to the inverter correctness theorem proved in chapter 3. It can be proved by first computing the switch model semantics of Inv using the defining equations for Sm, and then deriving the correctness result by a sequence of steps which is very similar to that in chapter 3. The theorem says that in the switch model of CMOS the behaviour of the design represented by the circuit term Inv is indeed that of an inverter—that is, in every environment e, the value on the output 'o' is the negation of the value on the input 'i'.

7.2.2 The threshold model semantics

In the threshold switching model, the values on circuit nodes are modelled by values of type *tri*. The semantics of *circ* for the threshold switching model is therefore a function Tm from *circ* to predicates on environments of type *str→tri*. The function Tm is defined by primitive recursion as follows:

$$
\begin{aligned}
&\vdash \mathsf{Tm}\ (\mathsf{Pwr}\ p)\ e &&= (e\ p = \mathsf{Hi})\\
&\vdash \mathsf{Tm}\ (\mathsf{Gnd}\ g)\ e &&= (e\ g = \mathsf{Lo})\\
&\vdash \mathsf{Tm}\ (\mathsf{Ntran}\ g\ s\ d)\ e &&= (e\ g = \mathsf{Hi}) \supset ((e\ d = \mathsf{Lo}) = (e\ s = \mathsf{Lo}))\\
&\vdash \mathsf{Tm}\ (\mathsf{Ptran}\ g\ s\ d)\ e &&= (e\ g = \mathsf{Lo}) \supset ((e\ d = \mathsf{Hi}) = (e\ s = \mathsf{Hi}))\\
&\vdash \mathsf{Tm}\ (\mathsf{Join}\ c_1\ c_2)\ e &&= \mathsf{Tm}\ c_1\ e \wedge \mathsf{Tm}\ c_2\ e\\
&\vdash \mathsf{Tm}\ (\mathsf{Hide}\ s\ c)\ e &&= \exists v.\ \mathsf{Tm}\ c\ \lambda st.\ ((st = s) \Rightarrow v\ |\ e\ st)
\end{aligned}
$$

This definition is similar to the recursive definition of Sm. The difference is that the function Tm is defined for environments of type *str→tri*, and the threshold switching model of CMOS behaviour is used in the defining equations for the primitive devices Pwr, Gnd, Ntran, and Ptran. The semantics of composition and hiding are the same as in the switch model.

Like the defining equations for Sm, the equations shown above for the meaning function Tm can be used to derive assertions about the behaviour of any CMOS circuit design. For example, one can prove that the inverter circuit represented by Inv has the threshold model semantics given by the following theorem:

$$\vdash \textsf{Tm Inv } e = ((e \text{ 'i'} = \textsf{Hi}) \supset (e \text{ 'o'} = \textsf{Lo})) \wedge ((e \text{ 'i'} = \textsf{Lo}) \supset (e \text{ 'o'} = \textsf{Hi}))$$

This says that in any environment in which the input 'i' has either the value Hi or the value Lo, the output 'o' must have the value Lo or the value Hi, respectively.

7.3   Defining satisfaction

The first step in formulating the abstraction relationship between the two models just introduced is to define what it means for a CMOS circuit design to satisfy a specification in a model. In the following definition of satisfaction, c is a circuit term representing a circuit design, M is a meaning function on circuit terms and S is a specification of required behaviour. The function $f{:}\alpha{\rightarrow}\beta$ is a data abstraction function, and C is a validity condition on the abstraction relationship.

$$\vdash \textsf{Sat } M\ C\ c\ f\ S = \forall e{:}str{\rightarrow}\alpha.\ C\ e \supset (M\ c\ e \supset S(f \circ e)) \qquad\qquad (7.2)$$

This definition formalizes correctness as a relationship of data abstraction between the design model for the CMOS circuit represented by c and the specification of required behaviour S. Expressed in the notation used in chapter 4, an abstraction relationship of this kind would look something like this:

$$\vdash C[c_1, \ldots, c_n] \supset M[c_1, \ldots, c_n] \underset{f}{\textsf{ sat }} S[a_1, \ldots, a_n]$$

The definition of Sat states that in a transistor model M, the circuit c is correct with respect to the specification S if for every environment e that is allowed by the semantics $M\ c$ and satisfies the validity condition C, the abstract environment $f \circ e$ satisfies S. Composition on the left with the data abstraction function translates environments of type $str{\rightarrow}\alpha$ into corresponding environments of type $str{\rightarrow}\beta$.

7.4   Correctness in the two models

In the switch model, a specification is a predicate on environments of type $str{\rightarrow}bool$. A formal specification Not for the inverter circuit shown above, for example, can be defined by the equation

$$\vdash \textsf{Not } e = (e \text{ 'o'} = \neg(e \text{ 'i'}))$$

The predicate Not stipulates what must hold of the environment of a correctly functioning inverter with input 'i' and output 'o'. Using the satisfaction relation Sat

just defined, a switch model correctness theorem for the inverter circuit Inv defined
on page 133 can be written

$\vdash$ Sat Sm true Inv id Not   where $\vdash$ true $e =$ T and $\vdash$ id $b = b$

The theorem states that the inverter circuit Inv is correct in the switch model Sm
with respect to the specification Not. The validity condition true is just true of every
switch model environment, and the data abstraction function id is just the identity
function on *bool*. This correctness theorem is therefore equivalent to

$\vdash \forall e.$ Sm Inv $e \supset (e$ 'o' $= \neg(e$ 'i'$))$

In analysing the formal relationship between the switch model defined by Sm and
the threshold switching model defined by Tm, only switch model correctness results
of the kind illustrated by this example will be considered. That is, correctness will
be stated using the identity data abstraction function id and the trivially-satisfied
validity condition true.

In the threshold model, a specification is a predicate on environments of type
$str \rightarrow tri$. To formulate the abstraction relationship between the models, correctness
results in the switch model must be related to equivalent correctness results in the
threshold switching model. This can be done by using the validity condition def and
the data abstraction function abs defined as shown below.

$\vdash$ def $e = \forall s. \neg(e\ s = $ X$)$

$\vdash$ (abs Hi $=$ T) $\wedge$ (abs Lo $=$ F)

The condition 'def e' states that a threshold switching model environment $e{:}str \rightarrow tri$
assigns only the strongly-driven values Hi or Lo to every string—that is, no wire s has
the degenerate logic level modelled by the third value 'X'. The function abs:$tri \rightarrow bool$
is just the data abstraction function defined in chapter 5.

Using def and abs, any switch model correctness theorem can be reformulated
as a correctness result with respect to an *abstract* specification in the threshold
switching model. Consider, for example, the switch model correctness theorem for
the inverter. An equivalent theorem stating correctness with respect to the abstract
specification Not can be expressed in the threshold model as shown below.

$\vdash$ Sat Tm def Inv abs Not

Expanding this theorem with the definitions of the satisfaction relation Sat, the
validity condition def, and the specification Not gives

$\vdash \forall e. (\forall s. \neg(e\ s = $ X$)) \supset ($Tm Inv $e \supset ($abs$(e$ 'o'$) = \neg($abs$(e$ 'i'$))))$

This says that in any well-behaved environment, where no external wire has the
degenerate value X, the inverter circuit modelled by Inv is correct with respect to
the abstract specification of intended behaviour for an inverter.

In general, any switch model correctness assertion 'Sat Sm true c id S', where c is a circuit term and $S:(str{\rightarrow}bool){\rightarrow}bool$ is a specification of required behaviour, can be expressed in the threshold model by a correctness assertion of the form 'Sat Tm def c abs S', where S is treated as an abstract specification of required behaviour. This translation is the basis for the formulation of the abstraction relationship between the two models discussed in the sections that follow.

7.5   Relating the models

The abstraction relationship between Sm and Tm is expressed formally in logic as a conditional equivalence between the correctness results provable in the two models. In particular, there is a condition on circuit terms Wb (defined later) such that the two models agree on the correctness results that can be proved about circuits that satisfy this condition:

$$\vdash \forall c.\ \text{Wb}\ c \supset \forall S.\ \text{Sat Sm true}\ c\ \text{id}\ S = \text{Sat Tm def}\ c\ \text{abs}\ S \qquad (7.3)$$

This theorem states that if a circuit term c satisfies Wb, then for any specification S, the design represented by c is correct with respect to S in the switch model exactly when it is correct with respect to S in the threshold model. The switch model is therefore an adequate basis for correctness proofs of circuits that satisfy the condition Wb. For these circuits, there is no point in using the more complex threshold switching model, since the two models agree on the specifications that these circuits satisfy.

Theorem 7.3 is an explicit and rigorous formulation of the notion that the switch model of CMOS behaviour is an abstraction of the threshold switching model. That the switch model is an abstraction (i.e. a simplification) of the threshold model is expressed by the fact that theorem 7.3 asserts that only some of the correctness results provable in the threshold model—namely ones based on the data abstraction function abs and qualified by the validity condition def—are also provable in the switch model. The predicate Wb expresses a validity condition on this abstraction relationship between the two models. For the class of circuits that satisfy Wb, the switch model is a *valid* abstraction of the more detailed threshold model, in the sense that it cannot be used to prove a correctness result that does not also hold in the more accurate threshold model.

The definition of the validity condition Wb and a sketch of the proof of theorem 7.3 are given two sections that follow. The proof has two parts. It is first shown that for any CMOS circuit design, correctness in the threshold model implies correctness in the switch model. The conditional equivalence given by theorem 7.3 is then derived by defining Wb and proving that the converse implication holds for circuits that satisfy this condition.

7.5.1 Correctness in Tm implies correctness in Sm

Theorem 7.3 says that for the class of circuit designs that satisfy the condition Wb all propositions about correctness in the two models are equivalent. In fact, for *any* circuit term c, a correctness result in the threshold model implies a correctness result in the simpler switch model:

$$\vdash \forall c\, S.\, \text{Sat Tm def } c \text{ abs } S \supset \text{Sat Sm true } c \text{ id } S \tag{7.4}$$

It is necessary to impose the condition Wb only in order to prove the converse implication. This is exactly what one would expect, for if a circuit can be proved correct using the detailed threshold model, then it must also be correct according to the more abstract—but less accurate—switch model.

The first step in the proof of theorem 7.4 is to define a representation function which is the right inverse of the data abstraction function abs. The required function rep:*bool*→*tri* is defined by cases on *bool* such that it has the following property:

$$\vdash (\text{rep T} = \text{Hi}) \wedge (\text{rep F} = \text{Lo})$$

With this function one can formulate the following key lemma about the satisfaction of an abstract specification in the threshold model of CMOS behaviour given by Tm:

$$\vdash \text{Sat Tm def } c \text{ abs } S = \forall e.\, \text{Tm } c \,(\text{rep} \circ e) \supset S\, e \tag{7.5}$$

The proof of this lemma is straightforward; the lemma follows immediately from the fact that the data representation and abstraction functions abs and rep have the properties shown below.

$$\vdash \text{def}(\text{rep} \circ e) \qquad \vdash \text{abs} \circ \text{rep} \circ e = e \qquad \vdash \text{def } e \supset (\text{rep} \circ \text{abs} \circ e = e)$$

These theorems show that there is a bijection between abstract environments of type *str*→*bool* and the set of all concrete environments of type *str*→*tri* that satisfy the validity condition def. Satisfaction of an abstract specification S qualified by def in the threshold model is therefore equivalent to satisfaction of S by an abstract environment e for which the corresponding concrete environment rep $\circ$ e is allowed by the threshold model semantics.

Using lemma 7.5, proving theorem 7.4 reduces to proving the following theorem about the relationship between satisfaction in the two models:

$$\vdash \forall c\, S.\, (\forall e.\, \text{Tm } c \,(\text{rep} \circ e) \supset S\, e) \supset (\forall e.\, \text{Sm } c\, e \supset S\, e)$$

The variable S in this theorem stands for an arbitrary predicate on switch model environments of type *str*→*bool*. It is straightforward to show that it is sufficient to consider only the strongest predicate that satisfies the left hand side of the implication—namely the predicate $\lambda e.\, \mathsf{Tm}\; c\; (\mathsf{rep} \circ e)$. The proof of theorem 7.4 can therefore be further reduced to proving the assertion

$$\vdash \forall c\, e.\, \mathsf{Sm}\; c\; e \supset \mathsf{Tm}\; c\; (\mathsf{rep} \circ e) \qquad\qquad (7.6)$$

This theorem says that for every environment e which is allowed by the switch model semantics, the corresponding environment $\mathsf{rep} \circ e$ is allowed by the threshold model semantics. This final lemma follows easily by structural induction on the circuit term c and completes the proof of theorem 7.4.

7.5.2 Conditional equivalence of the two models

The preceding section has shown that a correctness result in the threshold model implies a correctness result in the simpler switch model. The converse implication, however, does not always hold. Some CMOS circuit designs which can be proved correct with respect to a specification S in the switch model are not correct with respect to S in the threshold switching model. Formally, one can prove

$$\vdash \neg \forall c\, S.\, \mathsf{Sat}\; \mathsf{Sm}\; \mathsf{true}\; c\; \mathsf{id}\; S \supset \mathsf{Sat}\; \mathsf{Tm}\; \mathsf{def}\; c\; \mathsf{abs}\; S \qquad\qquad (7.7)$$

The CMOS circuit shown in figure 7.2 provides a counterexample by which this negative result can be proved. This circuit is intended to be an implementation of the one-bit comparator specified below.

$$\vdash \mathsf{Cmp}\; e = (e\; \text{'out'} = (e\; \text{'a'} = e\; \text{'b'}))$$

This specification describes a device with two boolean inputs 'a' and 'b' and one boolean output 'o'. The device compares the values on the input wires 'a' and 'b'. If they are equal, then the value on the output 'o' is *true*. Otherwise the value on the output 'o' is *false*.

The circuit shown in figure 7.2 is intended to implement the comparator behaviour specified by the predicate Cmp. It is, however, built from an *incorrect* exclusive-or gate Xor connected to an inverter by the internal wire 'w'. This Xor circuit is an example of a design that can be proved correct using the switch model, but which is in fact incorrect due to the threshold switching behaviour of its transistors [21].

According to the switch model, the circuit Cmpr defined in figure 7.2 is a correct implementation of the one-bit comparator specified by Cmp. One can prove the following correctness result for this circuit in the switch model:

$$\vdash \mathsf{Sat}\; \mathsf{Sm}\; \mathsf{true}\; \mathsf{Cmpr}\; \mathsf{id}\; \mathsf{Cmp}$$

According to the more accurate threshold switching model, however, the circuit

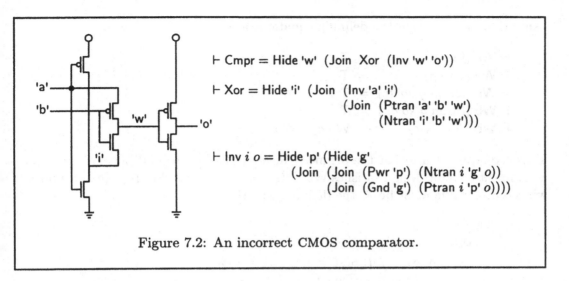

$\vdash$ Cmpr = Hide 'w' (Join Xor (Inv 'w' 'o'))

$\vdash$ Xor = Hide 'i' (Join (Inv 'a' 'i')
   (Join (Ptran 'a' 'b' 'w')
      (Ntran 'i' 'b' 'w')))

$\vdash$ Inv i o = Hide 'p' (Hide 'g'
   (Join (Join (Pwr 'p') (Ntran i 'g' o))
      (Join (Gnd 'g') (Ptran i 'p' o))))

Figure 7.2: An incorrect CMOS comparator.

represented by Cmpr is not correct with respect to the abstract specification Cmp. Formally, we have

$\vdash \neg$ Sat Tm def Cmpr abs Cmp

The problem with the comparator circuit is that for certain input values the value on the internal wire 'w' can be the degraded logic level X because of threshold effects. If the input 'a' is Lo and the input 'b' is Hi, then the value on the hidden wire 'w' can be either Hi or X. This means that the voltage on 'w' may be too low to drive the gates of the transistors in the output inverter. In the threshold model, the output 'o' is not forced to be the correct value Lo in this case, and the circuit therefore fails to satisfy the abstract specification given by Cmp. The problem is, of course, completely invisible to the switch model of CMOS behaviour.

The incorrectness of the comparator circuit can be detected in the threshold model because there is an environment e which satisfies the validity condition def e and the constraint Tm Cmpr e but does not satisfy the constraint Cmp (abs $\circ$ e) imposed by the specification. In particular, there is a threshold model environment e that satisfies both the validity condition and the model and makes the following assignment of values to the external wires of the device: e 'a' = Lo, e 'b' = Hi, and e 'o' = Hi. For this environment, not only does the threshold model allow the internal wire 'w' to have the value X, but it in fact *forces* the internal wire 'w' to have this value.

This observation motivates the following definition of the predicate Wb, which rules out circuits with internal wires that can be forced to have the value X and which therefore expresses a condition sufficient to make the two transistor models agree. For the circuit terms that model primitive devices and circuit terms constructed using the function Join, the defining equations are

$\vdash$ Wb (Pwr p) $=$ T
$\vdash$ Wb (Gnd p) $=$ T
$\vdash$ Wb (Ntran g so dr) $=$ T
$\vdash$ Wb (Ptran g so dr) $=$ T
$\vdash$ Wb (Join c_1 c_2) $=$ Wb c_1 $\wedge$ Wb c_2

These equations state that the primitive devices satisfy the condition Wb, and that
a composite circuit design satisfies Wb if its subcomponents do. To rule out internal
wires whose value must be X, the defining equation is

$\vdash$ Wb (Hide s c) $=$
    Wb c $\wedge$
    $\forall e.$ (Tm c e $\wedge$ $\forall st.$ $\neg(st = s)$ $\supset$ $\neg(e$ $st = $ X)) $\supset$
        $\exists v.$ $\neg(v = $ X) $\wedge$ Tm c ($\lambda st.$ (($st = s$) $\Rightarrow$ v | e st))

For a circuit 'Hide s c' to satisfy Wb it must be the case that the circuit c satisfies
Wb. Furthermore, whenever c is in an environment in which every external wire
except for s does not have the value X, it is possible for the wire s not to have the
value X as well. In other words, there is no well-behaved *external* environment e
that satisfies the validity condition def e but forces the internal wire s to have the
degenerate value X.

If Wb is defined as shown above, then the following theorem about satisfaction
in the two models of transistor behaviour can be proved:

$$\vdash \forall c. \text{ Wb } c \supset \forall S. \text{ Sat Sm true } c \text{ id } S \supset \text{ Sat Tm def } c \text{ abs } S \tag{7.8}$$

This says that for circuit terms c that satisfy Wb, a correctness result proved in
the switch model implies an equivalent correctness result in the threshold switching
model. This expresses the fact that the simple switch model is a valid abstraction
of the more detailed threshold model for a particular class of circuit designs.

The formal proof of theorem 7.8 proceeds as follows. By lemma 7.5, the proof
reduces to showing that

$$\vdash \forall c. \text{ Wb } c \supset \forall S. (\forall e. \text{ Sm } c \text{ } e \supset S \text{ } e) \supset (\forall e. \text{ Tm } c \text{ (rep} \circ e) \supset S \text{ } e)$$

Again, it is sufficient to consider the strongest specification S that satisfies the left
hand side of the implication, so the proof of theorem 7.8 further reduces to proving

$$\vdash \forall c. \text{ Wb } c \supset \forall e. \text{ Tm } c \text{ (rep} \circ e) \supset \text{ Sm } c \text{ } e \tag{7.9}$$

This theorem follows by structural induction on circuit terms. Only the step case
for the constructor Hide is at all difficult. The defining equation for Wb(Hide s c),

however, ensures that the hidden wire s is not forced to be the value X. If this is the case, then there is always a boolean internal value in the switch model such that the implication stated by theorem 7.9 holds.

From theorems 7.8 and 7.4, it follows immediately that correctness results in the two transistor models formalized by the meaning functions Tm and Sm are equivalent for circuit terms that satisfy Wb. For circuit designs that satisfy Wb, the simple switch model is an adequate basis for verification, since the threshold switching model can not be used to detect design errors in these circuits which will not also be found by using the simpler switch model.

7.6   Improving the results

The preceding sections have shown how a specially-defined concrete recursive type *circ* can be used to formulate and prove assertions about the relative accuracy of two hardware models. These assertions are essentially statements about the class of all design models built up using the alternative primitive specifications in each model. Using the recursive type *circ* to embed the syntax of design models within the logic itself allows these assertions to be formulated as *theorems* of the logic, rather than meta-theorems.

There are two ways in which the particular result obtained in this chapter might be improved. These are briefly discussed below.

7.6.1   A syntactic condition is needed

The predicate Wb is a condition on CMOS designs which is sufficient to ensure that they can be verified using the switch model. The predicate Wb was not, however, defined in a way that makes it useful in practice for determining when the switch model can be used. In the defining equations for Wb, the meaning function Tm is used to state the condition that hidden wires are not forced to have the value X. This means that for any particular circuit term c it is necessary to carry out a proof in the threshold model in order to determine if 'Wb c' holds. But this may be just as much work as simply proving a threshold model correctness theorem for c. For an equivalence result of the kind stated by theorem 7.3 to be useful in practice, a condition is needed that can be checked purely *syntactically*.

A syntactic condition that makes the two transistor models agree on correctness could be seen as a 'design rule' for CMOS circuits which ensures that they are *verifiable* using the simple switch model. One example of such a syntactic condition would be a predicate FC which is true of a circuit term exactly when it represents a fully complementary CMOS circuit design. If this predicate is defined formally and shown to satisfy

$$\forall c.\ \text{FC}\ c \supset \forall S.\ \text{Sat Sm true}\ c\ \text{id}\ S = \text{Sat Tm def}\ c\ \text{abs}\ S$$

then this would show that the switch model is adequate for fully complementary CMOS logic; the extra complexity of the threshold switching is not needed to model circuits designed using this conservative design style. Furthermore, if FC is a purely syntactic condition—i.e. that it describes only the *structure* of fully complementary circuit designs—then checking whether the simple switch model can be used for any particular design can be done without having to reason about its behaviour in the threshold model.

7.6.2   Weakening the validity condition

A second way in which the result proved in this chapter could be improved is by weakening the validity condition def introduced in section 7.4. This condition was defined in order to translate a switch model correctness statement of the form $\forall e.\, \mathsf{Sm}\ c\ e \supset S\ e$ into an equivalent threshold model correctness statement

$$\forall e.\, \mathsf{def}\ e \supset (\mathsf{Tm}\ c\ e \supset S\ (\mathsf{abs} \circ e))$$

The problem with a correctness statement of this kind is that the constraint imposed on the environment e by the validity condition def e is too strong. The predicate def is defined by

$$\vdash \mathsf{def}\ e = \forall s.\, \neg(e\ s = \mathsf{X})$$

This means that in a threshold model correctness statement of the general form shown above it is assumed that the environment e assigns only a strongly-driven value (i.e. either Hi or Lo) to every external wire of the CMOS circuit represented by the circuit term c. In particular, the validity condition not only ensures that the input wires of the circuit represented by c are strongly-driven, but it also makes the *assumption* that the degenerate value X will never appear on the output wires.

The effect of having this built-in assumption is that a threshold model correctness statement of the form shown above fails to distinguish between circuits whose output wires are always strongly driven and circuits that can have X on their output wires. A correctness theorem provable in the switch model may therefore be translated into a threshold model correctness statement which is also provable—but only by virtue of the assumption that outputs are always strongly driven. For example, the theorem

$$\vdash \forall e.\, \mathsf{def}\ e \supset (\mathsf{Tm}\ \mathsf{Xor}\ e \supset (\mathsf{abs}(e\ {'w'}) = \neg(\mathsf{abs}(\ e{'a'}) = \mathsf{abs}(e\ {'b'}))))$$

states the correctness of the *incorrect* exclusive-or circuit in figure 7.2 and can be proved in the threshold model even though the exclusive-or circuit does not ensure that the output wire 'w' is strongly driven for all input values. The problem becomes apparent only when this wire is hidden, as in the comparator circuit.

To overcome this problem, it is necessary to weaken the validity condition used to express threshold model correctness statements, so that it constrains only the inputs of a device to have the strongly-driven values Hi and Lo. This would improve the translation between the models by removing the unjustified assumption of strongly-driven outputs.

One way of formulating such a validity condition is to define a condition 'def c e' which is parameterized by a circuit term c and has the meaning 'the environment e assigns only strongly-driven values to the external wires of c which are directly connected to the gates of transistors'. A formal definition of this validity condition is given by the following primitive recursive definition on circuit terms.

$$
\begin{aligned}
&\vdash \text{def } (\text{Pwr } p)\ e &&= \text{T} \\
&\vdash \text{def } (\text{Gnd } g)\ e &&= \text{T} \\
&\vdash \text{def } (\text{Ntran } g\ s\ d)\ e &&= \neg(e\ g = \text{X}) \\
&\vdash \text{def } (\text{Ptran } g\ s\ d)\ e &&= \neg(e\ g = \text{X}) \\
&\vdash \text{def } (\text{Join } c_1\ c_2)\ e &&= \text{def } c_1\ e \wedge \text{def } c_2\ e \\
&\vdash \text{def } (\text{Hide } s\ c)\ e &&= \text{def } c\ \lambda st.\ ((st = s) \Rightarrow \text{Hi} \mid e\ st)
\end{aligned}
$$

This makes the condition def c e impose the constraint that all the *externally driven inputs* connected to the gates of N-type and P-type transistors in c must be strongly driven by the environment e. This constrains the values only on external wires that are known to be inputs to the circuit represented by the circuit term c.

For example, one can prove from this definition the following theorem:

$$\vdash \text{def Xor } e = \neg(e\ 'a' = \text{X}) \wedge \neg(e\ 'b' = \text{X})$$

The new validity condition for the exclusive-or circuit constrains only the input wires 'a' and 'b' to be strongly driven; it does not constrain the value on the output wire 'w' and therefore does not make the unjustified assumption that this value is not X. With this new validity condition, it is *not* possible to prove the correctness of the incorrect exclusive-or gate in the threshold switching model.

Using the new validity condition for expressing correctness statements in the threshold switching model, the following assertion can be formulated about the equivalence of correctness results in the two models, where

$$\forall c.\ \text{Wb } c \supset ((\forall e.\ \text{Sm } c\ e \supset S\ e) = (\forall e.\ \text{def } c\ e \supset (\text{Tm } c\ e \supset S\ (\text{abs} \circ e))))$$

In this theorem, the condition Wb on circuit terms would have to be stronger than the predicate defined in section 7.5.2, since CMOS circuits whose outputs are not strongly driven would now (correctly) be considered incorrect in the threshold switching model. A theorem of this kind would give an improved statement of the abstraction relationship between the two models of CMOS behaviour.

7.7   Other approaches

The approach to the formalization of abstraction between models in this chapter
is strongly influenced by the categorical ideas used by Winskel in [118] to relate
two transistor models. Winskel uses the notion of adjunction between partial order
categories to relate his static-configuration model of CMOS behaviour [117] to the
switch model of transistor behaviour described by Camilleri et al. in [21]. This
categorical approach provides the basic framework for organization of the proof of
theorem 7.3 given in this chapter. In particular, lemma 7.5 comes essentially from
the adjunction between satisfaction in the two models described by Winskel.

References

[1] P. Amblard, P. Caspi, and N. Halbwachs, 'Use of time functions to describe and explain circuit behaviour', in *IEE Proceedings*, vol. 133, part E, no. 5 (September 1986), pp. 271–275.

[2] P. B. Andrews, *An Introduction to Mathematical Logic and Type Theory: to Truth through Proof*, Computer Science and Applied Mathematics Series (Academic Press, 1986).

[3] J. C. Barros and B. W. Johnson, 'Equivalence of the Arbiter, the Synchronizer, the Latch and the Inertial Delay', *IEEE Transactions on Computers*, vol. C-32, no. 7 (July 1983), pp. 603–614.

[4] H. G. Barrow, 'VERIFY: A Program for Proving Correctness of Digital Hardware Designs', *Artificial Intelligence*, vol. 24, nos. 1–3 (December 1984), pp. 437–491.

[5] D. A. Basin and P. Del Vecchio, 'Verification of Combinational Logic in Nuprl', in *Hardware Specification, Verification and Synthesis: Mathematical Aspects: Mathematical Sciences Institute Workshop, Cornell, July 1989*, edited by M. Leeser and G. Brown, Lecture Notes in Computer Science, vol. 408 (Springer-Verlag, 1990), pp. 333–357.

[6] C. Berthet and E. Cerny, 'An Algebraic Model for Asynchronous Circuits Verification', *IEEE Transactions on Computers*, vol. 37, no. 7 (July 1988), pp. 835–847.

[7] G. Birtwistle, ed. *IV Higher Order Workshop, Banff 1990: Proceedings of the IV Higher Order Workshop, Banff, September 1990*, Workshops in Computing series (Springer-Verlag, 1991).

[8] G. Birtwistle and B. Graham, 'Verifying SECD in HOL', in *Formal Methods for VLSI Design: IFIP WG 10.2 Lecture Notes*, edited by J. Staunstrup (North-Holland, 1990), pp. 129–177.

[9] G. Birtwistle and P. A. Subrahmanyam, eds. *Current Trends in Hardware Verification and Automated Theorem Proving* (Springer-Verlag, 1989).

[10] G. Birtwistle and P. A. Subrahmanyam, eds. *VLSI Specification, Verification and Synthesis*, Kluwer International Series in Engineering and Computer Science (Kluwer, 1988).

[11] G. V. Bochmann, 'Hardware Specification with Temporal Logic: An Example', *IEEE Transactions on Computers*, vol. C-31, no. 3 (March 1982), pp. 223–231.

[12] D. Borrione, ed. *From HDL Descriptions to Guaranteed Correct Circuit Designs: Proceedings of the IFIP WG 10.2 Working Conference, Grenoble, September 1986* (North-Holland, 1987).

[13] R. Boulton, A. Gordon, M. Gordon, J. Harrison, J. Herbert, and J. Van Tassel, 'Experience with embedding hardware description languages in HOL', in *Theorem Provers in Circuit Design: Theory, Practice and Experience: Proceedings of the IFIP WG10.2 International Conference, Nijmegen, June 1992*, edited by V. Stavridou, T. F. Melham, and R. T. Boute (North-Holland, 1992), pp. 129–156.

[14] R. S. Boyer and J. S. Moore, *A Computational Logic*, ACM Monograph Series (Academic Press, 1979).

[15] B. C. Brock and W. A. Hunt, Jr., 'A Formal Introduction to a Simple HDL', in *Formal Methods for VLSI Design: IFIP WG 10.2 Lecture Notes*, edited by J. Staunstrup (North-Holland, 1990), pp. 285–329.

[16] B. C. Brock, W. A. Hunt, Jr., and W. D. Young, 'Introduction to a Formally Defined Hardware Description Language', in *Theorem Provers in Circuit Design: Theory, Practice and Experience: Proceedings of the IFIP WG10.2 International Conference, Nijmegen, June 1992*, edited by V. Stavridou, T. F. Melham, and R. T. Boute (North-Holland, 1992), pp. 3–35.

[17] J. R. Burch, E. M. Clarke, and D. E. Long, 'Representing Circuits More Efficiently in Symbolic Model Checking', in *ACM IEEE 28th Design Automation Conference: Proceedings* (IEEE Computer Society Press, 1991), pp. 403–407.

[18] J. R. Burch, E. M. Clarke, K. L. McMillan, D. L. Dill, and L. J. Hwang, 'Symbolic Model Checking: 10^{20} States and Beyond', in *Proceedings of the Fifth Annual IEEE Symposium on Logic in Computer Science* (IEEE Computer Society Press, 1990), pp. 428–439.

[19] H. Busch, 'Transformational Design in a Theorem Prover', in *Theorem Provers in Circuit Design: Theory, Practice and Experience: Proceedings of the IFIP WG10.2 International Conference, Nijmegen, June 1992*, edited by V. Stavridou, T. F. Melham, and R. T. Boute (North-Holland, 1992), pp. 175–196.

[20] A. J. Camilleri, 'Executing Behavioural Definitions in Higher Order Logic' (Ph.D. dissertation, University of Cambridge, 1988).

[21] A. Camilleri, M. Gordon, and T. Melham, 'Hardware Verification using Higher-Order Logic', in *From HDL Descriptions to Guaranteed Correct Circuit Designs: Proceedings of the IFIP WG 10.2 Working Conference, Grenoble, September 1986*, edited by D. Borrione (North-Holland, 1987), pp. 43–67.

[22] L. Cardelli, 'An Algebraic Approach to Hardware Description and Verification' (Ph.D. dissertation, University of Edinburgh, 1982).

[23] S.-K. Chin, 'Verified Functions for Generating Signed-Binary Arithmetic Hardware', *IEEE Transactions on Computer-Aided Design of Integrated Circuits and Systems*, vol. 11, no. 12 (December 1992), pp. 1529–1558.

[24] A. Church, 'A Formulation of the Simple Theory of Types', *The Journal of Symbolic Logic*, vol. 5 (1940), pp. 56–68.

[25] L. J. M. Claesen, ed. *VLSI Design Methods*, 2 vols. (North-Holland, 1990).

[26] W. F. Clocksin and C. S. Mellish, *Programming in Prolog*, third edition (Springer-Verlag, 1987).

[27] A. Cohn, 'Correctness Properties of the Viper Block Model: The Second Level', in *Current Trends in Hardware Verification and Automated Theorem Proving*, edited by G. Birtwistle and P. A. Subrahmanyam (Springer-Verlag, 1989), pp. 1–91.

[28] A. Cohn, 'The Notion of Proof in Hardware Verification', *Journal of Automated Reasoning*, vol. 5, no. 2 (June 1989), pp. 127–139.

[29] A. Cohn, 'A Proof of Correctness of the Viper Microprocessor: The First Level', in *VLSI Specification, Verification and Synthesis*, edited by G. Birtwistle and P. A. Subrahmanyam, Kluwer International Series in Engineering and Computer Science (Kluwer, 1988), pp. 27–71.

[30] G. Cousineau, M. Gordon, G. Huet, R. Milner, L. Paulson, and C. Wadsworth, *The ML Handbook* (INRIA, 1986).

[31] W. J. Cullyer, 'Implementing Safety-Critical Systems: The VIPER Microprocessor', in *VLSI Specification, Verification and Synthesis*, edited by G. Birtwistle and P. A. Subrahmanyam, Kluwer International Series in Engineering and Computer Science (Kluwer, 1988), pp. 1–25.

[32] I. S. Dhingra, 'Formalising an Integrated Circuit Design Style in Higher Order Logic' (Ph.D. dissertation, University of Cambridge, 1988).

[33] D. L. Dill and E. M. Clarke, 'Automatic verification of asynchronous circuits using temporal logic', *IEE Proceedings*, vol. 133, part E, no. 5 (September 1986), pp. 276–282.

[34] H. Eveking, 'The Application of CHDL's to the Abstract Specification of Hardware', in *Computer Hardware Description Languages and their Applications: Proceedings of the IFIP WG 10.2 Seventh International Conference, Tokyo, August 1985*, edited by C. J. Koomen and T. Moto-oka (North-Holland, 1985), pp. 167–178.

[35] H. Eveking, 'Behavioural Consistency Between Register-Transfer- and Switch-Level Descriptions', in *Design Methodologies for VLSI and Computer Architecture: Proceedings of the IFIP TC 10 Working Conference, Pisa, September 1988*, edited by D. A. Edwards (North-Holland, 1989), pp. 183–201.

[36] H. Eveking, 'Experience in Designing Formally Verifiable HDL's', in *Computer Hardware Description Languages and their Applications: Proceedings of the IFIP WG 10.2 Tenth International Symposium, Marseille, April 1991*, edited by D. Borrione and R. Waxman (North-Holland, 1991), pp. 321–334.

[37] H. Eveking, 'Formal Verification of Synchronous Systems', in *Formal Aspects of VLSI Design: Proceedings of the 1985 Edinburgh Workshop on VLSI*, edited by G. J. Milne and P. A. Subrahmanyam (North-Holland, 1986), pp. 137–151.

[38] M. P. Fourman, 'Formal System Design', in *Formal Methods for VLSI Design: IFIP WG 10.2 Lecture Notes*, edited by J. Staunstrup (North-Holland, 1990), pp. 191–236.

[39] M. P. Fourman and R. A. Hexsel, 'Formal Synthesis', in *IV Higher Order Workshop, Banff 1990: Proceedings of the IV Higher Order Workshop, Banff, September 1990*, edited by G. Birtwistle, Workshops in Computing series (Springer-Verlag, 1991), pp. 245–264.

[40] J. A. Goguen, J. W. Thatcher, and E. G. Wagner, 'An initial algebra approach to the specification, correctness, and implementation of abstract data types', in *Data Structuring*, vol. 4 of *Current Trends in Programming Methodology*, edited by R. T. Yeh, 4 vols. (Prentice-Hall, 1977–8), pp. 80–149.

[41] M. Gordon, 'HOL: A Machine Oriented Formulation of Higher Order Logic', Technical Report 68, Computer Laboratory, University of Cambridge, revised version (July 1985).

[42] M. J. C. Gordon, 'HOL: A Proof Generating System for Higher-Order Logic', in *VLSI Specification, Verification and Synthesis*, edited by G. Birtwistle and P. A. Subrahmanyam, Kluwer International Series in Engineering and Computer Science (Kluwer, 1988), pp. 73–128.

[43] M. Gordon, 'LCF_LSM: A system for specifying and verifying hardware', Technical Report 41, Computer Laboratory, University of Cambridge (1983).

[44] M. Gordon, 'Proving a Computer Correct with the LCF_LSM Hardware Verification System', Technical Report 42, Computer Laboratory, University of Cambridge (1983).

[45] M. Gordon, 'Why higher-order logic is a good formalism for specifying and verifying hardware', in *Formal Aspects of VLSI Design: Proceedings of the 1985 Edinburgh Workshop on VLSI*, edited by G. J. Milne and P. A. Subrahmanyam (North-Holland, 1986), pp. 153–177.

[46] M. Gordon, P. Loewenstein, and M. Shahaf, 'Formal Verification of a Cell Library: a case study in technology transfer', in *Formal VLSI Correctness Verification*, vol. 2 of *VLSI Design Methods*, edited by L. J. M. Claesen, 2 vols. (North-Holland, 1990), pp. 409–417.

[47] M. J. C. Gordon and T. F. Melham, eds. *Introduction to HOL: A theorem proving environment for higher order logic* (Cambridge University Press, 1993).

[48] M. J. Gordon, A. J. Milner, and C. P. Wadsworth, *Edinburgh LCF: A Mechanised Logic of Computation*, Lecture Notes in Computer Science, vol. 78 (Springer-Verlag, 1979).

[49] B. T. Graham, *The SECD Microprocessor: A Verification Case Study*, Kluwer International Series in Engineering and Computer Science (Kluwer, 1992).

[50] D. Gries, *The Science of Programming*, Texts and Monographs in Computer Science (Springer-Verlag, 1981).

[51] A. Gupta, 'Formal Hardware Verification Methods: A Survey', *Formal Methods in System Design*, vol. 1, nos. 2–3 (October 1992), pp. 151–238.

[52] J. V. Guttag, E. Horowitz, and D. R. Musser, 'Abstract Data Types and Software Validation', *Communications of the ACM*, vol. 21, no. 12 (December 1978), pp. 1048–1064.

[53] R. W. S. Hale, 'Modelling a Ring Network in Interval Temporal Logic', in *Microcomputers, Usage and Design: Proceedings of the eleventh EUROMICRO Symposium on Microprocessing and Microprogramming*, edited by K. Waldschmidt and B. Myhrhaug (North-Holland, 1985), pp. 77–84.

[54] R. W. S. Hale, 'Programming in Temporal Logic' (Ph.D. dissertation, University of Cambridge, 1988).

[55] F. K. Hanna, 'Overview of the Veritas Project', Internal Report, University of Kent (June 1983).

[56] F. K. Hanna and N. Daeche, 'Purely Functional Implementation of a Logic', in *8th International Conference on Automated Deduction, Oxford, July 1986, Proceedings*, edited by J. H. Siekmann, Lecture Notes in Computer Science, vol. 230 (Springer-Verlag, 1986), pp. 598–607.

[57] F. K. Hanna and N. Daeche, 'Specification and verification of digital systems using higher-order predicate logic', *IEE Proceedings*, vol. 133, part E, no. 5 (September 1986), pp. 242–254.

[58] F. K. Hanna and N. Daeche, 'Specification and Verification using Higher-Order Logic: A Case Study', in *Formal Aspects of VLSI Design: Proceedings of the 1985 Edinburgh Workshop on VLSI*, edited by G. J. Milne and P. A. Subrahmanyam (North-Holland, 1986), pp. 179–213.

[59] F. K. Hanna, N. Daeche, and M. Longley, 'Specification and Verification Using Dependent Types', *IEEE Transactions on Software Engineering*, vol. 16, no. 9 (September 1990), pp. 949–964.

[60] F. K. Hanna, N. Daeche, and M. Longley, 'VERITAS+: a Specification Language based on Type Theory', in *Hardware Specification, Verification and Synthesis: Mathematical Aspects: Mathematical Sciences Institute Workshop, Cornell, July 1989*, edited by M. Leeser and G. Brown, Lecture Notes in Computer Science, vol. 408 (Springer-Verlag, 1990), pp. 358–379.

[61] F. K. Hanna, M. Longley and N. Daeche, 'Formal Synthesis of Digital Systems', in *Formal VLSI Specification and Synthesis*, vol. 1 of *VLSI Design Methods*, edited by L. J. M. Claesen, 2 vols. (North-Holland, 1990), pp. 153–169.

[62] N. A. Harman and J. V. Tucker, 'Clocks, Retimings, and the Formal Specification of a UART', in *The Fusion of Hardware Design and Verification: Proceedings of the IFIP WG 10.2 Working Conference, Glasgow, July 1988*, edited by G. J. Milne (North-Holland, 1988), pp. 375–396.

[63] N. A. Harman and J. V. Tucker, 'The formal specification of a digital correlator', in *Theoretical Foundations of VLSI Design*, edited by K. McEvoy and J. V. Tucker, Cambridge Tracts in Theoretical Computer Science 10 (Cambridge University Press, 1990), pp 161–262.

[64] W. S. Hatcher, *The Logical Foundations of Mathematics*, Foundations and Philosophy of Science and Technology Series (Pergamon Press, 1982).

[65] J. M. J. Herbert, 'Application of Formal Methods to Digital System Design' (Ph.D. dissertation, University of Cambridge, 1986).

[66] J. Herbert, 'Formal Reasoning about the Timing and Function of Basic Memory Devices', in *Formal VLSI Correctness Verification*, vol. 2 of *VLSI Design*

Methods, edited by L. J. M. Claesen, 2 vols. (North-Holland, 1990), pp. 379–398.

[67] J. Herbert, 'Temporal Abstraction of Digital Designs' *The Fusion of Hardware Design and Verification: Proceedings of the IFIP WG 10.2 Working Conference, Glasgow, July 1988*, edited by G. J. Milne (North-Holland, 1988), pp. 1–25.

[68] C. A. R. Hoare, *Communicating Sequential Processes*, Prentice-Hall International Series in Computer Science (Prentice-Hall, 1985).

[69] C. A. R. Hoare, 'Proof of Correctness of Data Representations', *Acta Informatica*, vol. 1, no. 4 (1972), pp. 271–281.

[70] C. A. R. Hoare and M. J. C. Gordon, eds. *Mechanized Reasoning and Hardware Design*, Prentice-Hall International Series in Computer Science (Prentice-Hall, 1992).

[71] C. A. R. Hoare and M. J. C. Gordon, 'Partial Correctness of C-MOS Switching Circuits: An Exercise in Applied Logic', in *Proceedings of the Third Annual Symposium on Logic in Computer Science* (Computer Society Press, 1988), pp. 28–36.

[72] A. Hopper and R. M. Needham, 'The Cambridge Fast Ring Networking System', Technical Report 90, Computer Laboratory, University of Cambridge (1986).

[73] W. A. Hunt, Jr., 'FM8501: A Verified Microprocessor' (Ph.D. dissertation, University of Texas at Austin, 1985).

[74] W. A. Hunt, Jr., 'Microprocessor Design Verification', *Journal of Automated Reasoning*, vol. 5, no. 4 (December 1989), pp. 429–460.

[75] P. B. Jackson, 'Nuprl and its Use in Circuit Design', in *Theorem Provers in Circuit Design: Theory, Practice and Experience: Proceedings of the IFIP WG10.2 International Conference, Nijmegen, June 1992*, edited by V. Stavridou, T. F. Melham, and R. T. Boute (North-Holland, 1992), pp. 311–336.

[76] B. Jacobs and T. Melham, 'Translating Dependent Type Theory into Higher Order Logic', in *Typed Lambda Calculi and Applications: Proceedings of the International Conference, Utrecht, March 1993*, Lecture Notes in Computer Science, vol. 664 (Springer-Verlag, 1993).

[77] G. Jones and M. Sheeran, eds. *Designing Correct Circuits*, Workshops in Computing series (Springer-Verlag, 1991).

[78] J. J. Joyce, 'Formal Verification and Implementation of a Microprocessor', in *VLSI Specification, Verification and Synthesis*, edited by G. Birtwistle and P. A. Subrahmanyam, Kluwer International Series in Engineering and Computer Science (Kluwer, 1988), pp. 129–157.

[79] J. Joyce, G. Birtwistle, and M. Gordon, 'Proving a Computer Correct in Higher Order Logic', Technical Report 100, Computer Laboratory, University of Cambridge (December 1986).

[80] M. E. Leeser, 'Reasoning about the Function and Timing of Integrated Circuits with Prolog and Temporal Logic' (Ph.D. dissertation, University of Cambridge, 1987).

[81] M. Leeser, 'Using Nuprl for the verification and synthesis of hardware', in *Mechanized Reasoning and Hardware Design*, edited by C. A. R. Hoare and M. J. C. Gordon, Prentice Hall International Series in Computer Science (Prentice Hall, 1992), pp. 49–68.

[82] M. Leeser and G. Brown, eds. *Hardware Specification, Verification and Synthesis: Mathematical Aspects: Mathematical Sciences Institute Workshop, Cornell, July 1989*, Lecture Notes in Computer Science, vol. 408 (Springer-Verlag, 1990).

[83] A. C. Leisenring, *Mathematical Logic and Hilbert's ε-Symbol*, University Mathematical Series (Macdonald & Co., 1969).

[84] K. McEvoy and J. V. Tucker, eds. *Theoretical Foundations of VLSI Design*, Cambridge Tracts in Theoretical Computer Science 10 (Cambridge University Press, 1990).

[85] D. MacKenzie, 'The fangs of the VIPER', *Nature*, vol. 352 (August 1991), pp. 467–468.

[86] P. Martin-Löf, 'Constructive Mathematics and Computer Programming', in *Mathematical Logic and Programming Languages*, edited by C. A. R. Hoare and J. C. Shepherdson, Prentice-Hall International Series in Computer Science (Prentice-Hall, 1985), pp. 167–184.

[87] T. F. Melham, 'Abstraction Mechanisms for Hardware Verification', in *VLSI Specification, Verification and Synthesis*, edited by G. Birtwistle and P. A. Subrahmanyam, Kluwer International Series in Engineering and Computer Science (Kluwer, 1988), pp. 267–291.

[88] T. F. Melham, 'Automating Recursive Type Definitions in Higher Order Logic', in *Current Trends in Hardware Verification and Automated Theorem*

Proving, edited by G. Birtwistle and P. A. Subrahmanyam (Springer-Verlag, 1989), pp. 341–386.

[89] T. Melham, 'A Package for Inductive Relation Definitions in HOL', in *Proceedings of the 1991 International Workshop on the HOL Theorem Proving System and its Applications, Davis, August 1991*, edited by M. Archer, J. J. Joyce, K. N. Levitt, and P. J. Windley (IEEE Computer Society Press, 1992), pp. 350–357.

[90] G. J. Milne, 'CIRCAL: A calculus for circuit description', *Integration*, vol. 1, nos. 2–3 (October 1983), pp. 121–160.

[91] G. J. Milne, ed. *The Fusion of Hardware Design and Verification: Proceedings of the IFIP WG 10.2 Working Conference, Glasgow, July 1988* (North-Holland, 1988).

[92] G. J. Milne, 'Simulation and Verification: Related Techniques for Hardware Analysis', in *Computer Hardware Description Languages and their Applications: Proceedings of the IFIP WG 10.2 Seventh International Conference, Tokyo, August 1985*, edited by C. J. Koomen and T. Moto-oka (North-Holland, 1985), pp. 404–417.

[93] G. Milne and R. Milner, 'Concurrent Processes and Their Syntax', *Journal of the ACM*, vol. 26, no. 2 (April 1979), pp. 302–321.

[94] G. J. Milne and P. A. Subrahmanyam, eds. *Formal Aspects of VLSI Design: Proceedings of the 1985 Edinburgh Workshop on VLSI* (North-Holland, 1986).

[95] R. Milner, 'How to derive inductions in LCF', Internal Report, University of Edinburgh (August 1980).

[96] R. Milner, 'A Theory of Type Polymorphism in Programming', *Journal of Computer and System Sciences*, vol. 17, no. 3 (December 1978), pp. 348–375.

[97] R. Milner, 'The use of machines to assist in rigorous proof', in *Mathematical Logic and Programming Languages*, edited by C. A. R. Hoare and J. C. Shepherdson, Prentice-Hall International Series in Computer Science (Prentice-Hall, 1985), pp. 77–88.

[98] B. Q. Monahan, 'Data Type Proofs Using Edinburgh LCF' (Ph.D. dissertation, University of Edinburgh, 1985).

[99] B. C. Moszkowski, *Executing Temporal Logic Programs* (Cambridge University Press, 1986).

[100] B. C. Moszkowski, 'Reasoning about Digital Circuits' (Ph.D. dissertation, Stanford University, 1983).

[101] P. Narendran and J. Stillman, 'Formal Verification of the Sobel Image Processing Chip', in *Current Trends in Hardware Verification and Automated Theorem Proving*, edited by G. Birtwistle and P. A. Subrahmanyam (Springer-Verlag, 1989), pp. 92–127.

[102] L. C. Paulson, *Logic and Computation: Interactive Proof with Cambridge LCF*, Cambridge Tracts in Theoretical Computer Science 2 (Cambridge University Press, 1987).

[103] R. Piloty and D. Borrione, 'The Conlan Project: Concepts, Implementations, and Applications', *Computer*, vol. 18, no. 2 (February 1985), pp. 81–92.

[104] M. Sheeran, 'Describing and reasoning about circuits using relations', in *Theoretical Foundations of VLSI Design*, edited by K. McEvoy and J. V. Tucker, Cambridge Tracts in Theoretical Computer Science 10 (Cambridge University Press, 1990), pp. 263–298.

[105] M. Sheeran, 'Design and verification of regular synchronous circuits', *IEE Proceedings*, vol. 133, part E, no. 5 (September 1986), pp. 295–304.

[106] V. Stavridou, T. F. Melham, and R. T. Boute, eds. *Theorem Provers in Circuit Design: Proceedings of the IFIP WG10.2 International Conference, Nijmegen, June 1992*, IFIP Transactions vol. A-10 (North-Holland, 1992).

[107] J. Staunstrup, ed. *Formal Methods for VLSI Design: IFIP WG 10.2 Lecture Notes* (North-Holland, 1990).

[108] J. Staunstrup and R. Sharp, eds. *Designing Correct Circuits: Proceedings of the Second IFIP WG10.2/WG10.5 Workshop, Lyngby, January 1992*, IFIP Transactions vol. A-5 (North-Holland, 1992).

[109] P. A. Subrahmanyam, 'Towards a framework for dealing with system timing in Very High Level Silicon Compilers', in *VLSI Specification, Verification and Synthesis*, edited by G. Birtwistle and P. A. Subrahmanyam, Kluwer International Series in Engineering and Computer Science (Kluwer, 1988), pp. 159–215.

[110] N. Traub, 'A Formal Approach to Hardware Analysis' (Ph.D. dissertation, University of Edinburgh, 1987).

[111] D. Turner, 'An Overview of Miranda', *Sigplan Notices*, vol. 21, no. 12 (December 1986), pp. 158–166.

[112] J. Van Tassel and D. Hemmendinger, 'Towards Formal Verification of VHDL Specifications', in *Formal VLSI Correctness Verification*, vol. 2 of *VLSI Design Methods*, edited by L. J. M. Claesen, 2 vols. (North-Holland, 1990), pp. 399–408.

[113] T. J. Wagner, 'Hardware Verification' (Ph.D. dissertation, Stanford University, 1977).

[114] N. H. E. Weste and K. Eshraghian, *Principles of CMOS VLSI Design: A Systems Perspective*, VLSI Systems Series (Addison-Wesley, 1985).

[115] A. N. Whitehead and B. Russell, *Principia Mathematica*, second edition, 3 vols. (Cambridge University Press, 1925–27).

[116] Å. Wikström, *Functional Programming Using Standard ML*, Prentice-Hall International Series in Computer Science (Prentice-Hall, 1987).

[117] G. Winskel, 'Models and logic of MOS circuits', in *Logic of Programming and Calculi of Discrete Design: International Summer School Directed by F. L. Bauer, M. Broy, E. W. Dijkstra, C. A. R. Hoare*, edited by M. Broy, NATO ASI Series, Series F: Computer and Systems Sciences, vol. 36 (Springer-Verlag, 1987), pp. 367–413.

[118] G. Winskel, 'Relating two models of hardware', in *Category Theory and Computer Science*, edited by D. H. Pitt, A. Poigné, and D. E. Rydeheard, Lecture Notes in Computer Science, vol. 283 (Springer-Verlag, 1987), pp. 98–113.

[119] A. S. Wojcik, 'Formal Design Verification of Digital Systems', in *ACM IEEE 20th Design Automation Conference: Proceedings* (IEEE Computer Society Press, 1983), pp. 228–234.

[120] M. Yoeli, ed. *Formal Verification of Hardware Design* (IEEE Computer Society Press, 1990).

Index

Printed in the United States
By Bookmasters